Visual Basic 2005
A Developer's Notebook™

Matthew MacDonald

O'REILLY®

Beijing · Cambridge · Farnham · Köln · Paris · Sebastopol · Taipei · Tokyo

Visual Basic 2005: A Developer's Notebook™
by Matthew MacDonald

Published by O'Reilly Media, Inc., 1005 Gravenstein Highway North, Sebastopol, CA 95472.

O'Reilly books may be purchased for educational, business, or sales promotional use. Online editions are also available for most titles (*safari.oreilly.com*). For more information, contact our corporate/institutional sales department: (800) 998-9938 or *corporate@oreilly.com*.

Editor:	John Osborn
Production Editor:	Sanders Kleinfeld
Cover Designer:	Edie Freedman
Interior Designer:	David Futato

Printing History:

April 2005:	First Edition.

 This book uses RepKover™, a durable and flexible lay-flat binding.

ISBN: 0-596-00726-4
[M]

Contents

The Developer's Notebook Series

So, you've managed to pick this book up. Cool. Really, I'm excited about that! Of course, you may be wondering why these books have the odd-looking, college notebook sort of cover. I mean, this is O'Reilly, right? Where are the animals? And, really, do you *need* another series? Couldn't this just be a cookbook? How about a nutshell, or one of those cool hacks books that seems to be everywhere? The short answer is that a developer's notebook is none of those things—in fact, it's such an important idea that we came up with an entirely new look and feel, complete with cover, fonts, and even some notes in the margin. This is all a result of trying to get something into your hands you can actually use.

It's my strong belief that while the nineties were characterized by everyone wanting to learn everything (Why not? We all had six-figure incomes from dot-com companies), the new millennium is about information pain. People don't have time (or the income) to read through 600 page books, often learning 200 things, of which only about 4 apply to their current job. It would be much nicer to just sit near one of the uber-coders and look over his shoulder, wouldn't it? To ask the guys that are neck-deep in this stuff why they chose a particular method, how they performed this one tricky task, or how they avoided that threading issue when working with piped streams. The thinking has always been that books can't serve that particular need—they can inform, and let you decide, but ultimately a coder's mind was something that couldn't really be captured on a piece of paper.

This series says that assumption is patently wrong—and we aim to prove it.

A Developer's Notebook is just what it claims to be: the often-frantic scribbling and notes that a true-blue alpha geek mentally makes when working with a new language, API, or project. It's the no-nonsense code that solves problems, stripped of page-filling commentary that often serves more as a paperweight than an epiphany. It's hackery, focused not on what is nifty or might be fun to do when you've got some free time (when's the last time that happened?), but on what you need to simply "make it work." This isn't a lecture, folks—it's a lab. If you want a lot of concept, architecture, and UML diagrams, I'll happily and proudly point you to our animal and nutshell books. If you want every answer to every problem under the sun, our omnibus cookbooks are killer. And if you are into arcane and often quirky uses of technology, hacks books simply rock. But if you're a coder, down to your core, and you just want to get on with it, then you want a Developer's Notebook. Coffee stains and all, this is from the mind of a developer to yours, barely even cleaned up enough for print. I hope you enjoy it...we sure had a good time writing them.

Notebooks Are...

Example-driven guides

As you'll see in the "Organization" section, developer's notebooks are built entirely around example code. You'll see code on nearly every page, and it's code that *does something*—not trivial "Hello World!" programs that aren't worth more than the paper they're printed on.

Aimed at developers

Ever read a book that seems to be aimed at pointy-haired bosses, filled with buzzwords, and feels more like a marketing manifesto than a programming text? We have too—and these books are the antithesis of that. In fact, a good notebook is incomprehensible to someone who can't program (don't say we didn't warn you!), and that's just the way it's supposed to be. But for developers...it's as good as it gets.

Actually enjoyable to work through

Do you really have time to sit around reading something that isn't any fun? If you do, then maybe you're into thousand-page language references—but if you're like the rest of us, notebooks are a much better fit. Practical code samples, terse dialogue centered around practical examples, and even some humor here and there—these are the ingredients of a good developer's notebook.

About doing, not talking about doing

If you want to read a book late at night without a computer nearby, these books might not be that useful. The intent is that you're coding as you go along, knee deep in bytecode. For that reason, notebooks talk code, code, code. Fire up your editor before digging in.

Notebooks Aren't...

Lectures

We don't let just anyone write a developer's notebook—you've got to be a bona fide programmer, and preferably one who stays up a little too late coding. While full-time writers, academics, and theorists are great in some areas, these books are about programming in the trenches, and are filled with instruction, not lecture.

Filled with conceptual drawings and class hierarchies

This isn't a nutshell (there, we said it). You won't find 100-page indices with every method listed, and you won't see full-page UML diagrams with methods, inheritance trees, and flow charts. What you will find is page after page of source code. Are you starting to sense a recurring theme?

Long on explanation, light on application

It seems that many programming books these days have three, four, or more chapters before you even see any working code. I'm not sure who has authors convinced that it's good to keep a reader waiting this long, but it's not anybody working on *this* series. We believe that if you're not coding within ten pages, something's wrong. These books are also chock-full of practical application, taking you from an example in a book to putting things to work on your job, as quickly as possible.

Organization

Developer's Notebooks try to communicate different information than most books, and as a result, are organized differently. They do indeed have chapters, but that's about as far as the similarity between a notebook and a traditional programming book goes. First, you'll find that all the headings in each chapter are organized around a specific task. You'll note that we said *task*, not *concept*. That's one of the important things to get about these books—they are first and foremost about doing something. Each of these headings represents a single *lab*. A lab is just what it sounds like—steps to accomplish a specific goal. In fact, that's the first heading you'll see under each lab: "How do I do that?" This is the central question of each lab, and you'll find lots of down-and-dirty code and detail in these sections.

Some labs have some things not to do (ever played around with potassium in high school chemistry?), helping you avoid common pitfalls. Some labs give you a good reason for caring about the topic in the first place; we call this the "Why do I care?" section, for obvious reasons. For those times when code samples don't clearly communicate what's going on, you'll find a "What just happened" section. It's in these sections that you'll find concepts and theory—but even then, they are tightly focused on the task at hand, not explanation for the sake of page count. Finally, many labs offer alternatives, and address common questions about different approaches to similar problems. These are the "What about..." sections, which will help give each task some context within the programming big picture.

And one last thing—on many pages, you'll find notes scrawled in the margins of the page. These aren't for decoration; they contain tips, tricks, insights from the developers of a product, and sometimes even a little humor, just to keep you going. These notes represent part of the overall communication flow—getting you as close to reading the mind of the developer-author as we can. Hopefully they'll get you that much closer to feeling like you are indeed learning from a master.

And most of all, remember—these books are...

All Lab, No Lecture

—Brett McLaughlin, Series Creator

Preface

When Beta 1 of Visual Basic .NET hit the programming scene in 2001, the new tool challenged experienced Visual Basic developers to step up to an entirely new programming platform and a whole new way of writing code. Fortunately, four years later, it's clear that the rewards of moving to .NET make up for the steep learning curve developers experience when they try to do so. Developers who have made the jump have a powerful set of tools for building Windows and web applications—a set that other programming frameworks are hard-pressed to match.

Visual Basic 2005 and the platform it's built on, .NET 2.0, don't represent the same seismic change. Instead, Visual Basic 2005 and .NET 2.0 are the latest releases of what are now a mature language and platform. Microsoft architects have ironed out inconsistencies, corrected flaws, and added dozens of requested features, from VB 6's edit-and-continue debugger to new Windows and web controls for displaying data. Still, even the keenest developer could use a quick tour of Visual Basic 2005 and .NET 2.0 to come to terms with all the changes.

This book provides a series of hands-on labs that take you through the new features you'll find in Visual Basic 2005, the .NET Framework 2.0, and the Visual Studio 2005 development tool. *Visual Basic 2005: A Developer's Notebook* is perfect for developers who have worked with a previous version of .NET and need to quickly get up to speed with what's new. Best of all, you'll learn everything through concise, focused examples (all of which are just a short download away).

Who This Book Is For

This book is written for anyone who's asked the question "What's new in .NET 2.0?" or, even more importantly, "What does it let me do now that I couldn't do before?" As the latest in the Developer's Notebook series of books, this book answers these questions without requiring you to wade through pages of remedial VB lessons or .NET theory.

The most important requirement for this book is a solid familiarity with VB .NET 1.0 or 1.1, and experience building .NET applications. *Visual Basic 2005: A Developer's Notebook* covers very little of the material that an experienced VB .NET 1.1 programmer already knows. Instead, this book aims to help you build on your current knowledge, rather than waste your time covering old material. If you're a VB programmer who hasn't made the jump to .NET yet, you'll find the labs in this book interesting, but you'll need to supplement your .NET knowledge with another book first. Try one of the many great introductions, such as Jesse Liberty's *Programming Visual Basic .NET* (O'Reilly) or my own *The Book of VB .NET* (No Starch Press).

What You Need to Use This Book

To make the best use of this book, you'll need the following ingredients:

- Windows 2000 Professional, Windows XP, or Windows Server 2003.
- Visual Studio 2005. Alternatively, you can use a scaled-down Visual Studio version, but you won't be able to complete all the labs. For example, Visual Basic 2005 Express Edition allows you to build Windows applications, console applications, and DLL components (but not web applications), and Visual Web Developer 2005 Express Edition allows you to build only web applications.
- In addition, if you want to run the database examples in Chapter 5 without any changes, you'll need SQL Server 7.0 or later with the sample Northwind database. SQL Server Express will also work fine.

Because Visual Basic 2005 is currently in a beta cycle, it's inevitable that there will be some changes to the product after this book is printed. (In rare cases, entire features have disappeared from one build to the next!) As a result, it's possible that some recipes may not work as written. Usually, the difference is simply syntactic, such as a minor renaming of a property, constant, or method, or a reshuffling of a class from one namespace to another. Occasionally, a feature changes more dramatically, and significant code revisions are needed. To help manage the confusion, refer to *http://www.oreilly.com/catalog/vbadn* to download the latest sample code, which is updated regularly to keep in step with newer builds. As an early adopter, you already know that working with beta versions is awkward, frustrating, and more than a little exciting. But all in all, it's a small price to pay for getting an advance seat to see the changes to Visual Basic and the .NET platform!

About This Book

This book is divided into six chapters. Each chapter tackles a particular category of enhancements in the VB 2005 language and the .NET 2.0 Framework:

Chapter 1, Visual Studio
> Visual Studio sports a host of embellishments, including enhanced IntelliSense and a new code snippets feature that puts useful examples at your fingertips. But the star of the show is undoubtedly the return of the long-missed edit-and-continue debugging engine.

Chapter 2, The Visual Basic Language
> The VB 2005 language has some new keywords, some of which duplicate features found in C# (e.g., operator overloading), and others that leverage completely new .NET Framework features (e.g., generics). Learn about them all in this chapter.

Chapter 3, Windows Applications
> The Windows Forms toolkit hasn't changed much, but a handful of entirely new controls provide modern menus and toolbars, masked text editing, web page display, and, finally, a decent data grid.

Chapter 4, Web Applications
> ASP.NET boasts the most improvements of any part of the .NET Framework. In this chapter, you'll get an overview of many new features, including codeless data–binding, site navigation, and new solutions for personalization, all of which aim to dramatically reduce the amount of code you need to write.

Chapter 5, Files, Databases, and XML
> In this chapter, you'll see what's new when dealing with data. This includes streamlined file access classes, a few new ADO.NET frills, and a better way to work with XML.

Chapter 6, .NET 2.0 Platform Services
> The last chapter wraps up with a slew of miscellaneous topics that demonstrate new .NET Framework features. These features include support for FTP, access to the Windows user security system, and a new way to deploy applications with the ClickOnce technology.

Conventions Used in This Book

The following typographical conventions are used in this book:

Plain text
> Indicates menu titles, menu options, menu buttons, and keyboard accelerators (such as Alt and Ctrl).

Italic
> Indicates new terms, URLs, email addresses, filenames, file extensions, pathnames, directories, usernames and passwords, and Unix utilities.

Constant width
> Indicates commands, options, switches, variables, attributes, keys, functions, types, classes, namespaces, methods, modules, properties, parameters, values, objects, events, event handlers, XML tags, HTML tags, macros, the contents of files, and the output from commands.

Constant width bold
> Used to highlight key portions of code.

TIP

This icon signifies a tip, suggestion, or general note.

WARNING

This icon indicates a warning or caution.

Using Code Examples

This book is here to help you get your job done. In general, you may use the code in this book in your programs and documentation. You do not need to contact us for permission unless you're reproducing a significant portion of the code. For example, writing a program that uses several chunks of code from this book does not require permission. Selling or distributing a CD-ROM of examples from O'Reilly books *does* require permission. Answering a question by citing this book and quoting example code does not require permission. Incorporating a significant amount of example code from this book into your product's documentation *does* require permission.

We appreciate, but do not require, attribution. An attribution usually includes the title, author, publisher, and ISBN. For example: "*Visual Basic 2005: A Developer's Notebook*, by Matthew MacDonald. Copyright 2005 O'Reilly Media, Inc., 0-596-00726-4."

If you feel your use of code examples falls outside fair use or the permission given above, feel free to contact us at *permissions@oreilly.com*.

Safari® Enabled

 When you see a Safari® Enabled icon on the cover of your favorite technology book, it means the book is available online through the O'Reilly Network Safari Bookshelf.

Safari offers a solution that's better than e-books. It's a virtual library that lets you easily search thousands of top technology books, cut and paste code samples, download chapters, and find quick answers when you need the most accurate, current information. Try it for free at *http://safari.oreilly.com*.

How to Contact Us

Please address comments and questions concerning this book to the publisher:

O'Reilly Media, Inc.
1005 Gravenstein Highway North
Sebastopol, CA 95472
(800) 998-9938 (in the United States or Canada)
(707) 829-0515 (international or local)
(707) 829-0104 (fax)

We have a web page for this book, where we list errata, examples, and any additional information. You can access this page at:

http://www.oreilly.com/catalog/vbadn

To comment or ask technical questions about this book, send email to:

bookquestions@oreilly.com

For more information about our books, conferences, Resource Centers, and the O'Reilly Network, see our web site at:

http://www.oreilly.com

Acknowledgments

This book couldn't have been written without the help of the first rate team at O'Reilly, who invented this unique series and are always experimenting with new ideas. I'm deeply grateful to John Osborn for bringing me into this project and giving it (occasional) focus through a difficult beta cycle, and the excellent technical reviewers who reviewed it, including Jesse Liberty, Steve Saunders, and Dianne Siebold. I'm especially grateful to Erick Ellis at Microsoft and the Windows Forms team, who've been absolutely stellar in getting quick answers to my .NET questions. Thanks also to Jay Roxe and Jay Schmelzer of the Visual Basic team for their help in resolving last-minute problems. I also owe the usual thanks to my coterie, including Nora, Paul, Razia, Hamid, and my wife Faria.

CHAPTER 1

Visual Studio

The new features of Visual Basic 2005 are actually provided by three separate components: the enhanced Visual Studio 2005 IDE, a new version of the VB compiler (*vbc.exe*), and the revamped .NET 2.0 Framework. In this chapter, you'll start by taking Visual Studio 2005 for a spin.

Besides being noticeably faster at creating and opening projects, Visual Studio 2005 also offers a slew of minor improvements and a few truly useful new features. The change that's likely to draw the most applause from long-time VB programmers is the return of the run-edit-continue debugger, a much loved tool in Visual Basic 6 that never made the transition to .NET. Other innovative features include a new system of code snippets (which allows you to insert blocks of pre-made code into your projects with a couple of mouse clicks), smarter IntelliSense, tools for peering into complex objects while debugging, and the ability to quickly create rich data-bound forms.

Getting Started with Visual Studio 2005

Most developers get acquainted with new programming platforms by using a development tool such as Visual Studio. All of the labs in this book can be completed with Visual Studio—in fact, without it you're forced to type in an overwhelming amount of basic boilerplate code (and you're likely to run into endless syntax errors and countless other irritations).

Visual Basic 2005 developers have a choice of three versions of Visual Studio: Visual Studio 2005, Visual Basic 2005 Express, and Visual Web Developer 2005 Express Edition. You can use any of these products with

In this chapter:
- *Getting Started with Visual Studio 2005*
- *Code, Debug, and Continue Without Restarting Your Application*
- *Look Inside an Object While Debugging*
- *Diagnose and Correct Errors on the Fly*
- *Rename All Instances of Any Program Element*
- *Use IntelliSense Filtering and AutoCorrect*
- *Edit Control Properties in Place*
- *Call Methods at Design Time*
- *Insert Boilerplate Code Using Snippets*

At first glance, Visual Studio hasn't changed too radically in its latest incarnation. However, it's worth taking a moment to orient yourself to Microsoft's newest IDE.

this book; however, if you use an express edition, certain project types won't be supported, and as a result you won't be able to complete all the labs.

TIP

Visual Studio 2005 is the direct successor to Visual Studio .NET, and it provides the most complete set of tools and features. Visual Basic 2005 Express Edition allows you to build Windows applications, console applications, and DLL components (but not web applications). Visual Web Developer 2005 Express Edition allows you to build *only* web applications. However, all three of these programs are really variations of the same tool—Visual Studio. As a result, the menus, toolbars, and behavior of these applications are essentially the same.

How do I do that?

To get started and create a new project, select File → New Project from the Visual Studio menu. You'll see a slightly revamped New Project dialog box, as shown in Figure 1-1. Depending on the version of Visual Studio you're using, you may see a different set of available project types.

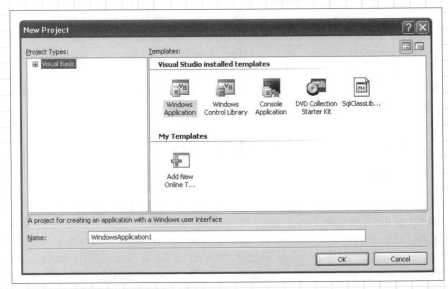

Figure 1-1. Creating a new project

To continue, select the Windows Application project type and click OK to create the new project. In the Solution Explorer, you'll see that the project contains a single form, an application configuration file, and a My Project node (which you can select to configure project and build settings). However, the list of assembly references won't appear in the Solution Explorer, unless you explicitly choose Project → Show All Files. Figure 1-2 shows both versions of the Solution Explorer.

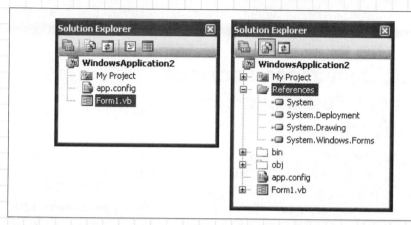

Figure 1-2. Two views of the Solution Explorer

To save your project, choose File → Save [ProjectName] from the menu. One change you're likely to notice is that Visual Studio no longer asks you to specify a directory path when you create a new project. That's because Visual Studio, in a bid to act more like Visual Basic 6, doesn't save any files until you ask it to.

TIP

This behavior actually depends on the Visual Studio environment settings. When you first install Visual Studio, you have the chance to choose your developer profile. If you choose Visual Basic Development Settings, you won't be asked to save your project when you first create it.

Of course, as a savvy programmer you know that files need to reside somewhere, and if you dig around you'll find a temporary directory like *C:\Documents and Settings\[UserName]\Local Settings\Application Data\ Temporary Projects\[ProjectName]* that's used automatically to store new, unsaved projects. Once you save a project, it's moved to the location you choose.

You can use the simple Windows application you created to try out the other labs in this chapter and tour Visual Studio's new features.

The process of creating web applications has also changed subtly in Visual Studio 2005, and you no longer need IIS and a virtual directory to test your web site. You'll learn more about web projects in Chapter 4.

What about...

...the real deal of differences between different Visual Studio flavors? You can get the final word about what each version does and does not support from Microsoft's Visual Studio 2005 developer center, at *http://lab. msdn.microsoft.com/vs2005*. This site provides downloads of the latest Visual Studio betas and white papers that explain the differences between the express editions and the full-featured Visual Studio 2005.

The single most requested feature from VB 6 returns to .NET: a debugger that lets you edit code without restarting your application.

Code, Debug, and Continue Without Restarting Your Application

Visual Basic 6 developers are accustomed to making changes on the fly, tweaking statements, refining logic, and even inserting entirely new blocks of code while they work. But the introduction of a new compile-time architecture with the .NET 1.0 common language runtime (CLR) caused this feature to disappear from Visual Studio .NET 2002 and 2003. Fortunately, it's returned in Visual Basic 2005, with a few enhancements and one major caveat—it won't work with ASP.NET.

How do I do that?

To see edit-and-debugging at its simplest, it's worth looking at an example where a problem sidelines your code—and how you can quickly recover. Figure 1-3 shows a financial calculator application that can calculate how long it will take you to become a millionaire, using Visual Basic's handy Pmt( ) function.

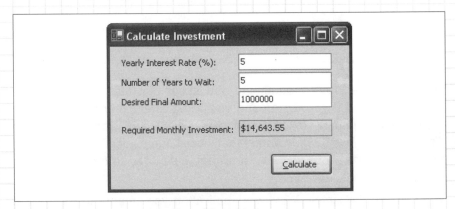

Figure 1-3. A simple form for a financial calculation

To create this program, first add four text boxes (the labels are optional), and then name them txtInterestRate, txtYears, txtFutureValue, and txtMonthlyPayment (from top to bottom). Then, add a button with the following event handler:

```
Private Sub btnCalculate_Click(ByVal sender As System.Object, _
    ByVal e As System.EventArgs) Handles btnCalculate.Click

    Dim InterestRate, Years, FinalValue, MonthlyPayment As Double
    InterestRate = Val(txtInterestRate.Text)
    FinalValue = Val(txtFutureValue.Text)
    MonthlyPayment = Pmt(InterestRate / 12 / 100, _
        Years * 12, 0, -FinalValue, DueDate.BegOfPeriod)
    txtMonthlyInvestment.Text = MonthlyPayment.ToString("C")

End Sub
```

Now run the application, enter some sample values, and click the button. You'll receive a runtime exception (with the cryptically worded explanation "Argument NPer is not a valid value") when your code tries to calculate the MonthlyPayment value. One way to discover the source of the problem is to move the mouse over all the parameters in the statement and verify that they reflect what you expect. In this case, the problem is that the Years variable is never set, and so contains the value 0.

Thanks to edit-and-continue debugging, you can correct this problem without restarting your application. When the error occurs, click the "Enable editing" link in the error window. Then, add the missing line:

```
Private Sub btnCalculate_Click(ByVal sender As System.Object, _
    ByVal e As System.EventArgs) Handles btnCalculate.Click

    Years = Val(txtYears.Text)
    ...

End Sub
```

Now, look for the yellow arrow in the margin that indicates where the debugger is in your code. Click and drag this yellow arrow up to the newly added line so that it will be executed next. When you press F5 or click the Start button, the code resumes from this point and the calculation completes without a hitch.

You don't need to wait for an error to occur to use edit-and-continue debugging. You can also set a breakpoint in your code or select Debug → Break from the menu at any time.

What about...

...changes that the edit-and-continue debugger doesn't support? For the most part, edit-and-continue debugging in Visual Basic 2005 supports a greater variety of edits than supported in Visual Basic 6. However, there are still some types of edits that require you to restart your application.

One example is if you delete the method in which your code is currently executing. For the full list, refer to the MSDN help, under the index entry "Edit and Continue → unsupported declaration edits" (which describes disallowed changes to declarations, like properties, methods, and classes) and "Edit and Continue → unsupported property and method body edits" (which describes disallowed changes inside your actual code routines).

To alert you when you make an unsupported edit, Visual Studio underlines the declaration of the current class with a green squiggly line. If you hover over that line, a ToolTip appears that explains the offending change. Figure 1-4 shows an example.

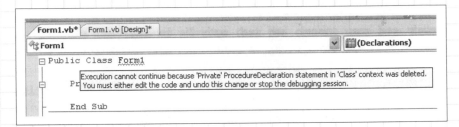

Figure 1-4. A ToolTip explaining an unsupported edit

At this point, you can either undo this change, or continue (knowing that you'll need to restart the program). If you attempt to continue execution (by pressing F5 or F8), Visual Studio asks whether you want to stop debugging or want to cancel the request and continue editing your code.

A more significant limitation of the new edit-and-continue feature is that it doesn't support ASP.NET web applications. However, Visual Basic (and C#) developers still receive *some* improvement in their web-application debugging experience. Visual Studio 2005 compiles each web page separately, rather than into a single assembly (as was the model in previous versions). As a result, when you find some misbehaving code in a web page, you can pause the debugger, edit the code, and refresh the web page by clicking Refresh in your browser. This behavior gives you an experience that's similar to edit-and-continue, but it only works on a per-page basis. Unfortunately, this feature won't help you if you're in the middle of debugging a complex routine inside a web page. In that case, you'll still need to re-request the web page after you make the change and start over.

Look Inside an Object While Debugging

Visual Studio has always made it possible for you to peer into variables while debugging your code, just by hovering over them with the mouse pointer. But there were always limitations. If the variable was an instance of an object, all you could see was the value returned by the ToString( ) method, which more often than not was simply the fully qualified name of the class itself. Moreover, you couldn't see the content of public properties and indexers. The Watch and Locals windows provided some improvement, but they weren't quite as convenient or intuitive. Visual Studio 2005 changes the picture with a new feature called *debugger DataTips*.

In Visual Studio 2005, it's even easier to take a look at the content of complex objects while debugging.

How do I do that?

To use debugger DataTips, it helps to have a custom class to work with. The code in Example 1-1 shows the declaration for two very simple classes that represent employees and departments, respectively.

Example 1-1. Two simple classes

```
Public Class Employee
    Private _ID As String
    Public ReadOnly Property ID( ) As String
        Get
            Return _ID
        End Get
    End Property

    Private _Name As String
    Public ReadOnly Property Name( ) As String
        Get
            Return _Name
        End Get
    End Property

    Public Sub New(ByVal id As String, ByVal name As String)
        _ID = id
        _Name = name
    End Sub
End Class

Public Class Department
    Private _Manager As Employee
    Public ReadOnly Property Manager( ) As Employee
        Get
            Return _Manager
```

Example 1-1. *Two simple classes (continued)*

```
        End Get
    End Property

    Private _DepartmentName As String
    Public ReadOnly Property Name() As String
        Get
            Return _DepartmentName
        End Get
    End Property

    Public Sub New(ByVal departmentName As String, ByVal manager As Employee)
        _DepartmentName = departmentName
        _Manager = manager
    End Sub
End Class
```

Now you can add some code that uses these objects. Add the following event handler to any form to create a new `Employee` and `Department` object when the form first loads.

```
Private Sub Form1_Load(ByVal sender As System.Object, _
    ByVal e As System.EventArgs) Handles MyBase.Load

    Dim Manager As New Employee("ALFKI", "John Smith")
    Dim Sales As New Department("Sales", Manager)

End Sub
```

Now place a breakpoint on the final `End Sub`, and run the application. When execution stops on the final line, hover over the `Sales` variable. An expanded ToolTip will appear that lists every private and public member of the object.

Even better, if one object references another, you can drill into the details of both objects. To try this out, click the plus sign (+) sign next to the `Manager` property to see the linked `Employee` object. Figure 1-5 shows the DataTip you'll see.

Using debugger DataTips, you can also edit simple data types on the fly. Just double click the property or variable, and edit the value. In Figure 1-5, the private variable `_Name` is currently being edited.

What about...

...working with exotic types of data? Using the .NET Framework, it's possible to create design-time classes that produce customized visualizations for specific types of data. While this topic is outside the scope of this book, you can see it at work with the three built-in visualizers for text, HTML, and XML data.

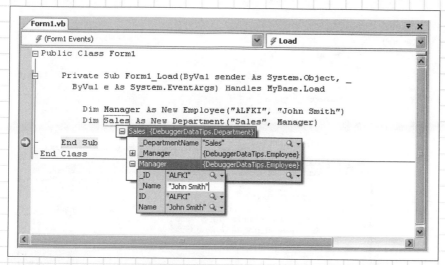

Figure 1-5. Peering into an object

For example, imagine you have a string variable that holds the content of an XML document. You can't easily see the whole document in the single-line ToolTip display. However, if you click the magnifying glass next to the content in the ToolTip, you'll see a list of all the visualizers you can use. Select XML Visualizer, and a new dialog box will appear with a formatted, color-coded, scrollable, resizable display of the full document content, as shown in Figure 1-6.

Where can I learn more?

For more information about debugger visualizers, look for the "Visualizers" index entry in the MSDN help.

Diagnose and Correct Errors on the Fly

Visual Studio does a great job of catching exceptions, but it's not always as helpful at resolving them. The new *Exception Assistant* that's hardwired into Visual Studio 2005 gives you a head start.

How do I do that?

You don't need to take any steps to activate the Exception Assistant. Instead, it springs into action as soon as your program encounters an unhandled exception.

Stumbled into a head-scratching exception? Visual Studio 2005 gives you a head start for resolving common issues with its Exception Assistant.

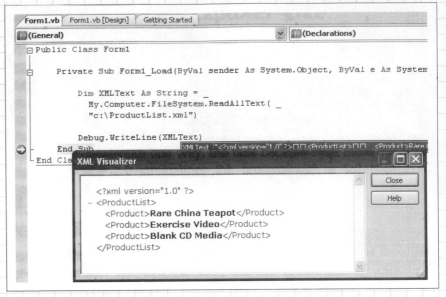

Figure 1-6. Viewing XML content while debugging

To see it in action, you need to create some faulty code. A good test is to add the following event handler to any form, which tries to open a non-existent file:

This example uses a new VB language feature—the My object. You'll learn much more about My objects in the next chapter.

```
Private Sub Form1_Load(ByVal sender As System.Object, _
    ByVal e As System.EventArgs) Handles MyBase.Load

    Dim XMLText As String = My.Computer.FileSystem.ReadAllText( _
      "c:\FileDoesNotExist")

End Sub
```

Now run the application. When the error occurs, Visual Studio switches into break mode and highlights the offending statement. The Exception Assistant then appears, with a list of possible causes for the problem. Each suggestion appears as a separate link in the pop-up window. If you click one of these links, the full MSDN help topic will appear. Figure 1-7 shows the result with the faulty file-reading code; the Exception Assistant correctly identifies the reason that the attempt to open the file failed.

If you want to see the low-level exception information, click the View Detail link at the bottom of the window. This pops up a dialog box with a PropertyGrid showing all the information of the associated exception object. This change alone is a great step forward from Visual Studio .NET 2003, where you needed to write a Catch exception handler and set a breakpoint to take a look at the underlying exception object.

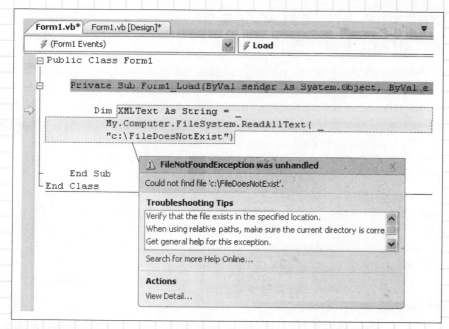

Figure 1-7. Getting help with an exception

What about...

...solving complex problems? The Exception Assistant isn't designed to help you sort through issues of any complexity. Instead, it works best at identifying the all-too-common "gotchas," such as trying to use a null reference (usually a result of forgetting to use the New keyword) and failing to convert a data type (often a result of an inadvertent type cast).

Where can I learn more?

For help in the real world, consult a colleague or one of the many .NET discussion groups. Some good choices include *http://lab.msdn.microsoft. com/vs2005/community* (for the latest on Visual Basic 2005) and—once Visual Basic 2005 enters its release phase—*http://www.windowsforms. net/Forums* (for Windows Forms questions), *http://www.asp.net/Forums* (for ASP.NET issues), and *http://discuss.develop.com/advanced-dotnet. html* (for more advanced .NET queries).

Rename All Instances of Any Program Element

Symbolic rename allows you to rename all instances of any element you declare in your program, from classes and interfaces to properties and methods, in a single step. This technique, which is decidedly not a simple text search-and-replace feature by virtue of its awareness of program syntax, solves many knotty problems found in previous releases of Visual Basic. For example, imagine you want to rename a public property named FirstName. If you use search-and-replace, you'll also inadvertently affect a text box named txtFirstName, an event handler named cmdFirstName_Click, a database field accessed through row("FirstName"), and even your code comments. With symbolic rename, the IDE takes care of renaming just what you want, and it completes all of its work in a single step.

How do I do that?

You can use symbolic rename from any code window. To understand how it works, create a form that has a single text box named TextBox1 and a button named cmdText. Finally, add the form code in Example 1-2.

Example 1-2. A simple form that uses the word "Text" heavily

```
Public Class TextTest

    Private Sub TextTest_Load(ByVal sender As System.Object, _
      ByVal e As System.EventArgs) Handles MyBase.Load
        ' Get the text from the text box.
        Dim Text As String = TextBox1.Text

        ' Convert and display the text.
        Text = ConvertText(Text)
        MessageBox.Show("Uppercase Text is: " & Text)
    End Sub

    Public Function ConvertText(ByVal Text As String) As String
        Return Text.ToUpper()
    End Function

End Class
```

This code performs a relatively mundane task: converting a user-supplied string to uppercase and displays it in a message box. What's notable is how many places it uses the word "Text." Now, consider what happens if you need to rename the local variable Text in the event handler for the

Form.Load event. Clearly, this is enough to confuse any search-and-replace algorithm. That's where symbolic rename comes in.

To use symbolic rename, simply right-click on the local Text variable, and select Rename from the context menu. In the Rename dialog box, enter the new variable name LocalText and click OK. All the appropriate instances in your code will be changed automatically without affecting other elements in your code (such as the text box, the comments, the literal text string, the form class name, the Text parameter in the ConvertText function, and so on). Here's the resulting code:

```
Public Class TextTest

    Private Sub cmdTest_Click(ByVal sender As System.Object, _
        ByVal e As System.EventArgs) Handles cmdText.Click
        ' Get the text from the text box.
        Dim LocalText As String = TextBox1.Text

        ' Convert and display the text.
        LocalText = ConvertText(LocalText)
        MessageBox.Show("Uppercase Text is: " & LocalText)
    End Sub

    Public Function ConvertText(ByVal Text As String) As String
        Return Text.ToUpper()
    End Function

End Class
```

Symbolic rename works with any property, class, or method name you want to change. Here are a few important points to keep in mind about how symbolic rename works:

- If you rename a class, all the statements that create an instance of that class are also changed.
- If you rename a method, all the statements that call that method are also changed.
- If you change a variable name that is the same as a method name, only the variable is changed (and vice versa).
- If you change a local variable name that is the same as a local variable name with different scope (for example, in another method), only the first variable is affected.

The symbolic rename feature isn't immediately impressive, but it's genuinely useful. Particularly noteworthy is the way it properly observes the scope of the item you want to rename. For example, when you rename a local variable, your changes don't spread beyond the current procedure. On the other hand, renaming a class can affect every file in your project.

Note that if you change the name of a control variable, your code will also be updated accordingly. However, there's one exception—the names of event handlers are never modified automatically. For example, if you change Button1 to Button2, all the code that interacts with Button1 will be updated, but the event handler subroutine Button1_Click will not be affected. (Remember, the name of the event handler has no effect on how it works in your application, as long as it's connected with the Handles clause.)

TIP

In Visual Studio 2005, when you rename a *.vb* file in the Solution Explorer, the name of the class in the file is also renamed, as long as the file contains a class that has the old name. For example, if you rename *Form1.vb* to *Form2.vb* and the file contains a class named Form1, that class will be renamed to Form2. Any code statements that create an instance of Form1 will also be updated, no matter where they reside in the project. However, if you've already changed the class name to something else (like MyForm), the class name won't be affected when you rename the file. In Visual Studio 2002 and 2003, the same action of renaming a form file has no effect on your code, so it's worth noting.

What about...

...support in Visual Basic 2005 for C# refactoring? Unfortunately, many of the additional refactoring features that Visual Studio provides to C# programmers don't appear in Visual Basic at all. Symbolic rename is one of the few new refactoring features that's alive and well for VB programmers in this release.

Use IntelliSense Filtering and AutoCorrect

Visual Studio 2005 makes IntelliSense more intelligent by restricting class names that aren't relevant and suggesting corrections you can apply to resolve syntax errors.

IntelliSense is one of the great conveniences of Visual Studio, and it continues to improve in Visual Studio 2005, with two new features that make it more useful: IntelliSense filtering and AutoCorrect. *IntelliSense filtering* restricts the number of options you see to those that make sense in the current context. *AutoCorrect* goes one step further by recommending ways to resolve syntax errors, rather than simply reporting them.

How do I do that?

There's no need for any extra steps when you use IntelliSense filtering—it's at work automatically. As you enter code, IntelliSense prompts you with lists of classes, properties, events, and more. In Visual Studio 2005, this list is tailored to your immediate needs, based on various contextual details. For example, if you're selecting an attribute to apply to a method, the IntelliSense list will show only classes that derive from the base `Attribute` class.

To see the new IntelliSense in action, start typing an exception-handling block. When you enter the `Catch` block, the IntelliSense list will show only classes that derive from the base `Exception` class (as shown in Figure 1-8). Select the Common or All tab at the bottom of the list, depending on whether you want to see the most commonly used classes or every possibility.

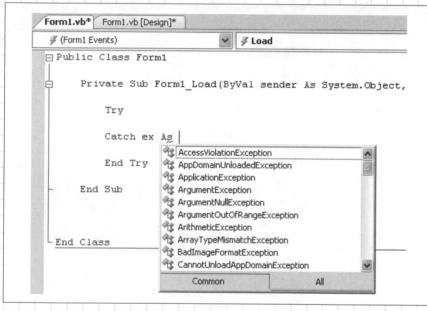

Figure 1-8. Filtering for Exception classes only

AutoCorrect is an IntelliSense improvement that targets syntax errors. Every time Visual Studio discovers a problem, it underlines the offending code in blue. You can hover over the problem to see a ToolTip with error information. With AutoCorrect, Visual Studio also adds a red error icon that, when clicked, shows a window with the suggested correction.

To see AutoCorrect in action, enter the following code (which attempts to assign a string to an integer without proper type-casting code):

```
Dim X As Integer
X = "2"
```

Assuming you have Option Strict switched on, you'll see a red error icon when you hover over this line. Click the red error icon. The AutoCorrect window that appears shows your code in blue, code to be added in red, and code to be removed crossed out with a solid line. Figure 1-9 shows the correction offered for this code snippet.

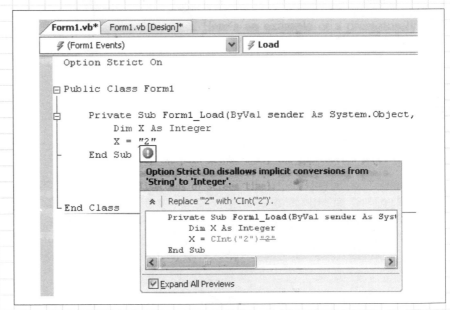

Figure 1-9. Intellisense AutoCorrect in action

Other problems that AutoCorrect can resolve include class names that aren't fully qualified, misspelled keywords, and missing lines in a block structure. In some cases, it will even show more than one possible correction.

What about...

...doing more? There's still a lot of additional intelligence that Intelli-Sense could provide, but doesn't. For example, when assigning a property from a class to a string variable, why not show only those properties that return string data types? Or when applying an attribute to a method, why not show attribute classes that can be applied only to methods? As computer processors become faster and have more and more idle cycles, expect to see new levels of artificial intelligence appearing in your IDE.

Edit Control Properties in Place

The Properties window in Visual Studio makes control editing easy, but not always fast. For example, imagine you want to tweak all the text on a form. In previous versions of Visual Studio, the only option was to select each control in turn and modify the Text property in the Properties window one at a time. Although this approach isn't necessarily awkward, it certainly isn't as easy as it could be. In Visual Studio 2005, you can adjust a single property for a series of controls directly on the form.

When you need to update a single property for a number of different controls, in-place property editing makes it easy.

How do I do that?

To try in-place property editing, create a new form and add an assortment of controls. (The actual controls you use don't really matter, but you should probably include some text boxes, buttons, and labels.) Then, select View → Property Editing View. Finally, choose the property you want to change from the drop-down list above the form design surface. By default, the Name property is selected, but Figure 1-10 shows an example with the Text property.

In property-editing view, an edit box appears over every control on the form with the contents of the selected property. You can edit the value of that property by simply clicking on the edit box and entering the new value. You can also jump from one control to the next by pressing the Tab key.

When you are finished with your work, again select View → Property Editing View, or click the Exit Mode link next to the property drop-down list.

What about...

...editing tab order? Visual Studio allows you to easily edit tab order by clicking controls in the order that you want users to be able to navigate through them. Select a form with at least one control, and choose

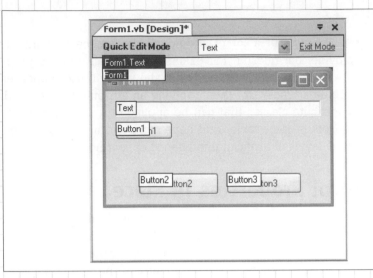

Figure 1-10. Editing a single property for multiple controls

View → Tab Order to activate this mode, which works the same as it did in Visual Studio 2003.

Call Methods at Design Time

Need to try out a freshly written code routine? Visual Studio 2005 lets you run it without starting your project.

Although Visual Studio .NET 2003 included the Immediate window, you couldn't use it to execute code at design time. Longtime VB coders missed this feature, which was a casualty of the lack of a background compiler. In Visual Studio 2005, this feature returns along with the return of a background compiler.

How do I do that?

You can use the Immediate window to evaluate simple expressions, and even to run subroutines in your code. To try out this technique, add the following shared method to a class:

```
Public Shared Function AddNumbers(ByVal A As Integer, _
   ByVal B As Integer) As Integer

    Return A + B

End Sub
```

By making this a shared method, you ensure that it's available even without creating an instance of the class. Now, you can call it easily in the design environment.

By default, the Immediate window isn't shown at design time. To show it, select Debug → Windows → Command from the menu. Statements inside the Immediate window usually start with ? (a shorthand for Print, which instructs Visual Studio to display the result). You can enter the rest of the statement like any other line of code, with the benefit of IntelliSense. Figure 1-11 shows an example in which the Command window is used to run the shared method just shown.

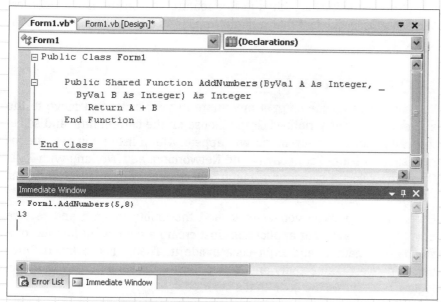

Figure 1-11. Executing code at design time

When you execute a statement like the one shown in Figure 1-11, there will be a short pause while the background compiler works (and you'll see the message "Build started" in the status bar). Then the result will appear.

The expression evaluation in the beta release of Visual Studio 2005 is a little quirky. Some evaluations won't work, and will simply launch your application without returning a result. Look for this to improve in future builds.

Where can I learn more?

The MSDN help includes more information about supported expression types at the index entry "expressions → about expressions."

Insert Boilerplate Code Using Snippets

Some code is common and generic enough that programmers everywhere write it again and again each day. Even though developers have the help of online documentation, samples, and books like the one you're reading, useful code never seems to be at your fingertips when you need it. Visual Studio 2005 includes a new code snippet feature that allows you to insert commonly used code and quickly adapt it to suit your purposes. Early beta builds of Visual Studio 2005 included a tool for building your own snippets. Although this feature isn't in the latest releases, Microsoft has suggested that it might appear as a separate add-on tool at a later time.

How do I do that?

You can insert a code snippet anywhere in your code. Just move to the appropriate location, right-click the mouse on the current line, and select Insert Snippet. A pop-up menu will appear with a list of snippet categories, such as Math, Connectivity and Networking, and Working with XML. Once you select a category, a menu will appear with a list of snippets. Once you select a snippet, the code will be inserted.

For example, suppose you want to add the ability to send and receive email messages to your application. Just create a new event handler or a standalone method, and right-click inside it. Then, choose Insert Snippet, and select Connectivity and Networking → Create an Email Message. Figure 1-12 shows the code that's inserted.

The shaded portions of code are literal values (like file paths and control references) that you need to customize to adapt the code to your needs. By pressing the Tab key, you can move from one shaded region to the next. Additionally, if you hover over a shaded region, a ToolTip will appear with a description of what content you need to insert.

What about...

...getting more snippets? The basic set of code snippets included with Visual Studio .NET is fairly modest. It includes some truly useful snippets (e.g., "Find a Node in XML Data") and some absurdly trivial ones (e.g., "Add a Comment to Your Code"). However, many useful topics, such as encryption, aren't dealt with at all.

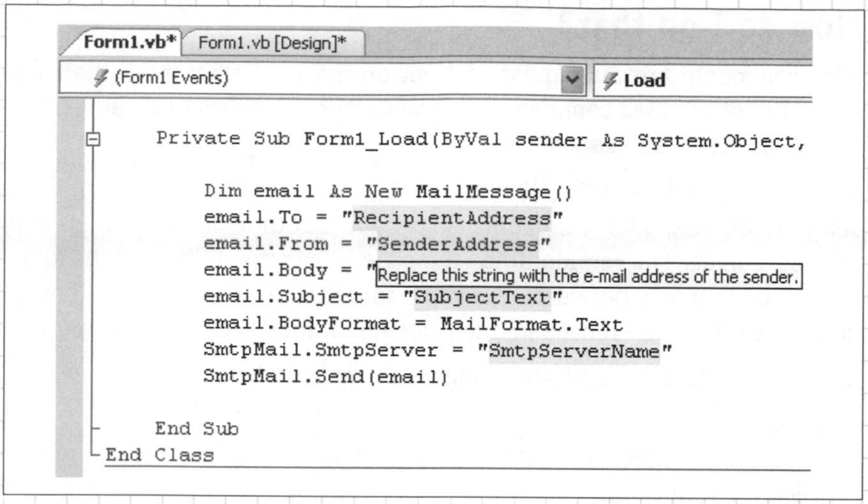

```
Form1.vb*   Form1.vb [Design]*

 (Form1 Events)                              Load

       Private Sub Form1_Load(ByVal sender As System.Object,

             Dim email As New MailMessage()
             email.To = "RecipientAddress"
             email.From = "SenderAddress"
             email.Body = "Replace this string with the e-mail address of the sender.
             email.Subject = "SubjectText"
             email.BodyFormat = MailFormat.Text
             SmtpMail.SmtpServer = "SmtpServerName"
             SmtpMail.Send(email)


       End Sub
  End Class
```

Figure 1-12. Customizing a code snippet

Where can I learn more?

Thanks to the pluggable nature of snippets, you may soon be able to add more snippets to your collection from community web sites, coworkers, third-party software developers, and even sample code from a book like this.

Create XML Documentation for Your Code

Properly commenting and documenting code takes time. Unfortunately, there's no easy way to leverage the descriptive comments you place in your code when it comes time to produce more detailed API references and documentation. Instead, you typically must create these documents from scratch.

Use XML comments to effortlessly create detailed code references, a feature C# programmers have had since .NET 1.0.

Visual Studio 2005 changes all this by introducing a feature that's been taken for granted by C# programmers since .NET 1.0—XML comments. With XML comments, you comment your code using a predefined format. Then, you can use other tools to extract these comments and use them to build other documents. These documents can range from help documentation to specialized code reports (for example, a list of unresolved issues, legacy code, or code review dates).

How do I do that?

XML comments are distinguished from ordinary comments by their format. First of all, XML comments start with three apostrophes (rather than just one). Here's an example:

```
''' <summary>This is the summary.</summary>
```

As you can see, XML comments also have another characteristic—they use tag names. The tag identifies the type of comment. These tags allow you to distinguish between summary information, information about a specific method, references to other documentation sections, and so on.

The most commonly used XML comment tags include:

`<summary>`
> Describes a class or another type. This is the highest-level information for your code.

`<remarks>`
> Allows you to supplement the summary information. This tag is most commonly used to give a high-level description of each type member (e.g., individual methods and properties).

`<param>`
> Describes the parameters accepted by a method. Add one `<param>` tag for each parameter.

`<returns>`
> Describes the return value of a method.

`<exception>`
> Allows you to specify which exceptions a class can throw.

`<example>`
> Lets you specify an example of how to use a method or other member.

`<see>`
> Allows you to create a link to another documentation element.

In addition, there are tags that are usually used just to format or structure blocks of text. You use these tags inside the other tags. They include:

`<para>`
> Lets you add structure to a tag (such as a `<remarks>` tag) by separating its content into paragraphs.

`<list>`
> Starts a bulleted list. You must tag each individual list item with the `<item>` tag.

`<c>`

   Indicates that text within a description should be marked as code. Use the `<code>` tag to indicate multiple lines as code.

`<code>`

   Allows you to embed multiple lines of code, as in an example of usage. For example, you would commonly put a `<code>` tag inside an `<example>` tag.

In addition, you can define custom tags that you can then use for your own purposes.

Visual Studio helps you out by automatically adding some XML tags—but only when you want them. For example, consider the code routine shown here, which tests if two files are exactly the same using a hash code. In order to use this sample as written, you need to import the `System.IO` and `System.Security.Cryptography` namespaces:

```
Public Function TestIfTwoFilesMatch(ByVal fileA As String, _
   ByVal fileB As String) As Boolean

     ' Create the hashing object.
     Dim Hash As HashAlgorithm = HashAlgorithm.Create()

     ' Calculate the hash for the first file.
     Dim fsA As New FileStream(fileA, FileMode.Open)
     Dim HashA() As Byte = Hash.ComputeHash(fsA)
     fsA.Close()

     ' Calculate the hash for the second file.
     Dim fsB As New FileStream(fileB, FileMode.Open)
     Dim HashB() As Byte = Hash.ComputeHash(fsB)
     fsB.Close()

     ' Compare the hashes.
     Return (Convert.ToString(HashA) = Convert.ToString(HashB))

   End Function
```

Now, position your cursor just before the function declaration, and insert three apostrophes. Visual Studio will automatically add a skeleton set of XML tags, as shown here:

```
''' <summary>
'''
''' </summary>
''' <param name="fileA"></param>
''' <param name="fileB"></param>
''' <returns></returns>
''' <remarks></remarks>
Public Function TestIfTwoFilesMatch(ByVal fileA As String, _
   ByVal fileB As String) As Boolean
   ...
```

Now, you simply need to fill in some sample content within the tags:

```
''' <summary>
''' This function tests whether two files
''' contain the exact same content.
''' </summary>
''' <param name="fileA">Contains the full path to the first file.</param>
''' <param name="fileB">Contains the full path to the second file.</param>
''' <returns>True if the files match, false if they don't.</returns>
''' <remarks>
''' The implementation of this method uses cryptographic classes
''' to compute a hash value. This may not be the most performant
''' approach, but it is sensitive to the minutest differences,
''' and can't be practically fooled.
''' </remarks>
```

To make a more realistic example, put the TestIfTwoFilesMatch() method into a class, and add XML documentation tags to the class declaration. Here's a typical example, which uses cross-references that point to the available methods in a list:

```
''' <summary>
''' This class contains methods for comparing files.
''' </summary>
''' <remarks>
'''       <para>This class is stateless. However, it's not safe to use
''' it if the file in question may already be help open by another
''' process.</para>
'''       <para>The methods in this class include:</para>
'''       <list type="bullet">
'''           <item><see cref="FileComparer.TestIfTwoFilesMatch"/>
''' TestifTwoFilesMatch() uses hash codes to compare two files.</item>
'''       </list>
''' </remarks>
Public Class FileComparer
    ...
End Class
```

Unlike other comments, XML comments are added to the metadata of your compiled assembly. They'll automatically appear in the Object Browser when you examine a type.

Additionally, once you've created your XML tags, you can export them to an XML document. Just double-click the My Project node in the Solution Explorer, choose the Compile tab, and ensure that the "Generate XML documentation file" option is selected. The XML documentation is automatically saved into an XML file with the same name as your project and the extension .xml (in the bin directory).

The generated document will include all of the XML comments, with none of the code. You can then feed this document into some other type of application. For example, you might create your own custom application to scan XML comment files and build specialized reports.

What about...

...creating help documentation? Although Visual Studio 2005 doesn't include any tools of its own, the open source NDoc application provides a solution (*http://ndoc.sourceforge.net*). NDoc scans code and uses the XML documentation tags it finds to build MSDN-style web pages or Visual Studio–style (MS Help 2.0) documentation. At the time of this writing, NDoc doesn't yet support .NET 2.0.

Where can I learn more?

The MSDN reference has much more information about XML comments, including guidelines for how to document types and how to use the standard set of tags. Look for the "XML documentation" index entry.

CHAPTER 2

The Visual Basic Language

When Visual Basic .NET first appeared, loyal VB developers were shocked to find dramatic changes in their favorite language. Suddenly, common tasks such as instantiating an object and declaring a structure required new syntax, and even basic data types like the array had been transformed into something new. Fortunately, Visual Basic 2005 doesn't have the same shocks in store. The language changes in the latest version of VB are refinements that simplify life *without* making any existing code obsolete. Many of these changes are language features imported from C# (e.g., operator overloading), while others are completely new ingredients that have been built into the latest version of the common language runtime (e.g., generics). In this chapter, you'll learn about all the most useful changes to the VB language.

Use the My Objects to Program Common Tasks

The new My objects provide easy access to various features that developers often need but don't necessarily know where to find in the sprawling .NET class library. Essentially, the My objects offer one-stop shopping, with access to everything from the Windows registry to the current network connection. Best of all, the My object hierarchy is organized according to use and is easy to navigate using Visual Studio IntelliSense.

In this chapter:

- Use the My Objects to Program Common Tasks
- Get Application Information
- Use Strongly Typed Resources
- Use Strongly Typed Configuration Settings
- Build Typesafe Generic Classes
- Make Simple Data Types Nullable
- Use Operators with Custom Objects
- Split a Class into Multiple Files
- Extend the My Namespace
- Skip to the Next Iteration of a Loop
- Dispose of Objects Automatically

How do I do that?

There are seven first-level My objects. Out of these, three core objects centralize functionality from the .NET Framework and provide computer information. These include:

My.Computer

> This object provides information about the current computer, including its network connection, the mouse and keyboard state, the printer and screen, and the clock. You can also use this object as a jumping-off point to play a sound, find a file, access the registry, or use the Windows clipboard.

My.Application

> This object provides information about the current application and its context, including the assembly and its version, the folder where the application is running, the culture, and the command-line arguments that were used to start the application. You can also use this object to log an application event.

My.User

> This object provides information about the current user. You can use this object to check the user's Windows account and test what groups the user is a member of.

Along with these three objects, there are another two objects that provide *default instances*. Default instances are objects that .NET creates automatically for certain types of classes defined in your application. They include:

My.Forms

> This object provides a default instance of each Windows form in your application. You can use this object to communicate between forms without needing to track form references in another class.

My.WebServices

> This object provides a default proxy-class instance for every web service. For example, if your project uses two web references, you can access a ready-made proxy class for each one through this object.

Finally, there are two other My objects that provide easy access to the configuration settings and resources:

My.Settings

This object allows you to retrieve custom settings from your application's XML configuration file.

My.Resources

This object allows you to retrieve *resources*—blocks of binary or text data that are compiled into your application assembly. Resources are typically used to store localized strings, images, and audio files.

WARNING

Note that the My objects are influenced by the project type. For example, when creating a web or console application, you won't be able to use My.Forms.

Some of the My classes are defined in the Microsoft.VisualBasic.MyServices namespace, while others, such as the classes used for the My.Settings and My.Resources objects, are created dynamically by Visual Studio 2005 when you modify application settings and add resources to the current project.

To try out the My object, you can use Visual Studio IntelliSense. Just type My, followed by a period, and take a look at the available objects, as shown in Figure 2-1. You can choose one and press the period again to step down another level.

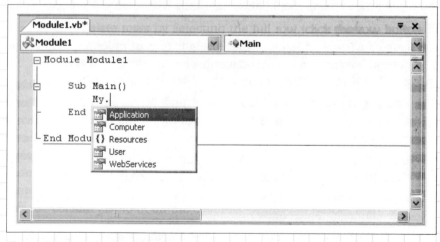

Figure 2-1. Browsing the My objects

To try a simple example that displays some basic information using the My object, create a new console project. Then, add this code to the Main( ) routine:

```
Console.WriteLine(My.Computer.Name)
Console.WriteLine(My.Computer.Clock.LocalTime)
Console.WriteLine(My.Application.CurrentDirectory)
Console.WriteLine(My.User.Identity.Name)
```

When you run this code, you'll see some output in the console window, which shows the computer name, current time, application directory, and user:

```
SALESSERVER
2005-10-1 8:08:52 PM
C:\Code\VBNotebook\1.07\MyTest\bin
MATTHEW
```

WARNING

The My object also has a "dark side." Use of the My object makes it more difficult to share your solution with non-VB developers, because other languages, such as C#, don't have the same feature.

Where can I learn more?

You can learn more about the My object and see examples by looking up the "My Object" index entry in the MSDN Help. You can also learn more by examining some of this book's other labs that use the My object. Some examples include:

- Using My.Application to retrieve details of your program, such as the current version and the command-line parameters used to start it (see the "Get Application Information" lab in this chapter).

- Using My.Resources to load images and other resources from the application assembly (see the "Use Strongly Typed Resources" lab in this chapter).

- Using My.Settings to retrieve application and user settings (see the "Use Strongly Typed Configuration Settings" lab in this chapter).

- Using My.Forms to interact between application windows (see the "Communicate Between Forms" lab in Chapter 3).

- Using My.Computer to perform file manipulation and network tasks in Chapters 5 and 6.

- Using My.User to authenticate the current user (see the "Test Group Membership of the Current User" lab in Chapter 6).

Get Application Information

The My.Application object provides a wealth of information right at your fingertips. Getting this information is as easy as retrieving a property.

How do I do that?

The information in the My.Application object comes in handy in a variety of situations. Here are two examples:

- You want to get the exact version number. This could be useful if you want to build a dynamic About box, or check with a web service to make sure you have the latest version of an assembly.

- You want to record some diagnostic details. This becomes important if a problem is occurring at a client site and you need to log some general information about the application that's running.

To create a straightforward example, you can use the code in Example 2-1 in a console application. It retrieves all of these details and displays a complete report in a console window.

Example 2-1. Retrieving information from My.Application

```
' Find out what parameters were used to start the application.
Console.Write("Command line parameters: ")
For Each Arg As String In My.Application.CommandLineArgs
    Console.Write(Arg & " ")
Next
Console.WriteLine()
Console.WriteLine()

' Find out some information about the assembly where this code is located.
' This information comes from metadata (attributes in your code).
Console.WriteLine("Company: " & My.Application.Info.CompanyName)
Console.WriteLine("Description: " & My.Application.Info.Description)
Console.WriteLine("Located in: " & My.Application.Info.DirectoryPath)
Console.WriteLine("Copyright: " & My.Application.Info.Copyright)
Console.WriteLine("Trademark: " & My.Application.Info.Trademark)
Console.WriteLine("Name: " & My.Application.Info.AssemblyName)
Console.WriteLine("Product: " & My.Application.Info.ProductName)
Console.WriteLine("Title: " & My.Application.Info.Title)
Console.WriteLine("Version: " & My.Application.Info.Version.ToString())
Console.WriteLine()
```

Using the My.Application object, you can get information about the current version of your application, where it's located, and what parameters were used to start it.

Before you test this code, it makes sense to set up your environment to ensure that you will see meaningful data. For example, you might want to tell Visual Studio to supply some command-line parameters when it launches the application. To do this, double-click the My Project icon in the Solution Explorer. Then, choose the Debug tab and look for the "Command line parameters" text box. For example, you could add three parameters by specifying the command line /a /b /c.

If you want to set information such as the assembly author, product, version, and so on, you need to add special attributes to the *AssemblyInfo.vb* file, which isn't shown in the Solution Explorer. To access it, you need to select Solution → Show All Files. You'll find the *AssemblyInfo.vb* file under the My Projects node. Here's a typical set of tags that you might enter:

```
<Assembly: AssemblyVersion("1.0.0.0")>
<Assembly: AssemblyCompany("Prosetech")>
<Assembly: AssemblyDescription("Utility that tests My.Application")>
<Assembly: AssemblyCopyright("(C) Matthew MacDonald")>
<Assembly: AssemblyTrademark("(R) Prosetech")>
<Assembly: AssemblyTitle("Test App")>
<Assembly: AssemblyProduct("Test App")>
```

New in VB 2005 is the ability to add application information in a special dialog box. To use this feature, double-click the My Project item in the Solution Explorer, select the Assembly tab, and click the Assembly Information button.

All of this information is embedded in your compiled assembly as metadata.

Now you can run the test application. Here's an example of the output you'll see:

```
Command line parameters: /a /b /c


Company: Prosetech
Description: Utility that tests My.Application
Located in: C:\Code\VBNotebook\1.08\ApplicationInfo\bin
Copyright: (C) Matthew MacDonald
Trademark: (R) Prosetech
Name: ApplicationInfo.exe
Product: Test App
Title: Test App
Version: 1.0.0.0
```

What about...

...getting more detailed diagnostic information? The `My.Computer.Info` object also provides a dash of diagnostic details with two useful properties. `LoadedAssemblies` provides a collection with all the assemblies that are currently loaded (and available to your application). You can also examine their version and publisher information. `StackTrace` provides a snapshot of the current stack, which reflects where you are in your code. For example, if your `Main( )` method calls a method named `A( )` that then calls method `B( )`, you'll see three of your methods on the stack—`B( )`, `A( )`, and `Main( )`—in reverse order.

Here's the code you can add to start looking at this information:

```
Console.WriteLine("Currently loaded assemblies")
For Each Assm As System.Reflection.Assembly In _
  My.Application.Info.LoadedAssemblies
    Console.WriteLine(Assm.GetName( ).Name)
Next
Console.WriteLine( )

Console.WriteLine("Current stack trace: " & My.Application.Info.StackTrace)
Console.WriteLine( )
```

Use Strongly Typed Resources

In addition to code, .NET assemblies can also contain *resources*—embedded binary data such as images and hardcoded strings. Even though .NET has supported a system of resources since Version 1.0, Visual Studio hasn't included integrated design-time support. As a result, developers who need to store image data usually add it to a control that supports it at design time, such as a `PictureBox` or `ImageList`. These controls insert the picture data into the application resource file automatically.

In Visual Studio 2005, it's dramatically easier to add information to the resources file and update it afterward. Even better, you can access this information in a strongly typed fashion from anywhere in your code.

Strongly typed resources let you embed static data such as images into your compiled assemblies, and access it easily in your code.

How do I do that?

In order to try using a strongly typed resource of an image in this lab, you need to create a new Windows application before continuing.

To add a resource, start by double-clicking the My Project node in the Solution Explorer. This opens up the application designer, where you can configure a host of application-related settings. Next, click the Resources tab. In the Categories drop-down listbox, select the type of resources you want to see (strings, images, audio, and so on). The string view shows a grid of settings. The image view is a little different—by default, it shows a thumbnail of each picture.

To add a new picture, select the Images category from the drop-down list and then select Add → Existing File from the toolbar. Browse to an image file, select it, and click OK. If you don't have an image file handy, try using one from the *Windows* directory, such as *winnt256.bmp* (which is included with most versions of Windows).

By default, the resource name has the same name as the file, but you can rename it after adding it. In this example, rename the image to EmbeddedGraphic (as shown in Figure 2-2).

Figure 2-2. Adding a picture as a strongly typed resource

The resources class is added in the My Project directory and is given the name Resources.Designer. vb. To see it, you need to choose Project → Show All Files. Of course, you should never change this file by hand

Using a resource is easy. All resources are compiled dynamically into a strongly typed resource class, which you can access through My. Resources. To try out this resource, add a PictureBox control to your Windows form (and keep the default name PictureBox1). Then, add the following code to show the image when the form loads:

```
Private Sub Form1_Load(ByVal sender As System.Object, _
    ByVal e As System.EventArgs) Handles MyBase.Load

    PictureBox1.Image = My.Resources.EmbeddedGraphic

End Sub
```

If you run the code, you'll see the image appear on the form. To make sure the image is being extracted from the assembly, try compiling the application and then deleting the image file (the code will still work seamlessly).

When you add a resource in this way, Visual Studio copies the resource to the *Resources* subdirectory of your application. You can see this directory, along with all the resources it contains, in the Solution Explorer. When you compile your application, all the resources are embedded in the assembly. However, there's a distinct advantage to maintaining them in a separate directory. This way, you can easily update a resource by replacing the file and recompiling the application. You don't need to modify any code. This is a tremendous benefit if you need to update a number of images or other resources at once.

You can also attach a resource to various controls using the Properties window. For example, when you click the ellipsis (...) in the Properties window next to the Image property for the PictureBox control, a designer appears that lists all the pictures that are available in the application's resources.

Another advantage of resources is that you can use the same images in multiple controls on multiple different forms, without needing to add more than one copy of the same file.

What about...

...the ImageList? If you're a Windows developer, you're probably familiar with the ImageList control, which groups together multiple images (usually small bitmaps) for use in other controls, such as menus, toolbars, trees, and lists. The ImageList doesn't use typed resources. Instead, it uses a custom serialization scheme. You'll find that although the ImageList provides design-time support and programmatic access to the images it contains, this access isn't strongly typed.

Use Strongly Typed Configuration Settings

Use error-proof configuration settings by the application designer.

Applications commonly need configuration settings to nail down details like file locations, database connection strings, and user preferences. Rather than hardcoding these settings (or inventing your own mechanism to store them), .NET lets you add them to an application-specific configuration file. This allows you to adjust values on a whim by editing a text file without recompiling your application.

In Visual Studio 2005, configuration settings are even easier to use. That's because they're automatically compiled into a custom class that provides strongly typed access to them. That means you can retrieve settings using properties, with the help of IntelliSense, instead of relying on string-based lookups. Even better, .NET enhances this model with the ability to use updatable, user-specific settings to track preferences and other information. You'll see both of these techniques at work in this lab.

How do I do that?

Every custom configuration setting is defined with a unique string name. In previous versions of .NET, you could retrieve the value of a configuration setting by looking up the value by its string name in a collection. However, if you use the wrong name, you wouldn't realize your error until you run the code and it fails with a runtime exception.

In Visual Studio 2005, the story is much improved. To add a new configuration setting, double-click the My Project node in the Solution Explorer. This opens up the application designer where you can configure a host of application-related settings. Next, click the Settings tab, which shows a list of custom configuration settings where you can define new settings and their values.

In a web application, configuration settings are placed in the web.config file. In other applications, application settings are recorded to a configuration file that takes the name of the application, plus the extension .config, as in MyApp.exe.config.

To add a custom configuration setting to your application, enter a new setting name at the bottom of the list. Then specify the data type, scope, and the actual content of the setting. For example, to add a setting with a file path, you might use the name UserDataFilePath, the type String, the scope Application (you'll learn more about this shortly), and the value c:\MyFiles. Figure 2-3 shows this setting.

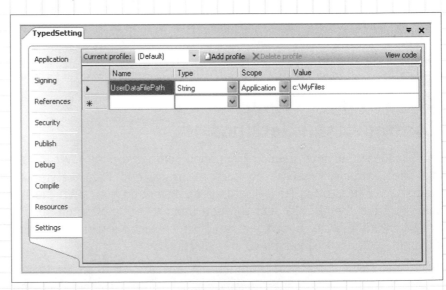

Figure 2-3. Defining a strongly typed application setting

When you add the setting, Visual Studio .NET inserts the following information into the application configuration file:

```
<configuration>
  <!-- Other settings are defined here. -->
  <applicationSettings>
    <WindowsApplication1.MySettings>
      <setting name="UserDataFilePath" serializeAs="String">
        <value>c:\MyFiles</value>
      </setting>
    </WindowsApplication1.MySettings>
  </applicationSettings>
</configuration>
```

At the same time behind the scenes, Visual Studio compiles a class that includes information about your custom configuration setting. Then, you can access the setting by name anywhere in your code through the My.Settings object. For example, here's code that retrieves the setting named UserDataFilePath:

```
Dim path As String
path = My.Settings.UserDataFilePath
```

In .NET 2.0, configuration settings don't need to be strings. You can also use other serializable data types, including integers, decimals, dates, and times (just choose the appropriate data type from the Types drop-down list). These data types are serialized to text in the configuration file, but you can retrieve them through My.Settings as their native data type, with no parsing required!

The application settings class is added in the My Project directory and is named Settings.Designer. vb. To see it, select Project → Show All Files.

What about...

...updating settings? The UserDataFilePath example uses an *application-scoped* setting, which can be read at runtime but can't be modified. If you need to change an application-scoped setting, you have to modify the configuration file by hand (or use the settings list in Visual Studio).

Your other choice is to create *user-scoped* settings. To do this, just choose User from the Scope drop-down list in the settings list. With a user-scoped setting, the value you set in Visual Studio is stored as the default in the configuration file in the application directory. However, when you change these settings, a new *user.config* file is created for the current user and saved in a user-specific directory (with a name in the form *c:\Documents and Settings\[UserName]\Local Settings\Application Data\[ApplicationName]\[UniqueDirectory]*).

The only trick pertaining to user-specific settings is that you *must* call My.Settings.Save( ) to store your changes. Otherwise, changes will only persist until the application is closed. Typically, you'll call My.Settings. Save( ) when your application ends.

To try out a user-scoped setting, change the scope of the UserDataFilePath setting from Application to User. Then, create a form that has a text box (named txtFilePath) and two buttons, one for retrieving the user data (cmdRefresh) and one for changing it (cmdUpdate). Here are the event handlers you'll use:

```
Private Sub cmdRefresh_Click(ByVal sender As System.Object, _
  ByVal e As System.EventArgs) Handles cmdRefresh.Click
    txtFilePath.Text = My.Settings.UserDataFilePath
End Sub

Private Sub cmdUpdate_Click(ByVal sender As System.Object, _
  ByVal e As System.EventArgs) Handles cmdUpdate.Click
    My.Settings.UserDataFilePath = txtFilePath.Text
End Sub
```

Finally, to make sure your changes are there the next time you run the application, tell .NET to create or update the *user.config* file when the form closes with this code:

```
Private Sub Form1_FormClosed(ByVal sender As Object, _
  ByVal e As System.Windows.Forms.FormClosedEventArgs) _
  Handles Me.FormClosed
    My.Settings.Save( )
End Sub
```

This rounds out a simple test form. You can run this application and try alternately retrieving the current setting and storing a new one. If you're interested, you can then track down the *user.config* file that has the changed settings for the current user.

Build Typesafe Generic Classes

Need to create a class that's flexible enough to work with any type of object, but able to restrict the objects it accepts in any given instance? With generics, VB has the perfect solution.

Programmers often face a difficult choice. On one hand, it's keenly important to build solutions that are as generic as possible, so that they can be reused in different scenarios. For example, why build a CustomerCollection class that accepts only objects of type Customer when you can build a generic Collection class that can be configured to accept objects of any type? On the other hand, performance and type safety considerations can make a generic solution less desirable. If you use a generic .NET Collection class to store Customer objects, for example, how can you be sure that someone won't accidentally insert another type of object into the collection, causing an insidious problem later on?

Visual Basic 2005 and .NET 2.0 provide a solution called *generics*. Generics are classes that are *parameterized by type*. In other words, generics allow you to create a class template that supports any type. When you instantiate that class, you specify the type you want to use, and from that point on, your object is "locked in" to the type you chose.

How do I do that?

An example of where the use of generics makes great sense is the System.Collections.ArrayList class. ArrayList is an all-purpose, dynamically self-sizing collection. It can hold ordinary .NET objects or your own custom objects. In order to support this, ArrayList treats everything as the base Object type.

The problem is that there's no way to impose any restrictions on how ArrayList works. For example, if you want to use ArrayList to store a collection of Customer objects, you have no way to be sure that a faulty piece of code won't accidentally insert strings, integers, or some other type of object, causing future headaches. For this reason, developers often create their own strongly typed collection classes—in fact, the .NET class library is filled with dozens of them.

Generics can solve this problem. For example, using generics you can declare a class that works with any type using the Of keyword:

```
Public Class GenericList(Of ItemType)
    ' (Code goes here)
End Class
```

In this case, you are creating a new class named GenericList that can work with any type of object. However, the client needs to specify what type should be used. In your class code, you refer to that type as ItemType. Of course, ItemType isn't really a type—it's just a placeholder for the type that you'll choose when you instantiate a GenericList object.

Example 2-2 shows the complete code for a simple typesafe ArrayList.

Example 2-2. A typesafe collection using generics

```
Public Class GenericList(Of ItemType)
    Inherits CollectionBase

    Public Function Add(ByVal value As ItemType) As Integer
        Return List.Add(value)
    End Function

    Public Sub Remove(ByVal value As ItemType)
        List.Remove(value)
    End Sub
```

Example 2-2. *A typesafe collection using generics (continued)*

```
    Public ReadOnly Property Item(ByVal index As Integer) As ItemType
        Get
            ' The appropriate item is retrieved from the List object and
            ' explicitly cast to the appropriate type, and then returned.
            Return CType(List.Item(index), ItemType)
        End Get
    End Property
End Class
```

The GenericList class wraps an ordinary ArrayList, which is provided through the List property of the CollectionBase class it inherits from. However, the GenericList class works differently than an ArrayList by providing strongly typed Add() and Remove() methods, which use the ItemType placeholder.

Here's an example of how you might use the GenericList class to create an ArrayList collection that only supports strings:

```
    ' Create the GenericList instance, and choose a type (in this case, string).
    Dim List As New GenericList(Of String)

    ' Add two strings.
    List.Add("blue")
    List.Add("green")

    ' The next statement will fail because it has the wrong type.
    ' There is no automatic way to convert a GUID to a string.
    ' In fact, this line won't ever run, because the compiler
    ' notices the problem and refuses to build the application.
    List.Add(Guid.NewGuid())
```

There's no limit to how many ways you can parameterize a class. In the GenericList example, there's only one type parameter. However, you could easily create a class that works with two or three types of objects, and allows you to make all of these types generic. To use this approach, just separate each parameter type with a comma (between the brackets at the beginning of a class).

For example, consider the following GenericHashTable class, which allows you to define the type of the items the collection will store (ItemType), as well as the type of the keys you will use to index those items (KeyType):

```
    Public Class GenericHashTable(Of ItemType, KeyType)
        Inherits DictionaryBase
        ' (Code goes here.)
    End Class
```

Another important feature in generics is the ability to apply *constraints* to parameters. Constraints restrict the types allowed for a given generic class. For example, suppose you want to create a class that supports only types that implement a particular interface. To do so, first declare the type or types the class accepts and then use the As keyword to specify the base class that the type must derive from, or the interface that the type must implement.

Here's an example that restricts the items stored in a GenericList to serializable items. This feature would be useful if, for example, you wanted to add a method to the GenericList that required serialization, such as a method that writes all the items in the list to a stream:

```
Public Class SerializableList(Of ItemType As ISerializable)
    Inherits CollectionBase
    ' (Code goes here.)
End Class
```

Similarly, here's a collection that can contain any type of object, provided it's derived from the System.Windows.Forms.Control class. The end result is a collection that's limited to controls, like the one exposed by the Forms.Controls property on a window:

```
Public Class ControlCollection(Of ItemType As Control)
    Inherits CollectionBase
    ' (Code goes here.)
End Class
```

Sometimes, your generic class might need the ability to create the parameter class. For example, the GenericList example might need the ability to create an instance of the item you want to store in the collection. In this case, you need to use the New constraint. The New constraint allows only parameter types that have a public zero-argument constructor, and aren't marked MustInherit. This ensures that your code can create instances of the parameter type. Here's a collection that imposes the New constraint:

```
Public Class GenericList(Of ItemType As New)
    Inherits CollectionBase
    ' (Code goes here.)
End Class
```

It's also worth noting that you can define as many constraints as you want, as long as you group the list of constraints in curly braces, as shown here:

```
Public Class GenericList(Of ItemType As {ISerializable, New})
    Inherits CollectionBase
    ' (Code goes here.)
End Class
```

Constraints are enforced by the compiler, so if you violate a constraint rule when using a generic class, you won't be able to compile your application.

What about...

...using generics with other code structures? Generics don't just work with classes. They can also be used in structures, interfaces, delegates, and even methods. For more information, look for the index entry "generics" in the MSDN Help. For more in-depth examples of advanced generic techniques, you can refer to a Microsoft whitepaper at *http://www.msdn. net/library/en-us/dnvs05/html/vb2005_generics.asp*.

Incidentally, the .NET Framework designers are well aware of the usefulness of generic collections, and they've already created several for you to use out of the box. You'll find them in the new Systems.Collections. Generic namespace. They include:

- List (a basic collection like the GenericList example)
- Dictionary (a name-value collection that indexes each item with a key)
- LinkedList (a linked list, where each item points to the next item in the chain)
- Queue (a first-in-first-out collection)
- Stack (a last-in-first-out collection)
- SortedList (a name-value collection that's kept in perpetually sorted order)

Most of these types duplicate one of the types in the System.Collections namespace. The old collections remain for backward compatibility.

Make Simple Data Types Nullable

With the new support for generics that's found in the .NET Framework, a number of new features become possible. One of these features—generic strongly typed collections—was demonstrated in the previous lab, "Build Typesafe Generic Classes." Now you'll see another way that generics can solve common problems, this time by using the new nullable data types.

How do I do that?

A null value (identified in Visual Basic by the keyword Nothing), is a special flag that indicates no data is present. Most developers are familiar with null object references, which indicate that the object has been defined but not created. For example, in the following code, the FileStream contains a null reference because it hasn't been instantiated with the New keyword:

```
Dim fs As FileStream
If fs Is Nothing
    ' This is always true because the FileStream hasn't
    ' been created yet.
    Console.WriteLine("Object contains a null reference.")
End If
```

Core data types like integers and strings *can't* contain null values. Numeric variables are automatically initialized to 0. Boolean variables are False. String variables are set to an empty string ("") automatically. In fact, even if you explicitly set a simple data type variable to Nothing in your code, it will automatically revert to the empty value (0, False, or ""), as the following code demonstrates:

```
Dim j As Integer = Nothing
If j = 0 Then
    ' This is always true because there is an
    ' implicit conversion between Nothing and 0 for integers.
    Console.WriteLine("Non-nullable integer j = " & j)
End If
```

This design sometimes causes problems, because there's no way to distinguish between an empty value and a value that was never supplied in the first place. For example, imagine you create code that needs to retrieve the number of times the user has placed an order from a text file. Later on, you examine this value. The problem occurs if this value is 0. Quite simply, you have no way to know whether this is valid data (the user placed no orders), or it represents missing information (the setting couldn't be retrieved or the current user isn't a registered customer).

Thanks to generics, .NET 2.0 has a solution—a System.Nullable class that can wrap any other data type. When you create an instance of Nullable you specify the data type. If you don't set a value, this instance contains a null reference. You can test whether this is true by testing the Nullable.HasType() method, and you can retrieve the underlying object through the Nullable.Value property.

Here's the sample code you need to create a nullable integer:

```
Dim i As Nullable(Of Integer)
If Not i.HasValue Then
    ' This is true, because no value has been assigned.
    Console.WriteLine("i is a null value")
End If

' Assign a value. Note that you must assign directly to i, not i.Value.
' The i.Value property is read-only, and it always reflects the
' currently assigned object, if it is not Nothing.
i = 100
If i.HasValue Then
    ' This is true, because a value (100) is now present.
    Console.WriteLine("Nullable integer i = " & i.Value)
End If
```

What about...

...using Nullable with full-fledged reference objects? Although you don't need this ability (because reference types can contain a null reference), it still gives you some advantages. Namely, you can use the slightly more readable HasValue( ) method instead of testing for Nothing. Best of all, you can make this change seamlessly, because the Nullable class has the remarkable ability to allow implicit conversions between Nullable and the type it wraps.

Where can I learn more?

To learn more about Nullable and how it's implemented, look up the "Nullable class" index entry in the MSDN Help.

Use Operators with Custom Objects

Tired of using clumsy syntax like ObjA. Subtract(ObjB) to perform simple operations on your custom objects? With VB's support for operator overloading, you can manipulate your objects as easily as ordinary numbers.

Every VB programmer is familiar with the arithmetic operators for addition (+), subtraction (-), division (/), and multiplication (*). Ordinarily, these operators are reserved for .NET numeric types, and have no meaning when used with other objects. However, in VB .NET 2.0 you can build objects that support all of these operators, as well as the operators used for logical operations and implicit conversion). This technique won't make sense for business objects, but it is extremely handy if you need to model mathematical structures such as vectors, matrixes, complex numbers, or—as demonstrated in the following example—fractions.

How do I do that?

To overload an operator in Visual Basic 2005, you need to create a special operator method in your class (or structure). This method must be declared with the keywords `Public Shared Operator`, followed by the symbol for the operator (e.g., +).

TIP

To *overload* an operator simply means to define what an operator does when used with a specific type of object. In other words, when you overload the + operator for a Fraction class, you tell .NET what to do when your code adds two Fraction objects together.

For example, here's an operator method that adds support for the addition (+) operator:

```
Public Shared Operator+(objA As MyClass, objB as MyClass) As MyClass
    ' (Code goes here.)
End Operator
```

Every operator method accepts two parameters, which represent the values on either side of the operator. Depending on the class and the operator, order may be important (as it is for division).

Once you've defined an operator, the VB compiler will call your code when it executes a statement that uses the operator with your class. For example, the compiler changes code like this:

```
ObjC = ObjA + ObjB
```

into this:

```
ObjC = MyClass.Operator+(ObjA, ObjB)
```

Example 2-3 shows how you can overload the Visual Basic arithmetic operators used to handle Fraction objects. A Fraction consists of two portions: a numerator and a denominator (known colloquially as "the top part and the bottom part"). The Fraction code overloads the +, -, *, and / operators, allowing you to perform fractional calculations without converting your numbers to decimals and losing precision.

Example 2-3. Overloading arithmetic operators in the Fraction class

```
Public Structure Fraction

    ' The two parts of a fraction.
    Public Denominator As Integer
    Public Numerator As Integer

    Public Sub New(ByVal numerator As Integer, ByVal denominator As Integer)
```

```
        Me.Numerator = numerator
        Me.Denominator = denominator
    End Sub

    Public Shared Operator +(ByVal x As Fraction, ByVal y As Fraction) _
      As Fraction
        Return Normalize(x.Numerator * y.Denominator + _
          y.Numerator * x.Denominator, x.Denominator * y.Denominator)
    End Operator

    Public Shared Operator -(ByVal x As Fraction, ByVal y As Fraction) _
      As Fraction
        Return Normalize(x.Numerator * y.Denominator - _
          y.Numerator * x.Denominator, x.Denominator * y.Denominator)
    End Operator

    Public Shared Operator *(ByVal x As Fraction, ByVal y As Fraction) _
      As Fraction
        Return Normalize(x.Numerator * y.Numerator, _
          x.Denominator * y.Denominator)
    End Operator

    Public Shared Operator /(ByVal x As Fraction, ByVal y As Fraction) _
      As Fraction
        Return Normalize(x.Numerator * y.Denominator, _
          x.Denominator * y.Numerator)
    End Operator

    ' Reduce a fraction.
    Private Shared Function Normalize(ByVal numerator As Integer, _
      ByVal denominator As Integer) As Fraction
        If (numerator <> 0) And (denominator <> 0) Then
            ' Fix signs.
            If denominator < 0 Then
                denominator *= -1
                numerator *= -1
            End If

            Dim divisor As Integer = GCD(numerator, denominator)
            numerator \= divisor
            denominator \= divisor
        End If

        Return New Fraction(numerator, denominator)
    End Function

    ' Return the greatest common divisor using Euclid's algorithm.
    Private Shared Function GCD(ByVal x As Integer, ByVal y As Integer) _
      As Integer
        Dim temp As Integer

        x = Math.Abs(x)
        y = Math.Abs(y)
```

Example 2-3. Overloading arithmetic operators in the Fraction class (continued)

```
            Do While (y <> 0)
                temp = x Mod y
                x = y
                y = temp
            Loop

            Return x
        End Function

        ' Convert the fraction to decimal form.
        Public Function GetDouble() As Double
            Return CType(Me.Numerator, Double) / _
                CType(Me.Denominator, Double)
        End Function

        ' Get a string representation of the fraction.
        Public Overrides Function ToString() As String
            Return Me.Numerator.ToString & "/" & Me.Denominator.ToString
        End Function

End Structure
```

The console code shown in Example 2-4 puts the fraction class through a quirk-and-dirty test. Thanks to operator overloading, the number remains in fractional form, and precision is never lost.

Example 2-4. Testing the Fraction class

```
Module FractionTest

    Sub Main()
        Dim f1 As New Fraction(2, 3)
        Dim f2 As New Fraction(1, 4)

        Console.WriteLine("f1 = " & f1.ToString())
        Console.WriteLine("f2 = " & f2.ToString())

        Dim f3 As Fraction
        f3 = f1 + f2      ' f3 is now 11/12
        Console.WriteLine("f1 + f2 = " & f3.ToString())

        f3 = f1 / f2      ' f3 is now 8/3
        Console.WriteLine("f1 / f2 = " & f3.ToString())

        f3 = f1 - f2      ' f3 is now 5/12
        Console.WriteLine("f1 - f2 = " & f3.ToString())

        f3 = f1 * f2      ' f2 is now 1/6
        Console.WriteLine("f1 * f2 = " & f3.ToString())
    End Sub

End Module
```

When you run this application, here's the output you'll see:

```
f1 = 2/3
f2 = 1/4
f1 + f2 = 11/12
f1 / f2 = 8/3
f1 - f2 = 5/12
f1 * f2 = 1/6
```

Usually, the parameters and the return value of an operator method use the same type. However, there's no reason you can't create more than one version of an operator method so your object can be used in expressions with different types.

What about...

...using operator overloading with other types? There are a number of classes that are natural candidates for operator overloading. Here are some good examples:

- Mathematical classes that model vectors, matrixes, complex numbers, or tensors.
- Money classes that round calculations to the nearest penny, and support different currency types.
- Measurement classes that have irregular units, like inches and feet.

Where can I learn more?

For more of the language details behind operator overloading and all the operators that you can overload, refer to the "Operator procedures" index entry in the MSDN Help.

Split a Class into Multiple Files

Have your classes grown too large to manage in one file? With the new Partial keyword, you can split a class into separate files.

If you've cracked open a .NET 2.0 Windows Forms class, you'll have noticed that all the automatically generated code is missing! To understand where it's gone, you need to learn about a new feature called *partial classes*, which allow you to split classes into several pieces.

How do I do that?

Using the new Partial keyword, you can split a single class into as many pieces as you want. You simply define the same class in more than one place. Here's an example that defines a class named SampleClass in two pieces:

```
Partial Public Class SampleClass
    Public Sub MethodA( )
        Console.WriteLine("Method A called.")
    End Sub
End Class

Partial Public Class SampleClass
    Public Sub MethodB( )
        Console.WriteLine("Method B called.")
    End Sub
End Class
```

In this example, the two declarations are in the same file, one after the other. However, there's no reason that you can't put the two SampleClass pieces in different source code files in the same project. (The only restrictions are that you can't define the two pieces in separate assemblies or in separate namespaces.)

When you build the application containing the previous code, Visual Studio will track down each piece of SampleClass and assemble it into a complete, compiled class with two methods, MethodA( ) and MethodB( ). You can use both methods, as shown here:

```
Dim Obj As New SampleClass( )
Obj.MethodA( )
Obj.MethodB( )
```

Partial classes don't offer you much help in solving programming problems, but they can be useful in breaking up extremely large, unwieldy classes. Of course, the existence of large classes in your application could be a sign that you haven't properly factored your problem, in which case you should really break your class down into separate, not partial, classes. One of the key roles of partial classes in .NET is to hide the designer code that is automatically generated by Visual Studio, whose visibility in previous versions has been a source of annoyance to some VB programmers.

For example, when you build a .NET Windows form in Visual Basic 2005, your event handling code is placed in the source code file for the form, but the designer code that creates and configures each control and connects its event handlers is nowhere to be seen. In order to see this code, you need to select Project → Show All Files from the Visual Studio menu. When you do, the file that contains the missing half of the class appears in the Solution Explorer as a separate file. Given a form named Form1, you'll actually wind up with a *Form1.vb* file that contains your code and a *Form1.Designer.vb* file that contains the automatically generated part.

What about...

...using the `Partial` keyword with structures? That works, but you can't create partial interfaces, enumerations, or any other .NET programming construct.

Where can I learn more?

To get more details on partial classes, refer to the index entry "Partial keyword" in the MSDN Help.

Extend the My Namespace

Do you use the My objects so much you'd like to customize them yourself? VB 2005 lets you plug in your own classes.

The My objects aren't defined in a single place. Some come from classes defined in the `Microsoft.VisualBasic.MyServices` namespace, while others are generated dynamically as you add forms, web services, configuration settings, and embedded resources to your project. However, as a developer you can participate in the My namespace and extend it with your own ingredients (e.g., useful calculations and tasks that are specific to your application).

How do I do that?

To plug a new class into the My object hierarchy, simply use a `Namespace` block with the name My. For example, you could add this code to create a new `BusinessFunctions` class that contains a company-specific function for generating custom identifiers (by joining the customer name to a new GUID):

```
Namespace My

    Public Class BusinessFunctions
        Public Shared Function GenerateNewCustomerID( _
          ByVal name As String) As String
            Return name & "_" & Guid.NewGuid.ToString()
        End Function
    End Class

End Namespace
```

Once you've created the `BusinessFunctions` object in the right place, you can make use of it in your application just like any other My object. For example, to display a new customer ID:

```
Console.WriteLine(My.BusinessFunctions.GenerateNewCustomerID("matthew"))
```

Note that the My classes you add need to use shared methods and properties. That's because the My object won't be instantiated automatically. As a result, if you use ordinary instance members, you'll need to create the My object on your own, and you won't be able to manipulate it with the same syntax. Another solution is to create a module in the My namespace, because all the methods and properties in a module are always shared.

You can also extend some of the existing My objects thanks to partial classes. For example, using this feature you could add new information to the My.Computer object or new routines to the My.Application object. In this case, the approach is slightly different. My.Computer exposes an instance of the MyComputer object. My.Application exposes an instance of the MyApplication object. Thus, to add to either of these classes, you need to create a partial class with the appropriate name, and add the instance members you need. You should also declare this class with the accessibility keyword Friend in order to match the existing class.

Here's an example you can use to extend My.Application with a method that checks for update versions:

Shared members are members that are always available through the class name, even if you haven't created an object. If you use shared variables, there will be one copy of that variable, which is global to your whole application.

```
Namespace My

    Partial Friend Class MyApplication
        Public Function IsNewVersionAvailable() As Boolean
            ' Usually, you would read the latest available version number
            ' from a web service or some other resource.
            ' Here, it's hardcoded.
            Dim LatestVersion As New Version(1, 2, 1, 1)
            Return Application.Info.Version.CompareTo(LatestVersion)
        End Function
    End Class

End Namespace
```

And now you can use this method:

```
If My.Application.IsNewVersionAvailable()
    Console.WriteLine("A newer version is available.")
Else
    Console.WriteLine("This is the latest version.")
End If
```

What about...

...using your My extensions in multiple applications? There's no reason you can't treat My classes in the same way that you treat any other useful class that you want to reuse in multiple applications. In other words, you can create a class library project, add some My extensions, and compile it to a DLL. You can then reference that DLL in other applications.

Of course, despite what Microsoft enthusiasts may tell you, extending the My namespace in that way has two potentially dangerous drawbacks:

- It becomes more awkward to share your component with other languages. For example, C# does not provide a My feature. Although you could still use a custom My object in a C# application, it wouldn't plug in as neatly.

- When you use the My namespace, you circumvent one of the great benefits of namespaces—avoiding naming conflicts. For example, consider two companies who create components for logging. If you use the recommended .NET namespace standard (CompanyName. ApplicationName.ClassName), there's little chance these two components will have the same fully qualified names. One might be Acme. SuperLogger.Logger while the other is ComponentTech.LogMagic. Logger. However, if they both extend a My object, it's quite possible that they would both use the same name (like My.Application. Logger). As a result, you wouldn't be able to use both of them in the same application.

Skip to the Next Iteration of a Loop

VB's new Continue keyword gives you a quick way to step out of a tangled block of code in a loop and head straight into the next iteration.

The Visual Basic language provides a handful of common *flow control* statements, which let you direct the execution of your code. For example, you can use Return to step out of a function, or Exit to back out of a loop. However, before VB 2005, there wasn't any way to skip to the next iteration of a loop.

How do I do that?

The Continue statement is one of those language details that seems like a minor frill at first, but quickly proves itself to be a major convenience. The Continue statement exists in three versions: Continue For, Continue Do, and Continue While, each of which is used with a different type of loop (For ... Next, Do ... Loop, or While ... End While).

To see how the Continue statement works consider the following code:

```
For i = 1 to 1000
    If i Mod 5 = 0 Then
        ' (Task A code.)
```

```
        Continue For
      End If
      ' (Task B code.)
    Next
```

This code loops 1,000 times, incrementing a counter i. Whenever i is divisible by five, the task A code executes. Then, the `Continue For` statement is executed, the counter is incremented, and execution resumes at the beginning of the loop, skipping the code in task B.

In this example, the continue statement isn't really required, because you could rewrite the code easily enough as follows:

```
    For i = 1 to 1000
      If i Mod 5 = 0 Then
        ' (Task A code.)
      Else
        ' (Task B code.)
      End If
    Next
```

However, this isn't nearly as possible if you need to perform several different tests. To see the real benefit of the `Continue` statement, you need to consider a more complex (and realistic) example.

Example 2-5 demonstrates a loop that scans through an array of words. Each word is analyzed, and the program decides whether the word is made up of letters, numeric characters, or the space character. If the program matches one test (for example, the letter test), it needs to continue to the next word without performing the next test. To accomplish this without using the `Continue` statement, you need to use nested loops, an approach that creates awkward code.

Example 2-5. Analyzing a string without using the Continue statement

```
' Define a sentence.
Dim Sentence As String = "The final number is 433."

' Split the sentence into an array of words.
Dim Delimiters() As Char = {" ", ".", ","}
Dim Words() As String = Sentence.Split(Delimiters)

' Examine each word.
For Each Word As String In Words
    ' Check if the word is blank.
    If Word <> "" Then
        Console.Write("'" + Word + "'" & vbTab & "= ")

        ' Check if the word is made up of letters.
        Dim AllLetters As Boolean = True
        For Each Character As Char In Word
            If Not Char.IsLetter(Character) Then
```

Example 2-5. Analyzing a string without using the Continue statement (continued)

```
                    AllLetters = False
                End If
            Next
            If AllLetters Then
                Console.WriteLine("word")
            Else
                ' If the word isn't made up of letters,
                ' check if the word is made up of numbers.
                Dim AllNumbers As Boolean = True
                For Each Character As Char In Word
                    If Not Char.IsDigit(Character) Then
                        AllNumbers = False
                    End If
                Next
                If AllNumbers Then
                    Console.WriteLine("number")
                Else
                    ' If the word isn't made up of letters or numbers,
                    ' assume it's something else.
                    Console.WriteLine("mixed")
                End If
            End If
        End If
    End If
Next
```

Now, consider the rewritten version shown in Example 2-6 that uses the Continue statement to clarify what's going on.

Example 2-6. Analyzing a string using the Continue statement

```
' Examine each word.
For Each Word As String In Words
    ' Check if the word is blank.
    If Word = "" Then Continue For
    Console.Write("'" + Word + "'" & vbTab & "= ")

    ' Check if the word is made up of letters.
    Dim AllLetters As Boolean = True
    For Each Character As Char In Word
        If Not Char.IsLetter(Character) Then
            AllLetters = False
        End If
    Next
    If AllLetters Then
        Console.WriteLine("word")
        Continue For
    End If

    ' If the word isn't made up of letters,
    ' check if the word is made up of numbers.
    Dim AllNumbers As Boolean = True
    For Each Character As Char In Word
```

Example 2-6. *Analyzing a string using the Continue statement (continued)*

```
        If Not Char.IsDigit(Character) Then
            AllNumbers = False
        End If
    Next
    If AllNumbers Then
        Console.WriteLine("number")
        Continue For
    End If

    ' If the word isn't made up of letters or numbers,
    ' assume it's something else.
    Console.WriteLine("mixed")
Next
```

What about...

...using Continue in a nested loop? It's possible. If you nest a For loop inside a Do loop, you can use Continue For to skip to the next iteration of the inner loop, or Continue Do to skip to the next iteration of the outer loop. This technique also works in reverse (with a Do loop inside a For loop), but it doesn't work if you nest a loop inside another loop of the same type. In this case, there's no unambiguous way to refer to the outer loop, and so your Continue statement always refers to the inner loop.

Where can I learn more?

For the language lowdown on Continue, refer to the index entry "continue statement" in the MSDN Help.

Dispose of Objects Automatically

In .NET, it's keenly important to make sure objects that use unmanaged resources (e.g., file handles, database connections, and graphics contexts) release these resources as soon as possible. Toward this end, such objects should always implement the IDisposable interface, and provide a Dispose( ) method that you can call to release their resources immediately.

The only problem with this technique is that you must always remember to call the Dispose( ) method (or another method that calls Dispose( ), such as a Close( ) method). VB 2005 provides a new safeguard you can apply to make sure Dispose( ) is always called: the Using statement.

Worried that you'll have objects floating around in memory, tying up resources until the garbage collector tracks them down? With the Using statement, you can make sure disposable objects meet with a timely demise.

How do I do that?

You use the Using statement in a block structure. In the first line, when you declare the Using block, you specify the disposable object you are using. Often, you'll also create the object at the same time using the New keyword. Then, you write the code that uses the disposable object inside the Using block. Here's an example with a snippet of code that creates a new file and writes some data to the file:

```
Using NewFile As New System.IO.StreamWriter("c:\MyFile.txt")
    NewFile.WriteLine("This is line 1")
    NewFile.WriteLine("This is line 2")
End Using

' The file is closed automatically.
' The NewFile object is no longer available here.
```

In this example, as soon as the execution leaves the Using block, the Dispose() method is called on the NewFile object, releasing the file handle.

What about...

...errors that occur inside a Using block? Thankfully, .NET makes sure it disposes of the resource no matter how you exit the Using block, even if an unhandled exception occurs.

The Using statement makes sense with all kinds of disposable objects, such as:

- Files (including FileStream, StreamReader, and StreamWriter)
- Database connections (including SqlConnection, OracleConnection, and OleDbConnection)
- Network connections (including TcpClient, UdpClient, NetworkStream, FtpWebResponse, HttpWebResponse)
- Graphics (including Image, Bitmap, Metafile, Graphics)

Where can I learn more?

For the language lowdown, refer to the index entry "Using block" in the MSDN Help.

Safeguard Properties with Split Accessibility

Most properties consist of a *property get procedure* (which allows you to retrieve the property value) and a *property set procedure* (which allows you to set a new value for the property). In previous versions of Visual Basic, the declared access level of both procedures needed to be the same. In VB 2005, you can protect a property by assigning to the set procedure a lower access level than you give to the get procedure.

In the past, there was no way to create a property that everyone could read but only your application could update. VB 2005 finally loosens the rules and gives you more flexibility.

How do I do that?

VB recognizes three levels of accessibility. Arranged from most to least permissive, these are:

- Public (available to all classes in all assemblies)
- Friend (available to all code in all the classes in the current assembly)
- Private (only available to code in the same class)

Imagine you are creating a DLL component that's going to be used by another application. You might decide to create a property called Status that the client application needs to read, and so you declare the property Public:

```
Public Class ComponetClass

    Private _Status As Integer
    Public Property Status() As Integer
        Get
            Return _Status
        End Get
        Set(ByVal value As Integer)
            _Status = value
        End Set
    End Property

End Class
```

The problem here is that the access level assigned to the Status property allows the client to change it, which doesn't make sense. You could make Status a read-only property (in other words, omit the property set procedure altogether), but that wouldn't allow other classes that are part of your applications and located in your component assembly to change it.

The solution is to give the property set procedure the Friend accessibility level. Here's what the code should look like, with the only change highlighted:

```
Public Property Status() As Integer
    Get
        Return _Status
    End Get
    Friend Set(ByVal value As Integer)
        _Status = value
    End Set
End Property
```

What about...

...read-only and write-only properties? Split accessibility doesn't help you if you need to make a read-only property (such as a calculated value) or a write-only value (such as a password that shouldn't remain accessible). To create a read-only property, add the ReadOnly keyword to the property declaration (right after the accessibility keyword), and remove the property set procedure. To create a write-only property, remove the property get procedure and add the WriteOnly keyword. These keywords are nothing new—they've been available since Visual Basic .NET 1.0.

Evaluate Conditions Separately with Short-Circuit Logic

With short-circuiting, you can combine multiple conditions to write more compact code.

In previous versions of VB, there were two logical operators: And and Or. Visual Basic 2005 introduces two new operators that supplement these: AndAlso and OrElse. These operators work in the same way as And and Or, except they have support for short-circuiting, which allows you to evaluate just one part of a long conditional statement.

How do I do that?

A common programming scenario is the need to evaluate several conditions in a row. Often, this involves checking that an object is not null, and then examining one of its properties. In order to handle this scenario, you need to use nested If blocks, as shown here:

```
If MyObject Is Nothing Then
    If MyObject.Value > 10 Then
        ' (Do something.)
    End If
End If
```

It would be nice to combine both of these conditions into a single line, as follows:

```
If MyObject Is Nothing And MyObject.Value > 10 Then
    ' (Do something.)
End If
```

Unfortunately, this won't work because VB always evaluates both conditions. In other words, even if MyObject is Nothing, VB will evaluate the second condition and attempt to retrieve the MyObject.Value property, which will cause a NullReferenceException.

Visual Basic 2005 solves this problem with the AndAlso and OrElse keywords. When you use these keywords, Visual Basic won't evaluate the second condition if the first condition is false. Here's the corrected code:

```
If MyObject Is Nothing AndAlso MyObject.Value > 10 Then
    ' (Do something.)
End If
```

What about...

...other language refinements? In this chapter, you've had a tour of the most important VB language innovations. However, it's worth pointing out a few of the less significant ones that I haven't included in this chapter:

- The IsNot keyword allows you to simplify awkward syntax slightly. Using it, you can replace syntax like If Not x Is Nothing with the equivalent statement If x IsNot Nothing.

- The TryCast() function allows you to shave a few milliseconds off type casting code. It works like CType() or DirectCast(), with one exception—if the object can't be converted to the requested type a null reference is returned instead. Thus, instead of checking an object's type and then casting it, you can use TryCast() right away and then check if you have an actual object instance.

- Unsigned integers allow you to store numeric values that can't be negative. That restriction saves on memory storage, allowing you to accommodate larger numbers. Unsigned numbers have always been in the .NET Framework, but now VB 2005 includes keywords for them (UInteger, ULong, and UShort).

CHAPTER 3

Windows Applications

.NET 1.0 introduced a whole new toolkit for writing Windows applications. This toolkit—called *Windows Forms*—quickly won the hearts of developers with its rich features for creating self-sizing windows, customized controls, and dynamic graphics. But for all its strengths, the Windows Forms toolkit left out a few features that many VB 6 developers had come to expect, including a masked edit control and a way to display HTML web pages. The Windows Forms toolkit also lacked some of the frills found in modern Windows applications, like Office XP–style toolbars and menus with thumbnail images. As you'll see in this chapter, .NET 2.0 includes all of these elements and more.

Use Office-Style Toolbars

With .NET 1.0 and 1.1, VB developers have had to content themselves with either the woefully out-of-date ToolBar control, or draw their own custom toolbars by hand. In .NET 2.0, the situation improves with a rich new ToolStrip control that sports a modern, flat look, correctly handles Windows XP themes, and supports a wide range of graphical widgets, such as buttons, labels, drop-down lists, drop-down menus, text boxes, and more.

How do I do that?

To use the System.Windows.Forms.ToolStrip control, just drag the ToolStrip from the Menus & Toolbars section of the Visual Studio toolbox onto a form. To control which side of the form the ToolStrip lines up with, set the Docking property. For example, Figure 3-1 shows a form, Form1, with two ToolStrip controls, one docked to the top of the form and the other to the right side.

Finally, a ToolStrip control whose looks are worthy of a modern Windows application.

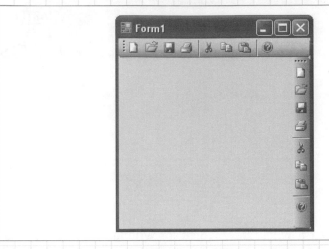

Figure 3-1. Three ToolStrip objects in one RaftingContainer

To add buttons to the ToolStrip, you can use the Visual Studio designer. Just click the ToolStrip smart tag and select Edit Items. You can choose new items from a drop-down list and configure their properties in a window like the one shown in Figure 3-2. Or, select Insert Standard Items to create standard ToolStrip buttons for document management (new, open, save, close) and editing (cut, copy, paste).

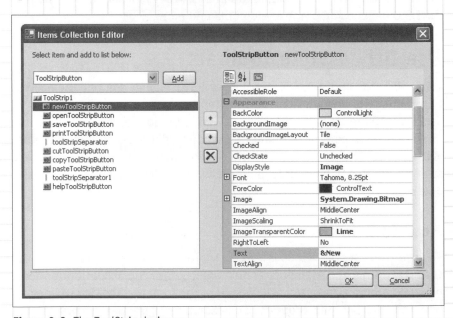

Figure 3-2. The ToolStrip designer

The key to mastering the ToolStrip control is learning about all the different widgets you can put inside it. These include:

ToolStripButton
> Represents an item on the toolbar that the user can click. It can include text or an image (or both). This is the most common ToolStrip item.

ToolStripLabel
> Represents a non-selectable item on the ToolStrip. It can include text or an image (or both).

ToolStripSeparator
> Divides adjacent items in a ToolStrip with a thin engraved line.

ToolStripDropDownButton *and* ToolStripSplitButton
> Represent a drop-down menu with items. The only difference is how the drop-down list is drawn. The ToolStripDropDownButton shows its items as a menu, with a thumbnail margin and the ability to check items. In both cases, the menu items are ToolStripMenuItem objects that are added to the collection exposed by the DropDownItems property.

ToolStripComboBox, ToolStripTextBox, *and* ToolStripProgressBar
> Allow you to add familiar .NET controls to a ToolStrip, such as ComboBox, TextBox, and ProgressBar. All of these items derive from ToolStripControlHost, which you can use to create your own ToolStrip controls (as described in the next section, "Add Any Control to a ToolStrip").

All the ToolStrip items derive from the ToolStripItem class. That means they all support a few basic properties (the most important include Text, Image, and ImageAlign, all of which set the display content). ToolStrip items all provide a Click event you can use to detect when the user clicks a toolbar button.

For example, if you want to react to a click of a ToolStrip item that you've named TestToolStripButton, you can use the following code:

```
Private Sub TestToolStripButton_Click(ByVal sender As Object, _
  ByVal e As System.EventArgs) Handles TestToolStripButton.Click

    MessageBox.Show("You clicked " & CType(sender, ToolStripItem).Name)
End Sub
```

Once you've created a ToolStrip and added at least one item, you can take advantage of a significant amount of out-of-the-box formatting. The

When the user clicks a button on the ToolStrip, that button's Click event fires. This is different than the legacy ToolBar control, which fired a generic Click event no matter which button was clicked.

following are just a few of the impressive features provided by ToolStrip:

- It matches the Office XP toolbar look, with a blue gradient background, etched sizing grips, and hot tracking (highlighting an item as the mouse moves over it).

- It correctly supports Windows XP themes. That means if you change the color scheme to Olive Green or Silver, all ToolStrip controls update themselves automatically, allowing your application to blend in with the scenery.

- It allows user customization. If you enable the ToolStrip. AllowReorder property, the user can rearrange the orders of buttons in a ToolStrip by holding down the Alt key and dragging items from one place to another, or even drag a button from one ToolStrip to another.

- It supports *overflow menus*. If you enable this feature (by setting ToolStrip.CanOverflow to True) and shrink the window so the entire ToolStrip no longer fits, a special drop-down menu appears at the right with all the extra buttons, as shown in Figure 3-3.

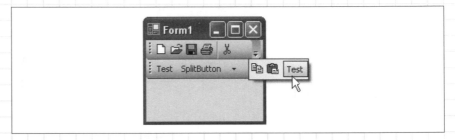

Figure 3-3. An overflow menu

In the previous example, the ToolStrip is fixed in place. If you want, you can give the user the ability to drag a ToolStrip, either to dock it in a different place or to rearrange several that appear together. To make this possible, you need to add a ToolStripContainer to your form, which shows up as a box with a blue gradient background (like the background of the ToolStrip). Although you can use more than one ToolStripContainer, usually you'll just use one and dock it to fill all or a portion of your window.

To add a ToolStripContainer and place a ToolStrip in it in one step, click the ToolStrip smart tag and then click the "Embed in ToolStripContainer" link.

The ToolStripContainer actually wraps four ToolStripPanel objects, one for each side. These objects are exposed through properties such as ToolStripContainer.LeftToolStripPanel, ToolStripContainer. TopToolStripPanel, and so on. Each panel can hold an unlimited number of ToolStrip objects, which are then docked to the corresponding side. The interesting part is that once you place a ToolStrip in a ToolStripContainer, the user gains the ability to drag a ToolStrip freely about its panel at runtime. Users can even drag a ToolStrip from one ToolStripPanel to another to change the side it's docked on (or even to an entirely separate ToolStripContainer in the same window).

TIP

If you want to prevent the user from docking the ToolStrip to the left side of the container, set the ToolStripContainer.LeftToolStripPanelVisible property to false. You can also use similar properties to prevent docking to the right, top, or bottom sides.

What about...

...updating the rest of your interface to look as good as the ToolStrip? .NET 2.0 actually provides four controls that sport the flat, modern look of Windows XP, and support Windows XP theming. These are ToolStrip, StatusStrip, MenuStrip, and ContextMenuStrip, which replace ToolBar, StatusBar, MainMenu, and ContextMenu. You can quickly refresh your application's interface just by updating these old standbys to the new controls.

TIP

In Visual Studio 2005, you won't see the legacy controls like ToolBar and StatusBar, because they're left out of the toolbox by default. If you want to use them, right-click the toolbox, choose Choose Items, and select these controls from the list.

Where can I learn more?

For more information, read about the ToolStrip classes in the MSDN help library reference. You can also refer to a few more recipes in this chapter:

- "Add Any Control to a ToolStrip" explains how to add other controls to a ToolStrip.
- "Add Icons to Your Menu" explains how to use the new MenuStrip control.

Add Any Control to a ToolStrip

The ToolStrip supports a wide range of ToolStripItem classes, allowing you to add everything from buttons and drop-down menus to textboxes and labels. However, in some situations you might want to go beyond the standard options and use other .NET controls, or even place your own custom controls in the ToolStrip. In order to make this work, you need to use the ToolStripControlHost.

How do I do that?

There's no way to add standard .NET controls directly to the ToolStrip, because the ToolStrip only supports classes that derive from ToolStripItem. You could create a class that derives from ToolStripItem to implement a custom ToolStrip element, but this approach is fairly complex and tedious. A much simpler approach is to use the ToolStripControlHost, which can wrap just about any .NET control.

To use the ToolStripControlHost with a non-ToolStripItem control, just pass the control object as a constructor argument when you create the ToolStripControlHost. Then, add the ToolStripControlHost object to the ToolStrip. You can use the code in Example 3-1 to add a CheckBox control to the ToolStrip.Items collection. Figure 3-4 shows the result.

Example 3-1. Adding a Checkbox control to a ToolStrip.Items collection

```
' Create a CheckBox.
Dim CheckStrip As New CheckBox()

' Set the CheckBox so it takes the size of its text.
CheckStrip.AutoSize = True
CheckStrip.Text = "Sample CheckBox in ToolStrip"

' Make sure the CheckbBox is transparent (so the
' ToolStrip gradient background shows through).
CheckStrip.BackColor = Color.FromArgb(0, 255, 0, 0)

' Create the ToolStripControlHost that wraps the CheckBox.
Dim CheckStripHost As New ToolStripControlHost(CheckStrip)

' Set the ToolStripControlHost to take the full width
' of the control it wraps.
CheckStripHost.AutoSize = True

' Add the wrapped CheckBox.
ToolStrip1.Items.Add(CheckStripHost)
```

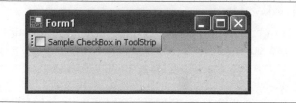

Figure 3-4. A ToolStrip with a CheckBox

What about...

...customizing the ToolStripControlHost? If you're using a ToolStripControlHost to host another control, you might want to add properties to the ToolStripControlHost to expose data from the hosted control. For example, you could add a Checked property to the ToolStripControlHost used in this example so that you could easily set or retrieve the checked state of the wrapped CheckBox control. In order to use this technique, you need to create a custom class that derives from ToolStripControlHost.

Where can I learn more?

The MSDN help reference includes an example with a ToolStripControlHost that hosts a date control. For more information, look up the index entry "ToolStrip → wrapping controls in."

Add Icons to Your Menu

Jazz up your dullest menus with thumbnail images.

Windows applications have been undergoing a gradual facelift since Windows XP and Office XP first appeared on the scene. Today, many modern Windows applications use a fine-tuned menu that sports a blue shaded margin on its left side, and an optional icon for each menu command. (To see what this looks like, you can jump ahead to Figure 3-5.)

If you wanted to create a polished-looking menu with this appearance in .NET 1.0 or 1.1, you needed to draw it yourself using GDI+ code. Although there are several surprisingly good examples of this technique available on the Internet, it's more than a little messy. In .NET 2.0, the situation improves dramatically. Even though the original MainMenu and ContextMenu controls are unchanged, two new controls—MenuStrip and ContextMenuStrip—provide the same functionality but render the menu with the new Office XP look.

How do I do that?

The MenuStrip and ContextMenuStrip classes leverage all the hard work that went into building the ToolStrip class. Essentially, a MenuStrip is a special container for ToolStripItem objects. The MenuStrip.Items property holds a collection of top-level menu headings (like File, Edit, View, and Help), each of which is represented by a ToolStripMenuItem object. Each ToolStripMenuItem has a DropDownItemsProperty, which exposes another collection of ToolStripMenuItem objects, one for each contained menu item.

Example 3-2 shows code that creates the familiar Windows File menu.

Example 3-2. Creating a Windows File menu

```
' Add the top-level items to the menu.
MenuStrip1.Items.AddRange(New ToolStripItem() _
  {fileToolStripMenuItem})

' Set the text for the File menu, and set "F" as the
' quick access key (so that Alt+F will open the menu.)
fileToolStripMenuItem.Text = "&File"

' Add the child items to the File menu.
fileToolStripMenuItem.DropDownItems.AddRange(New ToolStripItem() _
  {newToolStripMenuItem, openToolStripMenuItem, _
  toolStripSeparator, saveToolStripMenuItem, _
  saveAsToolStripMenuItem, toolStripSeparator1, _
  printToolStripMenuItem, printPreviewToolStripMenuItem, _
  toolStripSeparator2, exitToolStripMenuItem})

' Configure the File child items.
' Set the text and shortcut key for the New menu option.
newToolStripMenuItem.ShortcutKeys = CType((Keys.Control Or Keys.N), Keys)
newToolStripMenuItem.Text = "&New"

' Set the text and shortcut key for the Open menu option.
openToolStripMenuItem.ShortcutKeys = CType((Keys.Control Or Keys.O), Keys)
openToolStripMenuItem.Text = "&Open"

' (Code for configuring other omitted menu items.)
```

Usually, you won't enter this information by hand—instead, it's part of the designer code that Visual Studio generates automatically as you set the properties in the Properties window. However, it does show you how the menu works and what you'll need to do if you want to dynamically add new items at runtime.

As Example 3-2 reveals, the structure of a MenuStrip control is the same as the structure of its predecessor, the MainMenu control, with menu

---

objects containing other menu objects. The only difference is in the type of object used to represent menu items (it's now `ToolStripMenuItem` instead of `MenuItem`) and the name of the property used to hold the collection of contained menu items (`ToolStripMenuItem.DropDownItems` instead of `MenuItem.ChildItems`).

To reap the real benefits of the new `ToolStripMenuItem`, you need to use one property that wasn't available with ordinary `MenuItem` objects: the `Image` property, which sets the thumbnail icon that appears in the menu margin.

```
newToolStripMenuItem.Image = CType( _
    resources.GetObject("newToolStripMenuItem.Image"), _
    System.Drawing.Image)
```

Figure 3-5 shows the standard File menu.

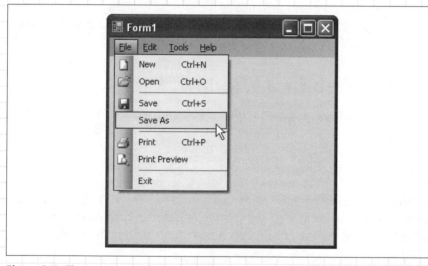

Figure 3-5. The new MenuStrip

Usually, you'll load all your images using the Visual Studio Properties Window at design time. In that case, they'll be embedded as a resource inside your assembly. Another option is to load them into an `ImageList` and then set the `ImageKey` or `IndexProperty` of `ToolStripMenuItem` to point to an image in the `ImageList`.

To quickly generate a basic menu framework (including the standard menu commands for the File, Edit, Tools, and Help menu), click the MenuStrip smart tag and select Insert Standard Items.

What about...

...painting a menu from scratch? Hopefully, you won't need to. The `ToolStripMenuItem` gives you a little bit more flexibility than the original `MenuItem` class—not only can you insert images, but you can also choose a nonstandard font by setting the `ToolStripMenuItem.Font` property. Here's an example:

```
fileToolStripMenuItem.Font = New Font("Verdana", 10, FontStyle.Regular)
```

This technique is useful when you want to show a list of fonts in some sort of document editing application, and you want to render the font names in their corresponding typefaces in the menu.

If you need to perform more radical alterations to how a menu is drawn, you'll need to use another renderer. The `MenuStrip`, like all the "strip" controls, provides a `RenderMode` and a `Renderer` property. The `RenderMode` property allows you to use one of the built-in renderers by choosing a value from the `ToolStripRenderMode` enumeration (such as `Professional`, `System`, and `Custom`). If you want to use a renderer of your own, select `Custom` and then supply a new renderer object in the `Renderer` property. This renderer could be an instance of a third-party class or an instance of a class you've created (just derive from `ToolStripRenderer` and override the methods to supply your specialized painting logic).

Put the Web in a Window

.NET's new managed WebBrowser control lets you show an HTML page or allow a user to browse a web site from inside your Windows application—with no interop headaches.

There's no shortage of reasons why you might want to integrate a web page window into your application. Maybe you want to show your company web site, create a customized browser, or display HTML product documentation. In .NET 1.0 and .NET 1.1, you could use a web browser window through COM interop, but there were a number of quirky or missing features. The new `WebBrowser` control in .NET 2.0 addresses these issues with easy web integration, support for printing and saving documents, and the ability to stop a user from navigating to the wrong web site.

How do I do that?

The `System.Windows.Forms.WebBrowser` control wraps an Internet Explorer window. You can drop the `WebBrowser` control onto any Windows form straight from the Visual Studio .NET toolbox.

The WebBrowser control supports everything IE does, including JavaScript, ActiveX controls, and plug-ins.

To direct the `WebBrowser` to show a page, you simply set the `Url` property to the target web page. All navigation in the `WebBrowser` is asynchronous, which means your code continues running while the page is downloading. To check if the page is complete, verify that the `ReadyState` property is `Completed` or, better yet, react to a `WebBrowser` event.

The WebBrowser events unfold in this order:

1. Navigating fires when you set a new Url or the user clicks a link. This is your chance to cancel the navigation before anything happens.

2. Navigated fires after Navigating, just before the web browser begins downloading the page.

3. The ProgressChanged event fires periodically during a download and gives you information about how many bytes have been downloaded and how many are expected in total.

4. DocumentCompleted fires when the page is completely loaded. This is your chance to process the page.

Example 3-3 shows the event-handling code for a form, WebForm, which hosts a WebBrowser along with a simple status bar and progress bar. The WebBrowser displays a local HTML file (note how the URL starts with file:///, not http://) and ensures that any external web links are opened in stand-alone Internet Explorer windows.

WebBrowser provides methods that duplicate the browser functions every web surfer is familiar with, such as Stop(), Refresh(), GoBack(), GoForward(), GoHome(), GoSearch(), Print(), ShowPrintDialog(), and ShowSaveAsDialog().

Example 3-3. Building a basic browser window

```
Public Class WebForm

    Private Sub WebForm_Load(ByVal sender As Object, ByVal e As EventArgs) _
        Handles MyBase.Load
        ' Prevent the user from dragging and dropping links onto this browser.
        Browser.AllowWebBrowserDrop = False

        ' Go to the local documentation page.
        Browser.Url = new Uri("file:///" & _
            My.Application.StartupPath & "\Doc.html")
    End Sub

    Private Sub Browser_Navigating(ByVal sender As Object, _
      ByVal e As WebBrowserNavigatingEventArgs) Handles Browser.Navigating
        If Not e.Url.IsFile Then
            ' Don't resolve this external link.
            ' Instead, use the Navigate() method to open a
            ' standalone IE window.
            e.Cancel = True
            Browser.Navigate(e.Url, True)
        End If
    End Sub

    Private Sub Browser_Navigated(ByVal sender As Object, _
      ByVal e As WebBrowserNavigatedEventArgs) Handles Browser.Navigated
        ' Show the progress bar.
        Progress.Visible = True
    End Sub
```

Example 3-3. Building a basic browser window (continued)

```
Private Sub Browser_ProgressChanged(ByVal sender As Object, _
  ByVal e As WebBrowserProgressChangedEventArgs) _
  Handles Browser.ProgressChanged
    ' Update the progress bar.
    Progress.Maximum = e.MaximumProgress
    Progress.Value = e.CurrentProgress
End Sub

Private Sub Browser_DocumentCompleted(ByVal sender As Object, _
  ByVal e As WebBrowserDocumentCompletedEventArgs) _
  Handles Browser.DocumentCompleted
    ' Hide the progress bar.
    Progress.Visible = False
End Sub

Private Sub Browser_StatusTextChanged(ByVal sender As Object, _
  ByVal e As EventArgs) Handles Browser.StatusTextChanged
    ' Display the text that IE would ordinarily show
    ' in the status bar.
    Status.Text = Browser.StatusText
End Sub

End Class
```

The WebBrowser window is stripped to the bare minimum and doesn't include a toolbar, address bar, or status bar (although you can add other controls to your form).

Figure 3-6 shows the form with its customized WebBrowser window. The window also includes a StatusStrip to display status text and a progress indicator when pages are being loaded.

Figure 3-6. An embedded web window

What about...

...other web surfing tricks? WebBrowser gives you almost all of the power of IE to use in your own applications. Here are a few more tricks you might want to try:

- Instead of setting the Url property, call the Navigate() method, which has two useful overloads. The first (shown in the previous example), allows you to launch a standalone browser window. The second allows you to load a document into a specific frame in the current page.

- Instead of using URLs, you can load an HTML document directly from another resource, using the DocumentStream or DocumentText property. The DocumentStream accepts a reference to any Stream object, while the DocumentText property accepts a string that contains the HTML data.

- Once you've loaded a document, you can explore it using the HTML document model that's built into .NET. The jumping-off point is the Document property, which returns an HtmlDocument object that models the current document, including its tags and content.

- You can direct the WebBrowser to a directory to give the user quick-and-dirty file browsing abilities. Keep in mind, however, that you won't be able to prevent them from copying, moving, or deleting files!

Where can I learn more?

For the full set of properties, look up the System.Windows.Forms. WebBrowser class in the MSDN class library reference.

Validate Input While the User Types

Visual Basic 6 and Access both provide developers with *masked editing controls*: text input controls that automatically format your input as you type it in based on a specific *mask*. For example, if you type 1234567890 into a masked input control that uses a telephone-number mask, the number is displayed as the string (123) 456-7890.

Masked input controls not only improve the presentation of certain values—they also prevent errors. Choosing the right mask ensures that certain characters will be rejected outright (for example, a telephone–

VB 6 programmers accustomed to the ActiveX MaskedEdit control were disappointed to find .NET did not include a replacement. In .NET 2.0, the new MaskedTextBox fills the gap.

number mask will not accept letters). Masked input controls also neatly avoid *canonicalization errors*, which occur when there is more than one way of representing the same information. For example, with the telephone number mask, the user will immediately realize that an area code is required, even if you don't specifically explain this requirement.

How do I do that?

Thanks to the wonders of COM Interop, it's still possible to use the VB 6 MaskedEdit control in .NET. However, the .NET MaskedTextBox control improves on several limitations and quirks in the MaskedEdit control, so it's still superior.

.NET 2.0 includes a new control named MaskedTextBox that extends the TextBox control. Once you've added a MaskedTextBox to a form, you can set the mask in two ways:

- You can choose one of the prebuilt masks.
- You can define your own custom mask.

To set a mask, click the MaskedTextBox smart tag and select Set Mask. The Input Mask dialog box appears, with a list of commonly used masks, including masks for phone numbers, zip codes, dates, and so on. When you select a mask from the list, the mask is displayed in the Mask text box. You can now customize the mask. You can also try the mask out using the Try It text box, as shown in Figure 3-7.

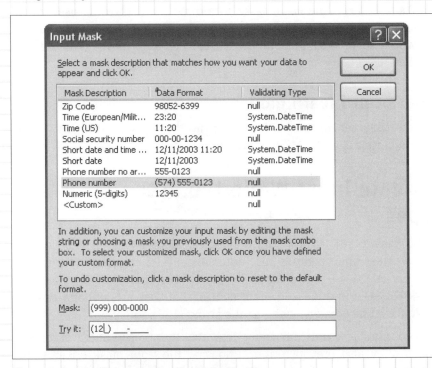

Figure 3-7. Selecting a mask for the MaskedTextBox

The mask you choose will be stored in the `MaskTextBox.Mask` property. Once you've chosen a mask, it will be applied whenever the user types in the `MaskedTextBox`. If you want to respond to user mistakes (like invalid characters) to provide more information, you can respond to the `MaskInputRejected` event.

If you want to build a custom mask, you need to understand a little more about how masking works. Essentially, a mask is built out of two types of characters: *placeholders*, which designate where the user must supply a character; and *literals*, which are used to format the value. For example, in the phone number mask (999)-000-000, the hyphens and brackets are literals. These characters are always present and can't be deleted, modified, or moved by the user. The number 0 is a placeholder that represents any number character, while the number 9 is a placeholder that represents an optional numeric character.

Table 3-1 lists and explains all the characters you can use to create a mask. You can use this as a reference to build your own masks.

Table 3-1. Mask characters

Character	Description
0	Required digit (0–9).
9	Optional digit or space. If left blank, a space is inserted automatically.
#	Optional digit, space, or plus/minus symbol. If left blank, a space is inserted automatically.
L	Required ASCII letter (a–z or A–Z).
?	Optional ASCII letter.
&	Required Unicode character. Allows anything that isn't a control key, including punctuation and symbols.
C	Optional Unicode character.
A	Required alphanumeric character (allows letter or number but not punctuation or symbols).
a	Optional alphanumeric character.
.	Decimal placeholder.
,	Thousands placeholder.
:	Time separator.
/	Date separator.
$	Currency symbol.
<	All the characters that follow will be converted automatically to lowercase as the user types them in. (There is no way to switch a subsequent portion of the text back to mixed-case entry mode once you use this character.)

Table 3-1. Mask characters (continued)

Character	Description
>	All the characters that follow will be converted automatically to uppercase as the user types them in.
\	Escapes a masked character, turning it into a literal. Thus, if you use \& it is interpreted as a literal character &, which will be inserted in the text box.
All other characters	All other characters are treated as literals, and are shown in the text box.

Finally, there are a few more properties that the MaskedTextBox provides (and you might want to take advantage of). These include:

BeepOnError

> If the user inputs an invalid character and BeepOnError is True, the MaskedTextBox will play the standard error chime.

PromptChar

> When the text box is empty, every required value is replaced with a prompt character. By default, the prompt character is the underscore (_), so a mask for a telephone number will display (___)-___-____ while empty.

MaskCompleted

> Returns True if there are no empty characters in the text box (meaning the user has entered the required value).

InputText

> InputText returns the data in the MaskedTextBox without any literal characters. For example, in a MaskedTextBox that allows the user to enter a telephone number, the Text property will return the fully formatted number, like (123)-456-7890, while InputText returns just the numeric content, or 1234567890.

What about...

...using masked editing in other input controls? It is possible, but not easy. The MaskedTextBox relies on a special MaskedEditProvider class in the System.ComponentModel namespace.

To create a different type of masked control, you need to create a custom control that uses the MaskedEditProvider internally. When your control receives a key press, you need to determine the attempted action and pass it on to the MaskedEditProvider using methods like Add( ), Insert( ),

Remove( ), and Replace( ). Then, you can retrieve the new display value by calling MaskedEditProvider.ToDisplayString( ), and refresh your custom control appropriately. The hard part is handling all of this low-level editing without causing flicker or losing the user's place in the input string. For more information, you can refer to the full example that's included with the downloadable code in the MaskedEditing project.

Create Text Boxes that Auto-Complete

With .NET's new auto-complete features, you can create intelligent text boxes able to suggest possible values based on recent entries or a default list.

In many of the nooks and crannies of the Windows operating system, you'll find AutoComplete text boxes. These text boxes suggest one or more values as you type.

Usually, AutoComplete values are drawn from your recent history. For example, when you type a URL into Internet Explorer's address bar, you'll see a list that includes URLs you've surfed to in the past. Now with .NET 2.0, you can harness the same AutoComplete features with your own custom lists or one of the lists maintained by the operating system.

How do I do that?

The TextBox and the ComboBox controls both support the AutoComplete feature in .NET 2.0. To use AutoComplete, first set the control's AutoCompleteMode property to one of the following values:

Append

> In this mode, the AutoComplete value is automatically inserted into the control as you type. However, the added portion is selected so that the new portion will be replaced if you continue typing. (Alternatively, you can just click delete to remove it.)

Suggest

> This is the friendliest mode. As you type, a drop-down list of matching AutoComplete values appears underneath the control. If one of these entries matches what you want, you can select it.

SuggestAppend

> This mode combines Append and Suggest. As with Suggest, a list of candidate matches is shown in a drop-down list. However, the first match is also inserted into the control and selected.

After choosing the type of AutoComplete, you need to specify what list will be used for suggestions. Do this by setting the AutoCompleteSource property to one of the following values:

FileSystem
> Includes recently entered file paths. Use FileSystemDirectories instead to include only directory paths.

HistoryList
> Includes URLs from Internet Explorer's history list.

RecentlyUsedList
> Includes all the documents in the user's "most recently used list," which appears in the Start menu (depending on system settings).

AllUrl
> Includes the URLs of all sites that the current user has visited recently, whether they were typed in manually by the user or linked to from a web page.

AllSystemSources
> Includes the full list of URLs and file paths.

ListItems
> Includes the items in the ComboBox.Items collection. This choice isn't valid with the TextBox.

CustomSource
> Includes the items in the AutoCompleteCustomSource collection. You need to add these items yourself.

Figure 3-8 shows an AutoComplete text box using AutoSuggestAppend as the AutoCompleteMode and AllUrl as the AutoCompleteSource.

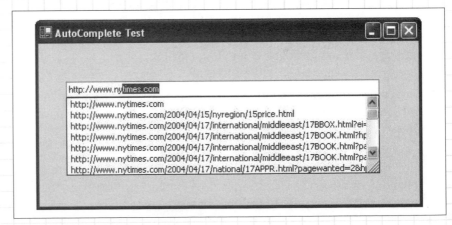

Figure 3-8. An AutoComplete text box

The TextBox and ComboBox controls both provide the same functionality. If you use AutoSuggest or AutoSuggestAppend with a ComboBox, the list of matches is displayed in a list under the control. However, this list shouldn't be confused with the list of entries that you've added to the ComboBox.Items property. When you click the drop-down arrow for the ComboBox, you'll see your list of items, *not* the list of AutoComplete suggestions. Both lists are completely separate, and there is no programmatic way for you to interact with the AutoComplete list. The only exception is if you create a ComboBox with an AutoCompleteSource of CustomSource or ListItems.

What about...

...using AutoComplete in other controls? Unfortunately, there's no managed way to do it in .NET. However, you can retrieve the information you need directly from the registry. For example, if you look in the *Software\ Microsoft\Internet Explorer\TypedURLs* section of the HKEY_CURRENT_USER registry key, you'll find the list of recently typed in URLs. To retrieve these items programmatically, refer to classes like the RegistryKey in the Microsoft.Win32 namespace.

Play a Windows System Sound

The Windows operating system alerts users to system events by mapping them to sounds recorded in specific audio files. The problem is that these files are stored in different locations on different computers. In .NET 1.0 and 1.1, there's no easy way to find the default system sounds and play them in your own application. A new SystemSounds class in .NET 2.0 addresses this problem, allowing you to play the most common sounds with a single line of code.

Need to sound the infamous Windows chime? With the new SystemSounds class, these audio files are right at your fingertips.

How do I do that?

The SystemSounds class in the System.Windows.Forms namespace provides five shared properties. Each of these properties is a separate SystemSound object that represents a specific operating-system event. Here's the full list:

- Asterisk
- Beep
- Exclamation
- Hand
- Question

To configure which WAV files are used for each sound, select the Sounds and Audio Devices icon in the Control Panel.

Using the SoundPlayer class, you can play WAV files without diving into the Windows API.

Once you decide which sound you want to use, you simply need to call its Play() method to play the sound. Here's an example:

```
SystemSounds.Beep.Play()
```

What about...

...playing arbitrary WAV files? The SystemSounds class works best if you just need an easy way to add a sound for simple user feedback. If you need to play an audio file of your own choosing, you need to use the SoundPlayer, as discussed in the next lab, "Play Simple WAV Audio."

Play Simple WAV Audio

Neither .NET 1.0 or .NET 1.1 provided a managed way to play audio. This shortcoming is finally addressed in .NET 2.0 with the new SoundPlayer class, which allows you to play audio synchronously or asynchronously.

How do I do that?

You can instantiate a SoundPlayer object programmatically, or you can add one to the component tray by dragging it from the toolbox at design time. Once you've created the SoundPlayer, you need to point it to the sound content you want to play. You do this by setting one of two properties:

SoundLocation
> If you have a file path or URL that points to a WAV file, specify this information in the SoundLocation property.

Stream
> If you have a Stream-based object that contains WAV audio content, use the Stream property.

Once you've set the Stream or SoundLocation property, you need to tell SoundPlayer to actually load the audio data by calling the Load() or LoadAsync() method. The Load() method pauses your code until all the audio is loaded into memory. On the other hand, LoadAsync() carries out its work on another thread and fires the LoadCompleted event once it's finished and the audio's available. Usually, you'll use Load() unless you have an extremely large audio file or it takes a long time to read the whole audio file (for example, when retrieving the audio over a slow network or Internet connection).

Finally, once the audio is available, you can call one of the following methods:

`PlaySync( )`
> Pauses your code until the audio playback is finished.

`Play( )`
> Plays the audio on another thread, allowing your code to continue with other tasks and making sure that your application's interface remains responsive.

`PlayLooping( )`
> Similar to `Play( )`, except that it loops the audio, repeating it continuously.

To halt asynchronous playback at any time, just call `Stop( )`.

The following code snippet shows an example that plays a sample sound synchronously:

```
Dim Player As New SoundPlayer( )
Player.SoundLocation = Application.StartupPath & "\mysound.wav"
Try
    Player.Load( )
    Player.PlaySync( )
Catch Err As Exception
    ' An error will occur here if the file can't be read
    ' or if it has the wrong format.
End Try
```

What about...

...other types of audio? Unfortunately, the SoundPlayer can only play the WAV audio format. If you want to play other types of multimedia, like MP3 or WMA files, you need to use a different solution, and there are no managed classes to help you out.

Two options include:

- Use COM Interop to access the Quartz library, which is a part of DirectX. The Quartz library allows you to play any file type supported by Windows Media Player, including MP3, WMA, and video formats like MPEG and AVI. For an example in C# code, refer to Microsoft's sample project at *http://msdn.microsoft.com/library/en-us/csref/html/vcwlkcominteroppart1cclienttutorial.asp*

- Use the managed DirectX 9.0 libraries. You'll need to install the DirectX client and SDK on the computer for this to work, but it gives you a great deal of power, including the ability to render three-dimensional graphics. See *http://msdn.microsoft.com/library/en-us/directx9_m/directx/dx9intro.asp* for an introduction.

Create a Windows Explorer–like Split Window

Split windows are easier than ever now that the SplitContainer control replaces the bare-bones Splitter.

.NET 1.0 gave developers the tools they needed to create split windows of the kind seen in Windows Explorer with the Splitter control. Unfortunately, creating these windows wasn't always easy, because it commonly required a combination of a Splitter and three Panel controls, all of which needed to be docked in the correct order. If you needed to split a window in more than one way, the task became even more awkward. Thankfully, .NET 2.0 streamlines the process with a SplitContainer control.

How do I do that?

A SplitContainer control is often used when the content in the two panels is related. When the user makes a selection in the first panel, the content in the second is refreshed.

Essentially, the SplitContainer control represents two panels separated by a splitter bar. The user can drag the bar to one side or another to change the relative amount of space given to each section. To help signal the availability of this functionality, the mouse pointer switches from a single- to a double-headed arrow icon when the user mouses over the splitter bar.

To create a simple interface with the SplitContainer, you should first decide how much screen real estate the SplitContainer will occupy. For example, if you need to reserve some space below the SplitContainer, start by docking a Panel to the bottom of the form. When you add the SplitContainer, its Dock property will automatically be set to DockStyle.Fill so that it fills whatever space is left over.

The SplitContainer always consists of two panels. If you set the Orientation property to Orientation.Vertical (the default), the splitter runs from top to bottom, creating left and right panels. The other option is Orientation.Horizontal, which creates top and bottom panels with a splitter bar running from left to right between them.

Once you've set the appropriate orientation, the next step is to add controls to each side of the SplitContainer. If you want a single control on each side, you simply need to drag the control to the appropriate panel in the SplitContainer and set the Dock property of the control to DockStyle.Fill, so that it fills all the available space between the splitter bar and the edges of the SplitContainer.

If you need to add more than one control in the same region of the SplitContainer, start by adding a Panel and setting the Dock property to DockStyle.Fill. Then, you can anchor other controls inside the Panel.

Once you've set up the `SplitContainer`, you don't need to write any code to manage the control resizing or user interaction. Figure 3-9 shows an example. (The complete SplitWindow project is available with the downloadable samples.)

You can also nest a `SplitContainer` inside another `SplitContainer`. This is most useful if you are using different orientations (for example, dividing a window into left and right regions and then dividing the region on the right into top and bottom compartments).

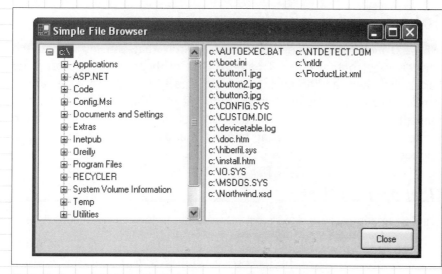

Figure 3-9. A vertically split window

What about...

...restricting how a `SplitContainer` can be resized? The `SplitContainer` provides several properties tailored for this purpose. For example, you can set the `Panel1MinSize` and `Panel2MinSize` properties with the minimum pixel width of the appropriate panels. Once you set these properties, the user won't be able to move the splitter bar to a position that shrinks the panel to less than its minimum allowed size. You can also stop resizing altogether by setting the `IsSplitterFixed` property to `False` (in which case you can still adjust the position of the splitter bar by programmatically modifying the `SplitterDistance` property).

Additionally, you can configure how the `SplitContainer` behaves when the whole form is resized. By default, the panels are sized proportionately. However, you can designate one of the panels as a *fixed panel* by setting the `FixedPanel` property. In this case, that panel won't be modified when the form is resized. (For example, in Windows Explorer the directory tree is in a fixed panel, and it doesn't change size when you expand or shrink the window.) Finally, you can even hide a panel temporarily by setting the `Panel1Collapsed` or `Panel2Collapsed` property to `True`.

Where can I learn more?

For more details on the SplitContainer and some how-to tips, look up "SplitContainer → Overview" in the index of the MSDN help reference.

Take Control of Window Layout

The new .NET layout controls give you a way to lay out controls in set patterns automatically, which can save a good deal of effort with highly dynamic or configurable interfaces.

.NET 2.0 includes two new container controls that can lay out all the controls they contain in a set pattern. Both of these controls extend the Panel class with additional layout logic. The FlowLayoutPanel arranges controls evenly over several rows (from left to right), or in multiple columns (from top to bottom). The TableLayoutPanel places its controls into a grid of invisible cells, allowing to you to keep consistent column widths and row heights.

How do I do that?

The layout controls are used most often in the following two scenarios:

- You have a dynamic interface that generates some of its elements programmatically. Using the layout controls, you can arrange a group of controls neatly without calculating a position for each control (and then setting the Location property accordingly).

- You have a localized interface that must adapt to different languages that require vastly different amounts of on-screen real estate. As a result, when the display text changes, the controls must also adjust their size. In this case, layout controls can help you make sure the controls remain properly arranged even when their size varies.

Example 3-4 demonstrates an implementation of the first scenario. It starts with a form that includes an empty FlowLayoutPanel. The FlowLayoutPanel has its BorderStyle set to BorderStyle.Fixed3D so the border is visible.

No controls are added to the FlowLayoutPanel at design time. Instead, several new buttons are added programmatically when a cmdGenerate button is clicked.

Example 3-4. Laying out buttons dynamically

```
Private Sub Button1_Click(ByVal sender As System.Object, _
    ByVal e As System.EventArgs) Handles Button1.Click
    For i As Integer = 0 To 10
        ' Create a new button.
        Dim Button As New Button
        Button.Text = "Dynamic Button #" & String.Format("{0:00}", i)
```

Example 3-4. Laying out buttons dynamically (continued)

```
        ' Size the button the width of the text.
        Button.AutoSize = True

        ' Add the button to the layout panel.
        FlowLayoutPanel1.Controls.Add(Button)
    Next
End Sub
```

Note that the code doesn't set the Location property for each button. That's because the FlowLayoutPanel won't use this information. Instead, it will arrange the buttons in the order they are added, spacing each button out from left to right and then top to bottom. (To reverse this order, change the FlowLayoutPanel.FlowDirection property.)

There is one piece of information that the FlowLayoutPanel *does* use. That's the Margin property of each container control. This sets the minimum border required between this control and the next. The code above doesn't change the Button.Margin property, because the default setting of 3 pixels is perfectly adequate.

There are actually four different components of the Margin property: Margin.Left, Margin.Right, Margin.Top, and Margin.Bottom. You can set these individually to specify different margins for the control on each side.

Figure 3-10 shows what the buttons look like once they've been added.

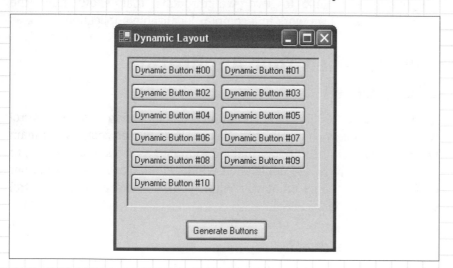

Figure 3-10. Laying out buttons dynamically

.NET also includes a TableLayoutPanel. This panel works like the FlowLayoutPanel, laying out controls automatically, but it aligns them according to invisible column and row grid lines. For example, if you have a number of controls that were sized differently, you can use the

TableLayoutPanel to ensure that each control is spaced out evenly in an imaginary cell.

What about...

...more advanced layout examples? There's a lot more you can do with a creative use of layout controls. Of course, just because you *can* doesn't mean you *should*. Microsoft architects recommend you use layout controls only in specialized scenarios where the anchoring and docking features of Windows Forms aren't enough. If you don't have a highly dynamic interface, layout managers may introduce more complexity than you need.

Where can I learn more?

To get started with more advanced uses of layout controls, refer to some of the information in the MSDN help library reference. Look up "Table-LayoutPanel control → about" in the index of the MSDN help reference. This displays general information about the TableLayoutPanel control and provides a link to two walkthroughs that show how the TableLayoutPanel can work in a complex localizable application.

Control When Your Application Shuts Down

In .NET 2.0, it's easier than ever to specify when your Windows application should call it quits.

In Visual Studio 2005, a new "Shutdown mode" option lets you control when your application should end. You can wrap up as soon as the main window is closed (the window that's designated as the *startup object*), or you can wait until *all* the application windows are closed. And if neither of these choices offers what you want, you can take complete control with the Application class.

How do I do that?

In Visual Studio, double-click the My Project item in the Solution Explorer. A tabbed window with application settings will appear, as shown in Figure 3-11. Click the Application tab, and look at the Windows Application Properties section at the bottom of the tab.

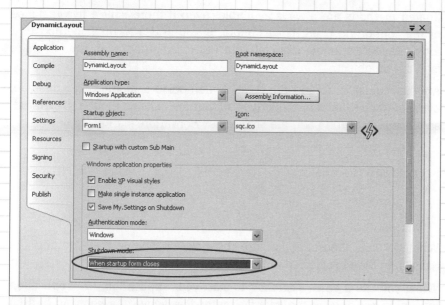

Figure 3-11. Application settings in Visual Studio 2005

You have two out-of-the-box choices for the "Shutdown mode" box:

When startup form closes

> This option matches the standard behavior of an application in .NET 1.0 and 1.1. As soon as the startup form is closed, the entire program shuts down, taking any other open windows with it. (The startup form is the form identified in the "Startup object" box.)

When last form closes

> This option matches the behavior of Visual Basic 6. Your application keeps on rolling as long as a window is open. When the last window is closed, the application follows suit, and shuts itself down.

If neither of these options is suitable, you can take matters into your own hands. First, select the "Startup with custom Sub Main" checkbox. Now, you need to add a subroutine named Main( ) to your application. You can place this subroutine in an existing form or class, as long as you make sure to add the Shared accessibility keyword. Here's an example:

```
Public Class MyForm

    Public Shared Sub Main
        ' (Startup code goes here.)
    End Sub

End Class
```

Shared methods are always available, even if there isn't a live instance of the containing class. For example, if you add a Main( ) method to a form, the .NET runtime can call your Main( ) method even though there isn't a form object.

Another choice is to add the Main( ) method to a *module*. In a module, every method, function, property, and variable acts as though it's shared, so you won't need to add the Shared keyword. Here's an example:

```
Public Module MyModule

    Public Sub Main
        ' (Startup code goes here.)
    End Sub

End Module
```

Using a module is a great choice if you have extensive initialization to perform, because it separates your startup code from your form code.

Whatever you choose, make sure the class or module that contains the Main( ) method is selected in the "Startup object" box.

When you use a Main( ) method to start your application, the application only runs as long as the Main( ) method is active. As soon as Main( ) ends, your application finishes. Here's an example of a prematurely terminated application:

```
Public Sub Main
    ' Show one form modelessly (without blocking the code).
    Form1.Show( )

    ' Show another form modelessly (at the same time as the first).
    Form2.Show( )

    ' After this line, the Main method ends, the application shuts
    ' itself down, and both windows close (after only being open a
    ' for a few milliseconds of screen time).
End Sub
```

And here's the correct code that shows two windows in sequence:

```
Public Sub Main
    ' Show one form modally (code stops until the window is closed).
    Form1.ShowDialog( )

    ' After the first window is closed, show the second modally.
    Form2.ShowDialog( )

    ' Now the application ends.
End Sub
```

In some cases, you might want to start your application with a Main( ) method to perform some basic initialization and show a few forms. Then, you might want to wait until all the forms are closed before the application ends. This pattern is easy to implement, provided you use the Application class. The basic idea is to call Application.Run( ) to keep your application alive indefinitely, and call Application.Exit( ) at some later point to end it. Here's how you could start the application with two visible windows:

```
Public Sub Main
    ' Show two forms modelessly (and at the same time).
    Form1.Show( )
    Form2.Show( )

    ' Keep the application going until you say otherwise.
    Application.Run( )
End Sub
```

To specify that the application should end when either window closes, use this code in the Form.Unload event handler of both forms:

```
Private Sub Form1_FormClosed(ByVal sender As Object, _
  ByVal e As FormClosedEventArgs) Handles Me.FormClosed
    Application.Exit( )
End Sub
```

What about...

...cleaning up when the application calls it quits? When your application ends you might want to release unmanaged resources, delete temporary files, or save some final settings. The Application class provides a solution with its ApplicationExit event. All you need to do is attach the event to a suitable event handler in the Main( ) method. Here's an example that uses a method named Shutdown( ):

```
AddHandler Application.ApplicationExit, AddressOf Shutdown
```

And here's the Shutdown( ) method that runs automatically just before the application ends:

```
Public Sub Shutdown(ByVal sender As Object, ByVal e As EventArgs)
    MessageBox.Show("Cleaning up.")
End Sub
```

The Application-ExitEvent always fires (and the code in an event handler for it always runs), even if the application has been derailed by an unhandled exception.

Where can I learn more?

For more information, refer to the Application class in the MSDN class library reference (it's in the System.Windows.Forms namespace).

Prevent Your Application from Starting Twice

There's no longer a need to write code to check whether your application is already running. VB 2005 will perform the check for you.

Want to make sure that the user can run no more than one copy of your application on the same computer? In VB .NET 1.0, you'd need to go through the awkward task of searching all the loaded processes to make sure your program wasn't already in memory. In VB 2005, the work is done for you.

How do I do that?

In Visual Studio, double-click the My Project item in the Solution Explorer. A tabbed window with application settings will appear. Click the Application tab, and look at the Windows Application Properties section at the bottom of the tab. Now click the "Make single instance application" checkbox and build the project.

If you try to start the application while it's already running, it will ignore you completely, and nothing will happen.

What about...

...showing a custom error message? If you need to show an error message, check for other instances without stopping the application, or otherwise tweak the code, then you'll need to perform the check youself by using the System.Diagnostics.Process class. Here's the code to get you started:

```
' Get the full name of the process for the current application.
Dim ModuleName, ProcessName As String
ModuleName = Process.GetCurrentProcess.MainModule.ModuleName
```

```
ProcessName = System.IO.Path.GetFileNameWithoutExtension(ModuleName)

' Check for other processes with this name.
Dim Proc() As System.Diagnostics.Process
Proc = Process.GetProcessesByName(ProcessName)
If Proc.Length > 1 Then
    ' (There is another instance running.)
Else
    ' (There are no other instances running.)
End If
```

Where can I learn more?

For more information, look up the "ProcessInfo class" index entry in the MSDN help, or look up "Process class sample" index entry for a full-fledged example.

Communicate Between Forms

In previous versions of .NET, you were responsible for tracking every open form. If you didn't, you might unwittingly strand a window, leaving it open but cut off from the rest of your application. VB 2005 restores the beloved approach of VB 6 developers, where there's always a *default instance* of your form ready, waiting, and accessible from anywhere else in your application.

VB 2005 makes it easy for forms to interact, thanks to the new default instances. This feature is a real timesaver—and a potential stumbling block.

How do I do that?

To access the default instance of a form, just use its class name. In other words, if you've created a form that's named (unimaginatively) Form1, you can show its default instance like this:

```
Form1.Show()
```

This automatically creates an instance of Form1 and then displays it. This instance of Form1 is designated as the default instance.

To communicate between forms, you simply add dedicated public methods. For example, if Form1 needs to be able to refresh Form2, you could add a RefreshData() method to Form2, like this:

```
Public Class Form2
    Private Sub RefreshData()
        MessageBox.Show("I've been refreshed!")
    End Sub
End Class
```

You could then call it like this:

```
Form2.RefreshData()
```

This calls the RefreshData( ) method of the default instance of Form2. The fact that RefreshData( ) is a method you added (not an inherited method, like the Show( ) method) makes no difference in how you use it.

You can also get at the forms using the My collection. For example, the code above is equivalent to this slightly longer statement:

```
My.Forms.Form2.RefreshData( )
```

You can always access the default instance of a form, even if it isn't currently visible. In fact, .NET creates the default instance of the form as soon as you access one of its properties or methods. If you only want to find out what forms are currently open, you're better off using the My.Application.OpenForms collection. Here's an example that iterates through the collection and displays the caption of each form:

```
For Each frm As Form In My.Application.OpenForms
    MessageBox.Show(frm.Text)
Next
```

You can also set a reference to the application's startup form using the My.Application.StartupForm property.

This handy trick just wasn't possible in earlier versions of .NET without writing your own code to manually track forms.

What about...

...potential problems? Conveniences such as default instances come at a price. In this case, you don't need to worry about wasted memory or any performance slowdown, since .NET is clever enough to create the forms as you need them. The real problem that you might face results from the fact that default instances confuse the concepts of classes and objects, making it all too easy to accidentally refer to different instances of the same form in different parts of your application.

For example, imagine you use this code to show a form:

```
Dim FormObject As New Form1
FormObject.Show( )
```

In this example, the form you've shown is an instance of Form1, but it isn't the default instance. That means that if another part of your code uses code like this:

```
Form1.Refresh( )
```

it won't have the effect you expect. The visible instance of Form1 won't be refreshed. Instead, the default instance (which probably isn't even visible) will be refreshed. Watch out for this problem—it can lead to exasperating headaches! (In all fairness to .NET, this isn't a new problem. Visual Basic 6 developers encountered the same headaches when creating forms dynamically. The difference is that Visual Basic 6 developers almost always rely on default instances, while .NET developers—until now—haven't.)

Improve Redraw Speeds for GDI+

Every control and form in .NET inherits from the base `Control` class. In .NET 2.0, the `Control` class sports a new property named `DoubleBuffered`. If you set this property to `True`, the form or control will automatically use double-buffering, which dramatically reduces flicker when you add custom drawing code.

Need to turbocharge your GDI+ animations? In .NET 2.0, the Form class can do the double-buffering for you.

How do I do that?

In some applications you need to repaint a window or control frequently. For example, you might refresh a window every 10 milliseconds to create the illusion of a continuous animation. Every time the window is refreshed, you need to erase the current contents and draw the new frame from scratch.

In a simple application, your drawing logic might draw a single shape. In a more complex animation, you could easily end up rendering dozens of different graphical elements at a time. Rendering these elements takes a small but significant amount of time. The problem is that if you paint each graphical element directly on the form, the animation will flicker as the image is repeatedly erased and reconstructed. To avoid this annoying problem, developers commonly use a technique known as *double-buffering*. With double-buffering, each new frame is fully assembled in memory, and only painted on the form when it's complete.

.NET 2.0 completely saves you the hassle of double-buffering. All you need to do is set the `DoubleBuffered` property of the form or control to `True`. For example, imagine you create a form and handle the `Paint` event to supply your own custom painting logic. If the form is set to use double-buffering, it won't be refreshed until the `Paint` event handler has finished, at which point it will copy the completed image directly onto the form. If `DoubleBuffered` is set to `False`, every time you draw an individual element onto the form in the `Paint` event handler, the form will be refreshed. As a result, the form will be refreshed dozens of times for anything but the simplest operations.

Example 3-5 features a form that makes use of custom drawing logic. When the user clicks the `cmdStart` button, a timer is switched on. This timer fires every few milliseconds and invalidates the form by calling its `Invalidate()` method. In response, Windows asks the application to repaint the window, triggering the `OnPaint()` method with the custom drawing code.

Example 3-5. An animated form

```
Public Class AnimationForm

    ' Indicates whether the animation is currently being shown.
    Private IsAnimating As Boolean = False

    ' Track how long the animation has been going on.
    Private StartTime As DateTime

    Private Sub Form_Paint(ByVal sender As Object, _
      ByVal e As System.Windows.Forms.PaintEventArgs) Handles MyBase.Paint

        ' Check if the animation is in progress.
        If IsAnimating Then

            ' Get reading to draw the current frame.
            Dim g As Graphics = e.Graphics
            g.SmoothingMode = System.Drawing.Drawing2D.SmoothingMode.HighQuality

            ' Paint the background.
            Dim BackBrush As New LinearGradientBrush( _
              New Point(0, 0), New Point(100, 100), _
              Color.Blue, Color.LightBlue)
            g.FillRectangle(BackBrush, New Rectangle(New Point(0, 0), _
              Me.ClientSize))
            g.FillRectangle(Brushes.LightPink, New Rectangle(New Point(10, 10), _
              New Point(Me.Width - 30, Me.Height - 50)))

            ' Calculate elapsed time.
            Dim Elapsed As Double = DateTime.Now.Subtract(StartTime).TotalSeconds

            Dim Pos As Double = (-100 + 24 * Elapsed ^ 2) / 10

            ' Draw some moving objects.
            Dim Pen As New Pen(Color.Blue, 10)
            Dim Brush As Brush = Brushes.Chartreuse
            g.DrawEllipse(Pen, CInt(Elapsed * 100), CInt(Pos), 10, 10)
            g.FillEllipse(Brush, CInt(Elapsed * 100), CInt(Pos), 10, 10)

            g.DrawEllipse(Pen, CInt(Elapsed * 50), CInt(Pos), 10, 10)
            g.FillEllipse(Brush, CInt(Elapsed * 50), CInt(Pos), 10, 10)

            g.DrawEllipse(Pen, CInt(Elapsed * 76), CInt(Pos) * 2, 10, 10)
            g.FillEllipse(Brush, CInt(Elapsed * 55), CInt(Pos) * 3, 10, 10)

            g.DrawEllipse(Pen, CInt(Elapsed * 66), CInt(Pos) * 4, 10, 10)
            g.FillEllipse(Brush, CInt(Elapsed * 72), CInt(Pos) * 3, 10, 10)

            If Elapsed > 10 Then
                ' Stop the animation.
                tmrInvalidate.Stop()
                IsAnimating = False
            End If
```

Example 3-5. An animated form (continued)

```
        Else
            ' There is no animation underway. Paint the background.
            MyBase.OnPaintBackground(e)
        End If

    End Sub


    Private Sub tmrInvalidate_Tick(ByVal sender As System.Object, _
        ByVal e As System.EventArgs) Handles tmrInvalidate.Tick
            ' Invalidate the form, which will trigger a refresh.
            Me.Invalidate()
    End Sub

    Private Sub cmdStart_Click(ByVal sender As System.Object, _
        ByVal e As System.EventArgs) Handles cmdStart.Click
            ' Start the timer, which will trigger the repainting process
            ' at regular intervals.
            Me.DoubleBuffered = True
            IsAnimating = True
            StartTime = DateTime.Now
            tmrInvalidate.Start()
    End Sub

    ' Ensure that the form background is not repainted automatically
    ' when the form is invalidated. This isn't necessary, because the
    ' Paint event will handle the painting for the form.
    ' If you don't override this method, every time the form is painted
    ' the window will be cleared and the background color will be painted
    ' on the surface, which causes extra flicker.
    Protected Overrides Sub OnPaintBackground( _
        ByVal pevent As System.Windows.Forms.PaintEventArgs)
            ' Do nothing.
    End Sub

End Class
```

Try running this example with and without double-buffering. You'll see a dramatic difference in the amount of flicker.

What about...

...owner-drawn controls? Double-buffering works exactly the same way with owner-drawn controls as with forms, because both the Form and Control classes provide the DoubleBuffered property and the Paint event. Of course, there's no point in double-buffering both a form and its controls, since that will only cause your application to consume unnecessary extra memory.

Where can I learn more?

Overall, the GDI+ drawing functions remain essentially the same in .NET 2.0. To learn more about drawing with GDI+, look up "GDI+ → Examples" in the index of the MSDN help library. You may also be interested in the "GDI+ Images" and "GDI+ Text" entries.

Handle Asynchronous Tasks Safely

Need to conduct a time-consuming task in the background without dealing with threading issues? The new Background-Worker class makes it easy.

One of .NET's most impressive features is its extensive support for multi-threaded programming. However, as most programmers discover at some point in their lives, multithreaded programming isn't necessarily easy.

One of the main challenges with Windows applications is that it's not safe to modify a form or control from a background thread, which means that after your background task is finished, there's no straightforward way to update your application's interface. You can use the Control. Invoke() method to marshal a method to the correct thread, but other problems then appear, such as transferring the information you need to make the update. Fortunately, all of these headaches can be avoided thanks to the new BackgroundWorker component.

How do I do that?

The BackgroundWorker component gives you a foolproof way to run a time-consuming task on a separate, dedicated thread. This ensures that your application interface remains responsive, and it allows your code to carry out other tasks in the foreground. Best of all, the underlying complexities of multithreaded programming are hidden. Once the background process is complete, you simply handle an event, which fires on the main thread. In addition, the BackgroundWorker supports progress reporting and canceling.

You can either create a BackgroundWorker object programmatically, or you can drag it onto a form from the Components tab of the toolbox. To start your background operation, you call the RunWorkerAsync() method. If you need to pass an input value to this process, you can supply it as an argument to this method (any type of object is allowed):

```
Worker.RunWorkerAsync(inputValue)
```

Next, you need to handle the DoWork event to perform the background task. The DoWork event fires on the background thread, which means at this point you can't interact with any other part of your application (unless you're willing to use locks or other techniques to safeguard access). Typically, the DoWork event handler retrieves the input value from the DoWorkEventArgs.Argument property and then carries out the time-consuming operation. Once the operation is complete, you simply set the DoWorkEventArgs.Result property with the result. You can use any data type or even a custom object. Here's the basic pattern you'll use:

```
Private Sub backgroundWorker1_DoWork(ByVal sender As Object, _
    ByVal e As DoWorkEventArgs) Handles backgroundWorker1.DoWork

    ' Get the information that was supplied.
    Dim Input As Integer = CType(e.Argument, Integer)

    ' (Perform some time consuming task.)

    ' Return the result.
    e.Result = Answer

End Sub
```

Finally, the BackgroundWorker fires a RunWorkerCompleted event to notify your application that the process is complete. At this point, you can retrieve the result from RunWorkerCompletedEventArgs and update the form accordingly:

```
Private Sub backgroundWorker1_RunWorkerCompleted( _
    ByVal sender As Object, ByVal e As RunWorkerCompletedEventArgs) _
    Handles backgroundWorker1.RunWorkerCompleted

    result.Text = "Result is: " & e.Result.ToString()

End Sub
```

Example 3-6 shows a form that puts all of these parts together. It performs a time-limited loop for a number of seconds that you specify. This example also demonstrates two more advanced techniques: cancellation and progress. To cancel the operation, you simply need to call the BackgroundWorker.CancelAsync() method. Your DoWork event-handling code can then check to see if the main form is attempting to cancel the operation and exit gracefully. To maintain progress information, your DoWork event-handling code needs to call the BackgroundWorker. ReportProgress() method and provide an estimated percent complete (where 0% means "just started" and 100% means "completely finished"). The form code can respond to the ProgressChanged event to read the new progress percentage and update another control, such as a ProgressBar. Figure 3-12 shows this application in action.

Example 3-6. An asynchronous form with the BackgroundWorker

```
Public Class AsyncForm

    Private Sub startAsyncButton_Click(ByVal sender As System.Object, _
      ByVal e As System.EventArgs) Handles startAsyncButton.Click

        ' Disable the Start button until
        ' the asynchronous operation is done.
        startAsyncButton.Enabled = False

        ' Enable the Cancel button while
        ' the asynchronous operation runs.
        cancelAsyncButton.Enabled = True

        ' Start the asynchronous operation.
        backgroundWorker1.RunWorkerAsync(Int32.Parse(txtWaitTime.Text))
    End Sub

    ' This event handler is where the actual work is done.
    Private Sub backgroundWorker1_DoWork(ByVal sender As Object, _
      ByVal e As DoWorkEventArgs) Handles backgroundWorker1.DoWork

        ' Get the information that was supplied.
        Dim Worker As BackgroundWorker = CType(sender, BackgroundWorker)

        Dim StartTime As DateTime = DateTime.Now
        Dim SecondsToWait As Integer = CType(e.Argument, Integer)
        Dim Answer As Single = 100
        Do
            ' Check for any cancellation requests.
            If Worker.CancellationPending Then
                e.Cancel = True
                Return
            End If

            ' Continue calculating the answer.
            Answer *= 1.01

            ' Report the current progress (percentage complete).
            Worker.ReportProgress(( _
              DateTime.Now.Subtract(StartTime).TotalSeconds / SecondsToWait) * 100)

            Thread.Sleep(50)
        Loop Until DateTime.Now > (StartTime.AddSeconds(SecondsToWait))

        e.Result = Answer
    End Sub

    ' This event handler fires when the background work
    ' is complete.
    Private Sub backgroundWorker1_RunWorkerCompleted( _
      ByVal sender As Object, ByVal e As RunWorkerCompletedEventArgs) _
      Handles backgroundWorker1.RunWorkerCompleted
```

Example 3-6. An asynchronous form with the BackgroundWorker (continued)

```vb
        ' Check what the result was, and update the form.
        If Not (e.Error Is Nothing) Then
            ' An exception was thrown.
            MessageBox.Show(e.Error.Message)
        ElseIf e.Cancelled Then
            ' Check if the user cancelled the operation.
            result.Text = "Cancelled"
        Else
            ' The operation succeeded.
            result.Text = "Result is: " & e.Result.ToString()
        End If

        startAsyncButton.Enabled = True
        cancelAsyncButton.Enabled = False
    End Sub

    ' This event handler updates the progress bar.
    Private Sub backgroundWorker1_ProgressChanged( _
      ByVal sender As Object, ByVal e As ProgressChangedEventArgs) _
      Handles backgroundWorker1.ProgressChanged

        Me.progressBar1.Value = e.ProgressPercentage
    End Sub

    Private Sub cancelAsyncButton_Click( _
      ByVal sender As System.Object, ByVal e As System.EventArgs) _
      Handles cancelAsyncButton.Click

        ' Cancel the asynchronous operation.
        Me.backgroundWorker1.CancelAsync()

        cancelAsyncButton.Enabled = False
    End Sub

End Class
```

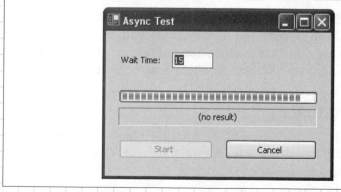

Figure 3-12. Monitoring a background task

What about...

...other scenarios where you can use the BackgroundWorker? This example used the BackgroundWorker with a long-running background calculation. Other situations in which the BackgroundWorker proves to be just as indispensable include:

- Contacting a web service
- Downloading a file over the Internet
- Retrieving data from a database
- Reading or writing large amounts of data

Where can I learn more?

The MSDN reference includes a detailed walkthrough for using the BackgroundWorker, and other topics that tackle multithreaded programming in detail. Look up the "background operations" index entry to see a slightly different approach that uses the BackgroundWorker to calculate Fibonacci numbers.

Use a Better Data-Bound Grid

.NET's DataGrid was a significant disappointment in an otherwise state-of-the-art framework. Now the Windows Forms team fills in the gaps with a first-rate grid.

The DataGrid that shipped with .NET 1.0 and 1.1 had a slew of limitations. It was difficult to customize, nearly impossible to extend, and had no support for important features like modifying or filling the DataGrid programmatically, accessing individual cells, or applying per-cell formatting. In many cases, VB developers avoided the DataGrid altogether and used third-party grids or even older COM-based controls like the MSFlexGrid. (In fact, third-party component developers regularly thanked Microsoft for making enhanced grid components an easy sell.)

In designing .NET 2.0, the Windows Forms team decided it would be nearly impossible to remedy the shortcomings without breaking backward compatibility. So, they chose to introduce an entirely new DataGridView control with support for all the missing features and more.

How do I do that?

You can bind the DataGridView to a DataTable object in the same way that you would bind a DataGrid. Here's the bare minimum code you might use to bind a table named Customers:

```
DataGridView1.DataSource = ds
DataGridView.DataMember = "Customers"
```

Of course, to put this code to work, you need to create the DataSet object ds and fill it with information. For a complete example that adds the necessary ADO.NET code for this step, refer to the downloadable content for this chapter.

When you use this code, the DataGridView creates one column for each field in the data source, and titles it using the field name. The grid also has a significant amount of out-of-the-box functionality. Some of the characteristics you'll notice include:

- The column headers are frozen. That means they won't disappear as you scroll down the list.

- You can edit values. Just double-click a cell or press F2 to put it in edit mode. (You can disable this feature by setting the DataColumn. ReadOnly property to True in the underlying DataTable.)

- You can sort columns. Just click the column header once or twice.

- You can automatically size columns. Just double-click on the column divider between headers to expand a column (the one on the left) to fit the current content.

- You can select a range of cells. You can highlight one or more cells, or multiple rows, by clicking and dragging. To select the entire table, click the square at the top-left corner.

- You can add rows by scrolling to the end of the grid and entering new values. To disable this feature, set the AllowUserToAddRows property to False.

- You can delete rows by selecting the full row (click the row button at the left) and pressing the Delete key. To disable this feature, set the AllowUserToDeleteRows property to False.

Before going any further with the DataGridView, there are two methods you'll want to consider using right away: AutoResizeColumns() and AutoResizeRows(). AutoResizeColumns() extends all columns to fit header text and cell data. AutoResizeRows() enlarges the row with multiple lines to fit header text and cell data (the DataGridView supports automatic wrapping). Both of these methods accept a value from an enumeration that allows you to specify additional options (such as extending the column just to fit all the columns, or just the header text):

```
' Create wider columns to fit data.
DataGridView1.AutoResizeColumns( _
  DataGridViewAutoSizeColumnsMode.AllCells)

' Create multi-line columns to fit data.
DataGridView1.AutoResizeRows( _
  DataGridViewAutoSizeRowsMode.HeaderAndColumnsAllCells)
```

You can also use the AutoResizeColumn( ) and AutoResizeRow( ) methods to change just a single column or row (specified as an index number).

Once you have created a DataGridView and populated it with data, you can interact with it through two useful collections: Columns and Rows. The Columns collection exposes a collection of DataGridViewCell objects, one for each column in the grid. You can set the order in which columns are displayed (by setting an index number in the DisplayIndex property), hide a column altogether (set Visible to false), or freeze a column so that it always remains visible even as the user scrolls to the side (set Frozen to true). You can also modify the column header text (HeaderText), the size (Width), and make it non-editable (ReadOnly). To look up a column, use the index number or the corresponding field name.

For example, here's the code you need to change some column properties in the OrderID column of a bound DataGridView:

```
' Keep this column visible on the left at all times.
DataGridView1.Columns("CustomerID").Frozen = True
DataGridView1.Columns("CustomerID").DisplayIndex = 0

' Configure the column appearance.
DataGridView1.Columns("CustomerID").HeaderText = "ID"
DataGridView1.Columns("CustomerID").Resizable = DataGridViewTriState.True
DataGridView1.Columns("CustomerID").MinimumWidth = 50
DataGridView1.Columns("CustomerID").Width = 50

' Don't allow the values in this column to be edited.
DataGridView1.Columns("CustomerID").ReadOnly = True
```

The Rows collection allows you to access individual DataGridViewRow objects by index number. Once you have a DataGridViewRow, you can examine its Cells collection to look up individual values in that row.

However, it's more likely that you'll want to access just those rows that correspond to the current user selection. The DataGridView actually provides three related properties that can help you:

SelectedRows

Provides a collection with one DataGridViewRow for each fully selected row. This makes sense if the SelectionMode only allows full row selection.

SelectedColumns

Provides a collection with one DataGridViewColumn for each fully selected column. This makes sense if the SelectionMode only allows full column selection.

SelectedCells

Always provides a collection with one DataGridViewCell for each selected cell, regardless of the selection mode. You can use this property if your selection mode allows individual cell selection or if you just want to process each cell separately.

For example, if you're using DataGridViewSelectionMode.FullRowSelect, you can use the following code to retrieve the current selection and display a specific field from each selected row when the user clicks a button:

```
Private Sub cmdSelection_Click(ByVal sender As System.Object, _
    ByVal e As System.EventArgs) Handles cmdSelection.Click

    For Each SelectedRow As DataGridViewRow In DataGridView1.SelectedRows
        MessageBox.Show(SelectedRow.Cells("CustomerID").Value)
    Next

End Sub
```

For a full example that puts all of these ingredients together, refer to the BetterDataGrid example in the downloadable samples.

You can control the type of selection that's allowed by setting the DataGridView. SelectionMode property. Different values allow selection for individual cells, rows, or columns. DataGridView. MultiSelect determines whether more than one item can be selected at a time.

What about...

...doing more with the DataGridView? The features described so far provide a snapshot of DataGridView basics, but they only scratch the surface of its customizability features. For more information, refer to the following two labs in this chapter ("Format the DataGridView" and "Add Images and Controls to the DataGridView").

Format the DataGridView

Formatting the .NET 1.x DataGrid ranges from awkward to nearly impossible. However, thanks to its multi-layered model, formatting the DataGridView is far easier. This model builds on a single class, the DataGridViewCellStyle, which encapsulates key formatting properties. You can assign different DataGridViewCellStyle objects to separate rows, columns, or even distinct cells.

By using a few simple style properties, you can configure the appearance of the entire grid, individual columns, or rows with important data.

How do I do that?

The DataGridView already looks better than the DataGrid in its default state. For example, you'll notice that the column headers have a modern, flat look and become highlighted when the user moves the mouse over them. However, there's much more you can do with the help of the `DataGridViewCellStyle` class.

The `DataGridViewCellStyle` collects all the formatting properties of the `DataGridView`. It defines appearance-related settings (e.g., color, font), and data formatting (e.g., currency, date formats). All in all, the `DataGridViewCellStyle` provides the following key properties:

Alignment
: Sets how text is justified inside the cell.

BackColor and ForeColor
: Set the color of the cell background and the color of the cell text.

Font
: Sets the font used for the cell text.

Format
: A format string that configures how numeric or date data values will be formatted as strings. You can use the standard .NET format specifiers and your own custom format strings. For example, C designates a currency value. (For more information, look up the index entry "numeric format strings" in the MSDN help.)

NullText
: A string of text that will be substituted for any null (missing) values.

SelectionBackColor and SelectionForeColor
: Set the cell background colors and text colors for selected cells.

WrapMode
: Determines if text will flow over multiple lines (if the row is high enough to accommodate it) or if it will be truncated. By default, cells will wrap.

The interesting part is that you can create and set `DataGridViewCellStyle` objects at different levels. When the `DataGridView` displays a cell, it looks for style information in several places. Here's the order from highest to lowest importance:

1. DataGridViewCell.Style
2. DataGridViewRow.DefaultCellStyle
3. DataGridView.AlternatingRowsDefaultCellStyle
4. DataGridView.RowsDefaultCellStyle
5. DataGridViewColumn.DefaultCellStyle
6. DataGridView.DefaultCellStyle

In other words, if DataGridView finds a DataGridViewCellStyle object assigned to the current cell (option 1), it always uses it. If not, it checks the DataGridViewCellStyle for the row, and so on.

The following code snippet performs column-specific formatting. It ensures that all the values in the CustomerID column are given a different font, alignment, and set of colors. Figure 3-13 shows the result.

```
Dim Style As DataGridViewCellStyle = _
    DataGridView1.Columns("CustomerID").DefaultCellStyle
Style.Font = New Font(DataGridView1.Font, FontStyle.Bold)
Style.Alignment = DataGridViewContentAlignment.MiddleRight
Style.BackColor = Color.LightYellow
Style.ForeColor = Color.DarkRed
```

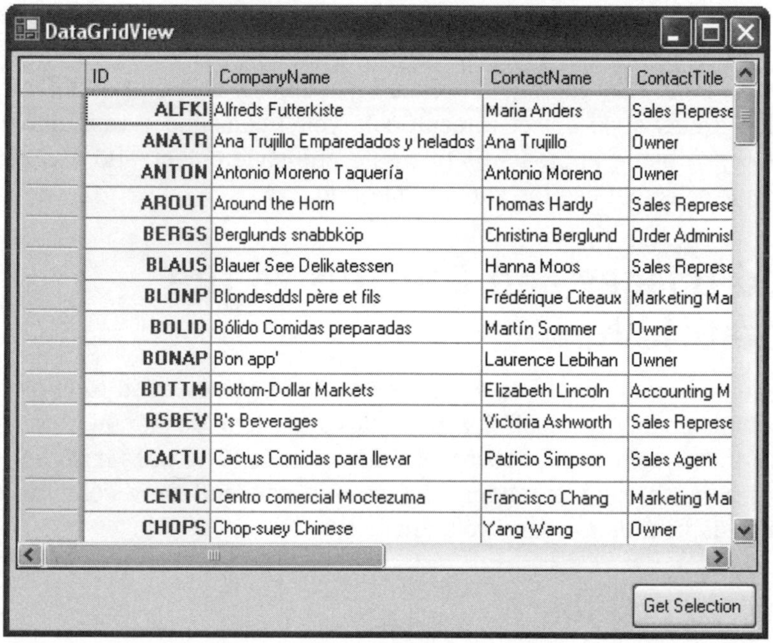

Figure 3-13. A DataGridView with a formatted column

If you use the design-time data-binding features of Visual Studio, you can avoid writing this code altogether. Just click the Edit Columns link in the Properties Window and use the designer to choose the formatting.

What about...

...the easiest way to apply custom cell formatting? Sometimes, you want to call attention to cells with certain values. You could handle this task by iterating over the entire grid, looking for those cells that interest you. However, you can save time by responding to the DataGridView. CellFormatting event. This event occurs as the grid is being filled. It gives you the chance to inspect the cell and change its style before it appears.

Here's an example that formats a cell to highlight high prices:

```
Private Sub DataGridView1_CellFormatting(ByVal sender As System.Object, _
    ByVal e As System.Windows.Forms.DataGridViewCellFormattingEventArgs) _
    Handles DataGridView1.CellFormatting

        ' Check if this is the right column.
        If DataGridView1.Columns(e.ColumnIndex).Name = "Price" Then
            ' Check if this is the right value.
            If e.Value > 100 Then
                e.CellStyle.ForeColor = Color.Red
                e.CellStyle.BackColor = Color.Yellow
            End If
        End If

End Sub
```

Keep in mind that you should reuse style objects if at all possible. If you assign a new style object to each cell, you'll consume a vast amount of memory. A better approach is to create one style object, and assign it to multiple cells that use the same formatting.

Add Images and Controls to the DataGridView

There's a lot more that you can do with the DataGridView, including adding static buttons and images.

To create a custom column with the DataGrid, you needed to implement the functionality yourself by deriving a custom DataGridColumnStyle class that would need dozens of lines of code. The DataGridView provides a much simpler model. In fact, you can add new columns right alongside your data-bound columns!

How do I do that?

In many scenarios, it's useful to display a button next to each row in a grid. Clicking this button can then remove a record, add an item to a shopping cart, or call up another window with more information. The DataGridView makes this easy with the DataGridViewButtonColumn class. You simply need to create a new instance, specify the button text, and add it to the end of the grid:

```
' Create a button column.
Dim Details As New DataGridViewButtonColumn()
Details.Name = "Details"
```

```
' Turn off data-binding and show static text.
' (You could use a property from the table by setting
' the DataPropertyName property instead.)
Details.UseColumnTextForButtonValue = False
Details.Text = "Details..."

' Clear the header.
Details.HeaderText = ""

' Add the column.
DataGridView1.Columns.Insert(DataGridView1.Columns.Count, Details)
```

Once you've performed this easy task, you can intercept the CellClick event to perform another action (Figure 3-14 shows the result of this simple test):

```
Private Sub DataGridView1_CellClick(ByVal sender As System.Object, _
    ByVal e As System.Windows.Forms.DataGridViewCellEventArgs) _
    Handles DataGridView1.CellClick

    If DataGridView1.Columns(e.ColumnIndex).Name = "Details" Then
        MessageBox.Show("You picked " & _
        DataGridView1.Rows(e.RowIndex).Cells("CustomerID").Value)
    End If

End Sub
```

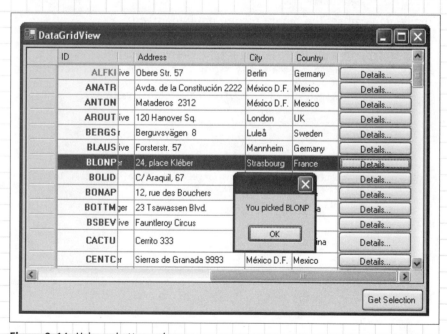

Figure 3-14. Using a button column

Creating an image column is just as easy. In this case, you simply create and add a new DataGridViewImageColumn object. If you want to show the same static image in each cell, simply set the Image property with the Image object you want to use.

A more sophisticated technique is to show a separate image for each record. You can draw this record from a binary field in the database, or read it from a file specified in a string field. In either case, the technique is basically the same. First of all, you hide the column that contains the real data (the raw binary information for the picture, or the path to the file) by setting its Visible property to False. Then, you create a new DataGridViewImageColumn:

```
DataGridView1.DataSource = ds
DataGridView1.DataMember = "pub_info"

' Hide the binary data.
DataGridView1.Columns("logo").Visible = False

' Add an image column.
Dim ImageCol As New DataGridViewImageColumn()
ImageCol.Name = "Image"
ImageCol.Width=200
DataGridView1.Columns.Add(ImageCol)
```

Finally, you can set the binary picture data you need:

In many cases, DataGridView is intelligent enough to recognize image data types and use them seamlessly in image columns, with no conversion required. However, if any extra work is required (e.g., converting or removing extra header information), you need to use the technique shown here.

```
For Each Row As DataGridViewRow In DataGridView1.Rows
    ' First, you must convert the binary data to a memory stream.
    ' Then, you can use the memory stream to create an Image object.
    Try
        Dim ImageBytes() As Byte = Row.Cells("logo").Value

        Dim ms As New MemoryStream(ImageBytes)
        Dim img As Image = Image.FromStream(ms)

        ' Finally, bind the image column.
        Dim ImageCell As DataGridViewImageCell = CType(Row.Cells("Image"), _
          DataGridViewImageCell)
        ImageCell.Value = img

        ' Now you can release the original information to save space.
        Row.Cells("logo").Value = New Byte() {}

        Row.Height = 100
    Catch
        ' Ignore errors from invalid images.
    End Try

Next
```

Figure 3-15 shows the DataGridView with image data.

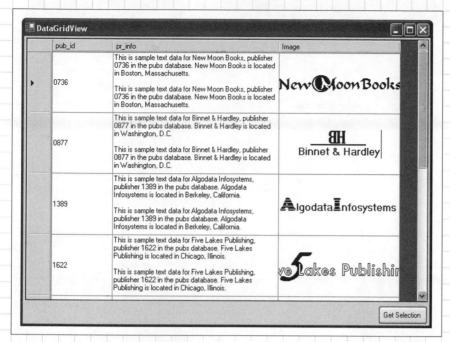

Figure 3-15. Using an image column

Where can I learn more?

So, you want to do even *more* with the DataGridView control? Because it is one of the key showpieces of the new .NET Windows Forms toolkit, there's a lot of online documentation for the DataGridView. Look up the index entry "DataGridView control (Windows Forms)" in the MSDN help, and you'll find nearly 100 entries detailing distinct features you can add to solutions that use the DataGridView!

Web Applications

Of all the changes in .NET, no part of the framework has undergone as many tweaks, tune-ups, and enhancements as ASP.NET, the popular platform for building web applications. Microsoft developers have piled on new features in an aggressive attempt to reduce the amount of code you need to write by at least 75 percent. Remarkably, they may have achieved their goal.

In this chapter, you'll see some of the most exciting and accessible changes available to VB 2005 programmers who build web applications with ASP.NET 2.0. You'll learn about new shortcuts for data binding, techniques for managing layout and web site navigation, and new tools for security and personalization. However, you won't learn about every feature that's been added to ASP.NET. We've left out, for example, the new web-part framework that provides a slew of controls for building portal web sites. For a more detailed look at the new features you'll find in ASP.NET 2.0, consider *ASP.NET 2.0: A Developer's Notebook* (O'Reilly).

Create a Web Application in Visual Studio 2005

Visual Studio .NET was the first product to equip ASP developers with a professional IDE, along with debugging and syntax-checking tools. However, creating ASP.NET projects still never seemed quite as easy as creating projects for ordinary Windows and console applications. Part of the trouble was managing the interaction between Visual Studio and Internet Information Services (IIS). Happily, Visual Studio 2005 dramatically improves the design-time experience for web applications by providing a new way to work with web projects.

In this chapter:
- *Create a Web Application in Visual Studio 2005*
- *Administer a Web Application*
- *Bind to Data Without Writing Code*
- *Bind Web Controls to a Custom Class*
- *Display Interactive Tables Without Writing Code*
- *Display Records One at a Time*
- *Achieve a Consistent Look and Feel with Master Pages*
- *Add Navigation to Your Site*
- *Easily Authenticate Users*
- *Determine How Many People Are Currently Using Your Web Site*

How do I do that?

To create a new web project in Visual Studio 2005 or Visual Studio Web Developer 2005 (Visual Studio 2005 Express isn't up to the task), select File → New → Web Site, *not* File → New → Project. You'll see the New Web Site dialog box (see Figure 4-1), in which you need to choose the location where the web project will be placed, and its development language. In the future, you'll also be able to open a new project based on a starter kit from this window.

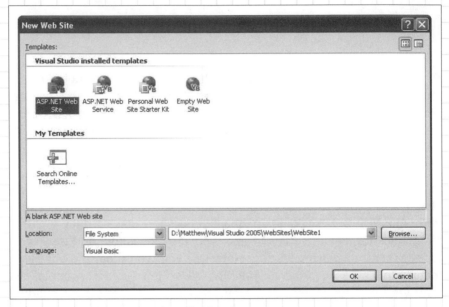

Figure 4-1. Creating a new web application directory

Visual Studio starts you out with a new directory containing two files: *default.aspx* (the entry point for your web application) and *default.aspx. vb* (the code-behind file). There are no project (*.vbproj*) or solution (*.sln*) files, which keeps the file structure simpler and makes it easier to deploy just what you need. Instead, Visual Studio automatically shows all the files and subdirectories in the web application directory.

As you start working with your web application, you'll find that Visual Studio has a few more surprises in store. One is the ability to automatically create a *web.config* file when you need it. To try this out, click the Start button to launch your application for the first time. At this point, Visual Studio notices that you don't have a *web.config* file. It then asks you if you'd like to add one automatically to enable debugging (Figure 4-2).

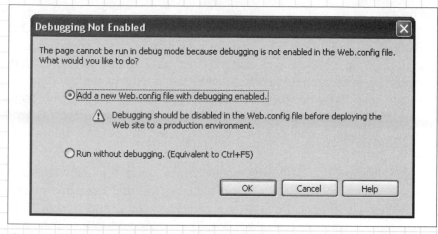

Figure 4-2. Automatically adding a new web.config file

The *web.config* file that Visual Studio creates is noticeably cleaner than the automatically generated version in Visual Studio .NET 2003. It only contains the information you need (in this case, the debugging settings). As you make other configuration changes to your application using Visual Studio, additional sections are added automatically. Once again, Visual Studio places the emphasis on simplicity and transparency.

When you run your web pages, Visual Studio's integrated web server starts automatically (look for a small icon in the system tray). As a result, you don't need to use IIS to test a web site. Visual Studio's scaled-down web server provides better security because it only serves requests that originate from the local computer. It also shuts down once you exit Visual Studio. Best of all, it allows you to create your web pages and web services where you want them, without worrying about creating the right virtual directory first.

You can try out all the labs in this chapter using the bare-bones web application you've created in this lab.

What about...

...the web page coding model? If you've spent much time programming ASP.NET web pages, you're probably aware that there are different ways to separate source code from visual content. In previous versions of Visual Studio, code-behind was the only standard that was supported (which conflicted with the default and exclusive setting of Web Matrix, another Microsoft web application IDE, which used inline code). The happy news is that Visual Studio 2005 supports both of these code models.

By default, when you add new web pages, Visual Studio 2005 uses a slightly simpler form of code-behind. Instead of using inheritance, this updated code-behind relies on another new feature called *partial classes* (see the lab "Split a Class into Multiple Files" in Chapter 2 for more information). Because partial classes provide the ability to merge separate files into one class, the code-behind file you use to handle web page events doesn't need boilerplate initialization code and web control declarations. Instead, it *only* contains your code, which makes it quite a bit shorter.

You can also use a *code-beside* model, which stores the *.aspx* tags and the code in the same file. To insert a new page that uses this model, select Web Site → Add New Item, select Web Form, and uncheck the "Place code in separate file" checkbox. Then, click Add to insert the file. The new file uses the code-beside approach but can be designed and coded just as easily as a code-behind page.

Don't be distracted by the fact that there is no file named precompile.axd in your virtual directory. All .axd requests invoke ASP.NET extensions that are configured in the machine. config configuration file.

To support these two models, Visual Studio needed to change its compilation model for ASP.NET files. Now, web pages and web services aren't compiled until you access them for the first time. (In previous versions of Visual Studio, the entire web site is compiled each time you launch the application by clicking the Start button.) However, you can still precompile your application after you deploy it in a production environment to ensure the best performance for the first set of requests. To do so, just execute a request for the *precompile.axd* extension in the root virtual directory once you deploy your application. For example, if your web application is stored in the virtual directory named *WebApplication*, you would use this URL from the web server computer:

```
http://localhost/WebApplication/precompile.axd
```

Where can I learn more?

ASP.NET gives you still more compilation and deployment options, which you can learn more about from the whitepaper at *http://msdn.microsoft. com/library/en-us/dnvs05/html/codecompilation.asp*.

Administer a Web Application

Thanks to the new Web Site Administration Tool, there's no need to edit the web.config configuration file by hand.

Many settings that control the behavior of an ASP.NET application are found in its *web.config* file, a special XML document that's placed in the virtual directory of a web application. In the past, ASP.NET developers were forced to edit the *web.config* settings by hand. But your life is about to get simpler thanks to a new ASP.NET 2.0 graphical interface called the Web Site Administration Tool (WAT).

How do I do that?

The Web Site Administration Tool (WAT) is installed on your computer with the .NET Framework 2.0. It allows you to configure ASP.NET web application settings using a dedicated web page.

To run the WAT to configure the current web project in Visual Studio, select Website → ASP.NET Configuration. Internet Explorer will automatically log you on under the current user account. Try it. Figure 4-3 shows you the screen you'll see.

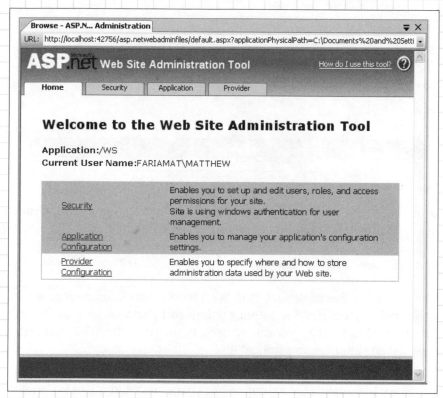

Figure 4-3. The Web Site Administration Tool

To try out WAT, click the Application tab and then click the "Create application settings" link. A pair of text boxes will appear that allow you to define the name and value of a new setting (see Figure 4-4). Enter "AppName" and "My Test ASP.NET Application" respectively, and click Save.

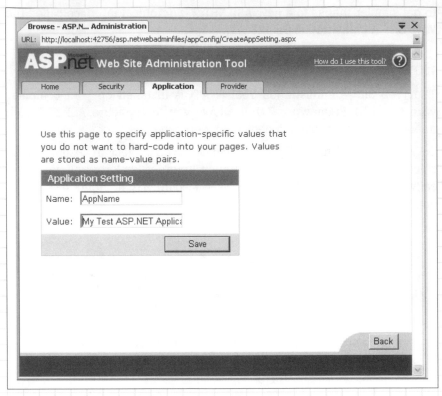

Figure 4-4. Configuring an application's setting through WAT

Now, open the *web.config* file to see the result. You'll find a new <appSettings> section with the following setting defined:

```
<appSettings>
  <add key="AppName" value="My Test ASP.NET Application" />
</appSettings>
```

This illustrates the basic way that WAT works—you interact with a web page, and it generates the settings you need behind the scenes. To edit or remove this setting, you simply need to return to the WAT and select the "Manage application settings" link.

If you want, you can complete this example by writing a simple routine to display the application setting in your page. Just add a label control to your web page and insert the following code in the Page_Load( ) event handler:

```
Label1.Text = "You are running " & _
   ConfigurationSettings.AppSettings("AppName")
```

Of course, using the WAT to generate application settings is only the beginning. You can also use the WAT to perform the following tasks:

Security
> Use this tab to set the authentication mode, define authorization rules, and manage users. You'll learn about this tab in the upcoming lab "Easily Authenticate Users."

Application
> Use this tab to set application settings (as demonstrated in this lab) and configure web site counters and debugging.

Provider
> Use this tab to configure where user role and personalization information is stored. By default, ASP.NET uses Access to store this information in the *AspNetDB.mdb* in the *App_Data* subdirectory (in Beta 1) or in a SQL Server database (in Beta 2).

What about...

...making changes to the configuration settings of a web application programmatically? Impressively, ASP.NET includes an extensive set of classes for exactly this purpose in the System.Web.Configuration and System.Web.Administration namespaces. You can use these classes to retrieve or alter web application settings in your web page or web service code. In fact, the entire Web Site Administration Tool is written as an ASP.NET application, and you'll find the source code (in C#) in the following directory:

```
c:\[Windows Directory]\Microsoft.NET\Framework\[Version]\
ASP.NETWebAdminFiles
```

Where can I learn more?

To learn more about the WAT, look for the index entry "Web Site Administration Tool" in the MSDN Help.

Bind to Data Without Writing Code

Most serious web applications need to retrieve records from a database. In .NET, the database access framework of choice is ADO.NET. However, writing the code to perform common database operations with ADO.NET, such as opening a connection and fetching a table of results, can be tedious and repetitive, which is not what VB programmers have come to expect. To simplify such tasks, ASP.NET 2.0 introduces several new *data*

With the new ASP.NET data provider controls, you can generate and bind all your database code at design time, without writing a single line of code.

source controls that greatly simplify the task of retrieving data and binding it to a web page.

How do I do that?

To use a new ASP.NET 2.0 data source control, all you need to do is to drag it from the Visual Studio toolbox to a web page, configure a few of its properties, and then bind it to other controls that display the data it exposes. When you run the web page, the data source control performs the heavy lifting, contacting your database and extracting the rows you need.

ASP.NET ships with several data source controls, and more are planned. Although the list has changed from build to build, the latest release includes:

SqlDataSource
> Interacts with a SQL Server database (Version 7.0 or later).

XmlDataSource
> Interacts with XML data from a file or some other data source.

ObjectDataSource
> Interacts with a custom object that you create. The next lab, "Bind Web Controls to a Custom Class," provides more details about this technique.

Other data sources are planned to allow easy retrieval of everything from directory listings to web service data.

To try out no-code data binding, drag a new SqlDataSource onto the design surface of a web page from the Data section of the toolbox. Then, click the control's smart tag and choose Configure Data Source. Visual Studio will walk you through a short wizard in which you specify the connection string for your database (which is then set in the ConnectionString property) and the query you want to perform (which is then set in the SelectCommand property). Find your database server, and select the Northwind database. Although you can build the query dynamically by selecting the columns in a table, for this example just specify the SQL string "SELECT ContactName FROM Customers".

When you're finished, Visual Studio will have added a SqlDataSource control tag to your web page, which looks something like this:

```
<asp:SqlDataSource ID="SqlDataSource1" Runat="server"
  SelectCommand="SELECT ContactName FROM Customers"
  ConnectionString=
  "Data Source=127.0.0.1;Integrated Security=SSPI;Initial
Catalog=Northwind">
</asp:SqlDataSource>
```

This data source defines a connection to the Northwind database, and a Select operation that retrieves a list of all contact names in the Customers table.

Binding a control to your data source is easy. To try this out, drag a BulletedList control onto your web page, which you can use to show the list of contact names from the Customers table. Click the smart tag, and select Connect to Data Source. You can then choose the data source you want to use (which is the data source created in the last step) and the field you want to display (which is ContactName).

Here's the finished tag:

```
<asp:BulletedList ID="BulletedList1" Runat="server"
   DataSourceID="SqlDataSource1"
   DataTextField="ContactName">
</asp:BulletedList>
```

Remember, to modify any ASP.NET control, you have two choices. You can select it and make changes in the Properties window, or you can switch to Source view and edit the control tag.

Amazingly enough, these two control declarations are all you need to create this data-bound page. When you run the page, the BulletedList will request data from the SqlDataSource, which will fetch it from the database using the query you've defined. You don't need to write a line of code.

For a little more sophistication, you could use another control to filter the list of contacts by some other piece of criteria, like country of residence. This raises a new problem—namely, how can you update the query in the SqlDataSource.SelectCommand according to the value entered in the other control?

ASP.NET solves this problem neatly with parameters. To try it out, start by adding a new data source that fetches a list of customer countries from the database. Here's an example that works in this case:

```
<asp:SqlDataSource ID="Countries" Runat="server" ConnectionString="..."
   SelectCommand="SELECT DISTINCT Country FROM Customers">
</asp:SqlDataSource>
```

Next, add a DropDownList control named lstCountries to expose the country list. You can use the same approach as when you wired up the BulletedList, or you can type the tag in by hand. Here's the completed tag you need:

```
<asp:DropDownList ID="lstCountries" Runat="server"
   DataValueField="Country" DataTextField="Country"
   DataSourceID="Countries" AutoPostBack="True">
</asp:DropDownList>
```

Now you can modify the query that creates the customer list. First, you insert a named parameter into your query. Remember to place an @ symbol at the beginning of the parameter name so SqlDataSource can recognize it. In this example, use @Country. (The @ denotes a named parameter when using the SQL Server provider.)

Here's what the revised data source tag should look like:

```
<asp:SqlDataSource ID="SqlDataSource1" Runat="server"
  SelectCommand="SELECT ContactName FROM Customers WHERE Country='@Country'
...
</asp:SqlDataSource>
```

Next, you add a definition that links the parameter to the appropriate control. Once again, you can configure this information in Visual Studio or by hand. In Visual Studio, select the SqlDataSource control and click the ellipses next to the SelectQuery property in the Properties window. (Truthfully, there is no real SelectQuery. That's just the way Visual Studio exposes the SelectCommand and SelectParameters properties to make it easier to edit them as a single unit at design time.) In this case, you need to create a new control parameter that retrieves the SelectedValue property of the lstCountries control.

Here's the revised data source tag once you've added the parameter definition:

```
<asp:SqlDataSource ID="SqlDataSource1" Runat="server"
  SelectCommand="SELECT ContactName FROM Customers WHERE Country=@Country"
  ConnectionString=
  "Data Source=127.0.0.1;Integrated Security=SSPI;Initial Catalog=Northwind"

  <SelectParameters>
    <asp:ControlParameter Name="Country"
      ControlID="lstCountries" PropertyName="SelectedValue">
    </asp:ControlParameter>
  </SelectParameters>
</asp:SqlDataSource>
```

Note that the name of the control parameter matches the name of the parameter in the SQL expression, with one minor quirk: the leading @ symbol is always left out.

Figure 4–5 shows the completed page. When you select a country from the drop-down list, the bulleted customer list is refreshed with the matching customers automatically. You now have a fair bit of functionality, and still have not written any code.

This example should already suggest possibilities where you can use multiple data source controls. For example, imagine you want to provide a master-detail view of orders by customer. You could use one data source to fill a listbox with customers. When the user selects a customer, you could then use your other data source to perform a query for the linked orders and show it in a different control.

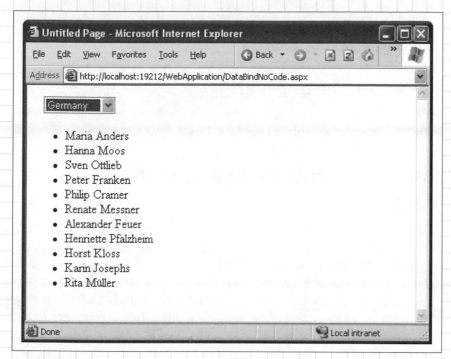

Figure 4-5. Linked data-bound controls with no code

What about...

...reasons *not* to use the new code-free data-binding controls? Many right-thinking developers steer clear of data-binding techniques because they embed database details into the user-interface code. In fact, that's exactly what this example does, which has negative consequences for maintainability, optimization, and debugging. Quite simply, with database details strewn everywhere in a large site, it's hard to stay consistent.

ASP.NET developers haven't forgotten about this side of things. With a little care, you can use the data source providers and still centralize your database logic. One of the best ways to do so is to use the ObjectDataSource control, which allows you to link to a custom class that you've created with data access code. The next lab, "Bind Web Controls to a Custom Class," demonstrates this technique.

Data sources also provide a useful place to add more advanced functionality. One of the most interesting examples is caching. If you set EnableCaching to True, the data source control will automatically insert the retrieved data into the ASP.NET cache and reuse it in future requests, potentially reducing your database load dramatically. You can configure the amount of time an item is cached by setting the CacheDuration and CacheExpirationPolicy properties.

Where can I learn more?

For more on caching and other advanced scenarios, look up the index entry "data source controls" in the MSDN help library.

Want to use data source binding without scattering database details throughout dozens of web pages? The ObjectData-Source control provides the solution.

Bind Web Controls to a Custom Class

Well-designed applications rigorously separate their data access logic from the rest of their code. In ASP.NET 2.0, you can achieve this separation while still using the new ASP.NET data source controls for convenient no-code-required design-time data binding. The secret is to use the new ObjectDataSource control, which knows how to fetch results from a data access class. You can then bind other controls to the ObjectDataSource for quick and easy web page display.

How do I do that?

To use the ObjectDataSource control, you must first create a custom class that retrieves the data from the database. The database class will contain one method for every database operation you want to perform. Methods that retrieve results from the database can return DataTable or DataSet objects, collections, or custom classes.

Example 4-1 shows a database class called CustomerDB that provides a single GetCustomers() method. The GetCustomers() method queries the database and returns a collection of CustomerDetails objects. The CustomerDetails object is also a custom object. It simply wraps all the details of a customer record from the database.

Example 4-1. A custom database class

```
Imports System.Data.SqlClient
Imports System.Collections.Generic

Public Class CustomerDB

    Private ConnectionString As String = _
    "Data Source=localhost;Initial Catalog=Northwind;Integrated Security=SSPI"

    Public Function GetCustomers() As List(Of CustomerDetails)
```

Example 4-1. *A custom database class (continued)*

```vb
        Dim Sql As String = "SELECT * FROM Customers"

        Dim con As New SqlConnection(ConnectionString)
        Dim cmd As New SqlCommand(Sql, con)
        Dim Reader As SqlDataReader
        Dim Customers As New List(Of CustomerDetails)
        Try
            con.Open()
            Reader = cmd.ExecuteReader()
            Do While Reader.Read()
                Dim Customer As New CustomerDetails()
                Customer.ID = Reader("CustomerID")
                Customer.Name = Reader("ContactName")
                Customers.Add(Customer)
            Loop
        Catch Err As Exception
            Throw New ApplicationException( _
                "Exception encountered when executing command.", Err)
        Finally
            con.Close()
        End Try

        Return Customers
    End Function

End Class

Public Class CustomerDetails

    Private _ID As String
    Private _Name As String

    Public Property ID() As String
        Get
            Return _ID
        End Get
        Set(ByVal Value As String)
            _ID = Value
        End Set
    End Property

    Public Property Name() As String
        Get
            Return _Name
        End Get
        Set(ByVal Value As String)
            _Name = Value
        End Set
    End Property

End Class
```

There are a couple of important points to note about this example. First, the database class must be stateless to work correctly. If you need any information, retrieve it from the custom application settings in the *web.config* file. Second, notice how the `CustomerDetails` class uses property procedures instead of public member variables. If you use public member variables, the `ObjectDataSource` won't be able to extract the information from the class and bind to it.

TIP

Example 4-1 uses a generic collection. For more information on this new CLR feature, refer to the lab "Build Typesafe Generic Classes" in Chapter 2.

To use the custom data access class in a data-binding scenario, you first need to make it a part of your web application. You have two options:

- Place it in a separate class library project and then compile it to a DLL file. Then, in the web application, add a reference to this assembly. Visual Studio will copy the DLL file into the *Bin* subdirectory of your web application.

- Put the source code in an ordinary *.vb* file in the *App_Code* subdirectory of your web application. ASP.NET automatically compiles any source code that's in this directory and makes it available to your web application. (To make sure it's compiled, choose Build → Build Website before going any further.)

Once you've taken one of these steps, drag an `ObjectDataSource` from the data tab of the Visual Studio toolbox onto the design surface of a web page. Click the control's smart tag and choose Configure Data Source. A wizard will appear that lets you choose your class from a drop-down list (a step that sets the `TypeName` property) and asks which method you want to call when performing a query (which sets the `MethodName` property).

Here's what the completed `ObjectDataSource` control tag looks like in the *.aspx* page of this example:

```
<asp:ObjectDataSource ID="ObjectDataSource1" Runat="server"
  TypeName="CustomerDB" SelectMethod="GetCustomers">
</asp:ObjectDataSource>
```

You are now able to bind other controls to the properties of the CustomerDetails class. For example, this BulletedList exposes the CustomerDetails.Name information for each object in the collection:

```
<asp:BulletedList ID="BulletedList1" Runat="server"
  DataTextField="Name" DataSourceID="ObjectDataSource1">
</asp:BulletedList>
```

When you run the application, the BulletedList requests data from the ObjectDataSource. The ObjectDataSource creates an instance of the CustomerDB class, calls GetCustomers(), and returns the data.

What about...

...updating a database through an ObjectDataSource? Not a problem. Both the ObjectDataSource and the SqlDataSource controls discussed in the previous lab, "Bind to Data Without Writing Code" support inserting, updating, and deleting records. With SqlDataSource, you simply need to set properties such as DeleteCommand, InsertCommand, and UpdateCommand with the appropriate SQL. With the ObjectDataSource, you set properties such as DeleteMethod, InsertMethod, and UpdateMethod by specifying the corresponding method names in your custom data access class. In many cases, you'll also need to specify additional information using parameters, which might map to other controls, query string arguments, or session information. For example, you might want to delete the currently selected record, or update a record based on values in a set of text boxes. To accomplish this, you need to add parameters, as described in the previous lab "Bind to Data Without Writing Code."

Once you've configured these operations (either by hand or by using the convenient design-time wizards), you can trigger them by calling the Delete(), Insert(), and Update() methods. Other controls that plug in to the data source control framework can also make use of these methods. For example, if you configure a SqlDataSource object with the information it needs to update records, you can enable GridView editing without needing to add a line of code. You'll see an example of this technique with the DetailsView control in the upcoming lab "Display Records One at a Time."

Where can I learn more?

For more information, look up the index entry "data source controls" in the MSDN help library. To learn about the new GridView, refer to the next lab, "Display Interactive Tables Without Writing Code."

Display Interactive Tables Without Writing Code

The new GridView control lets you create and display tables of data that users can sort, page through, and edit without requiring you to write a single line of code.

The ASP.NET 1.0 and 1.1 DataGrid control was tremendously popular, but implementing some of its most desirable features often required writing a lot of boilerplate code. For example, if you wanted to let users page through rows of data, it was up you to query the database after every postback, retrieve the requested page, and set the range of rows that you wanted to display. With the new GridView control, these headaches are a thing of the past.

In preparing for ASP.NET 2.0, Microsoft architects chose not to release a new version of the current DataGrid in order to simplify backward compatibility. Instead, the new GridView control duplicates and extends the functionality of the DataGrid, while making its features available to developers through a much simpler programming model.

How do I do that?

To use the new GridView control, drag it from the Data section of the Visual Studio toolbox onto the design surface of a web page. For hassle-free data binding, you can add a SqlDataSource control (described in the lab "Bind to Data Without Writing Code") or use an ObjectDataSource control in conjunction with a custom data access object, as explained in "Bind Web Controls to a Custom Class." In this case, we'll use a SqlDataSource control and the select query shown here to retrieve all fields and records in the Customers table of the Northwind database. Here's the final data source tag:

```
<asp:SqlDataSource ID="CusomtersList" Runat="server"
  SelectCommand="SELECT * FROM Customers"
  ConnectionString=
  "Data Source=127.0.0.1;Integrated Security=SSPI;Initial
Catalog=Northwind">
</asp:SqlDataSource>
```

You should be able to see the columns of your grid at design time. If you don't, choose Refresh Schema on the SqlDataSource smart tag (to set the column information from the database) and then choose Refresh Schema on the GridView smart tag.

Now, set the GridView.DataSourceID property to the name of the SqlDataSource (in this example, CustomersList). This binds the GridView to the SqlDataSource.

At this point, you can run your page and see a simple HTML table with a full list of customers. However, to make your table look respectable, there are a number of additional steps you'll want to take. These include:

- Setting the Font property to use a more attractive font. A common choice that's supported by most web browsers is Verdana (use a size of X-Small or XX-Small).

- Applying some formatting with styles. You can set colors, fonts, and sizes for the FooterStyle, HeaderStyle, RowStyle, and more using the Properties window. Or, to change the complete look in a hurry, click the GridView smart tag and choose AutoFormat. When you choose one these presets, all the GridView styles are set automatically.

Making the GridView look respectable is only part of the work. You can also switch on various GridView features using options in the GridView smart tag. Here are some links you can click to get quick results:

Enable Paging

This option sets the AllowPaging property to True. The GridView will then split long lists of records into separate pages (each with the number of rows designated in the PageSize property). Users can move from page to page by clicking numbered links that appear at the bottom of the GridView.

Enable Sorting

This option sets AllSorting to True. The GridView will then provide column hyperlinks. When the user clicks one, the whole table will be resorted in alphabetic order (or ascending numeric order) according to that column.

Enable Selection

This option adds a Select link in a new column at the left side of the grid. Users can click this link to select the row (at which point the SelectedIndex property will be set accordingly).

Enable Deleting

This option adds a Delete link in a new column at the left side of the grid. Users can click this link to delete the row from the database. You'll only see this option if you've defined a DeleteCommand for the attached data source.

Enable Editing

This option adds an Edit link in a new column at the left side of the grid. Users can click this link to put a row in edit mode (at which point an Update and Cancel link will appear, allowing them to push the change to the database or roll it back). You'll only see this option if you've defined an UpdateCommand for the attached data source.

Figure 4-6 shows a table that supports paging and sorting by column, which was generated by GridView without using a single line of custom code.

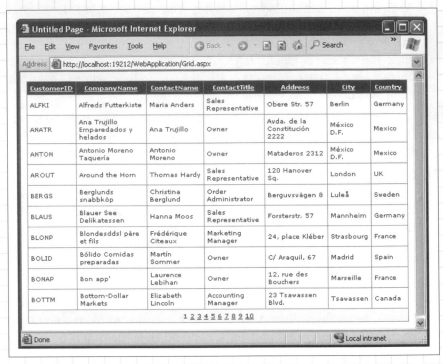

Figure 4-6. A GridView with sorting and paging enabled

What about...

...fine-tuning the GridView display? For example, you might want to tweak the sort order, the text used for the selection and editing links, the column titles, or the order of columns. You might also need to set default text and format strings. To perform any of these tasks, you simply customize the column objects that the GridView generates based on the format of the data source records. The easiest way to do so is to select Edit Columns link on the GridView smart tag and use the Fields dialog to customize the properties of each column. Try it.

Chapter 4: Web Applications

Display Records One at a Time

The new DetailsView control gives you a convenient way to let users view, edit, insert, and delete individual records.

While the GridView control is a perfect tool for presenting the records of a database as rows of data in a table, it becomes less convenient when you have records with many fields (especially if some fields are quite long), and you want to let users manipulate or add to the data they contain. One solution is to show only selected fields in a grid, but there are times when you need to display an entire record on a page and give the user the ability both to edit individual records and to add new records to the database. In ASP.NET, the handy new DetailsView gives you all the functionality you need to deal with individual records for free (i.e., without having to write your own code).

How do I do that?

The new DetailsView control works in much the same way as the GridView control described in the previous lab, "Display Interactive Tables Without Writing Code." The difference is that the DetailsView displays a single record at a time. By default, all the fields are displayed in a table, each field in a row of its own, listing from top to bottom.

To add a DetailsView to a web page, simply drag it onto the design surface from the Visual Studio Toolbox Data tab. Next, click its smart tag and select Configure Data Source to attach it to a data source control. You can also use the Auto Forms link in the smart tag to apply a rich set of styles to the grid it displays.

Because the DetailsView can only show a single record, you need to take extra steps to make sure it shows the right one. To do this, you need to use a *filter expression* (a SQL expression that limits the records you see according to the criteria you specify). You add the filter expression to the data source by setting the FilterExpression and FilterParameters properties of the DetailsView.

For example, consider the page that is shown in Figure 4-7. *GridAndDetails.aspx* contains both a GridView showing select information about the first five records and a DetailsView showing all fields of the selected record.

This page needs two data sources, one for the GridView (which is defined in the same way as described in the lab "Display Interactive Tables Without Writing Code.") and one for the DetailsView. The DetailsView data source definition looks like this:

```
<asp:SqlDataSource ID="SingleCustomerSource" Runat="server"
  SelectCommand="SELECT CustomerID, CompanyName, ContactName, ContactTitle,
```

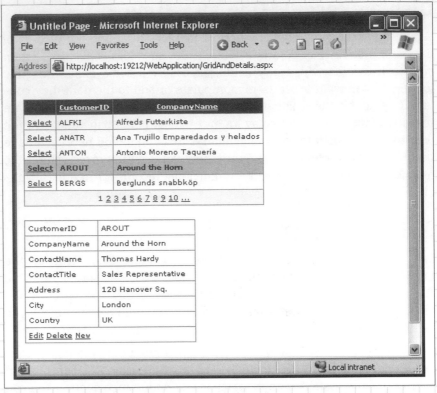

Figure 4-7. Connecting a GridView and DetailsView

```
Address, City, Country FROM Customers WHERE CustomerID=@CustomerID"
  ConnectionString=
"Data Source=127.0.0.1;Integrated Security=SSPI;Initial Catalog=Northwind"
>

  <SelectParameters>
    <asp:ControlParameter Name="CustomerID" ControlID="GridView1"
      PropertyName="SelectedValue">
    </asp:ControlParameter>
  </SelectParameters>

</asp:SqlDataSource>
```

This SELECT query selects only the single row that matches the CustomerID that's selected in the GridView control.

It's easy to hook up a basic DetailsView like the one shown in Figure 4-7. But life becomes even better if you do the work to add editing, deleting, and inserting abilities to the DetailsView. You can add all of these frills with the click of a button, provided you first make sure the connected data source has all the information it needs. For example, if you want to create a SqlDataSource that supports deleting, you need to configure the DeleteCommand and DeleteParameters properties. To create a data source that supports inserting new records, you need to add an InsertCommand and InsertParameters.

Adding these extra details is surprisingly easy. All you need to do is understand a few rules:

- All updates are performed through parameterized commands that use named placeholders instead of values.
- The parameter name is the same as the field name, with a preceding @ symbol. For example, the ContactName field becomes the @ContactName parameter.
- When you write the Where clause for your query, you need to precede the parameter name with the text original_. This indicates that you want to use the original value (which ignores any changes the user may have made). For example, @CustomerID becomes @original_CustomerID.

If you follow these rules, the DetailsView control will hook up the parameter values automatically. To try this out, follow these steps.

First, write a parameterized command that uses named placeholders instead of values. For example, here's a parameterized DeleteCommand for deleting the currently selected record, which follows the list of rules above:

```
DELETE Customers WHERE CustomerID=@original_CustomerID
```

This command deletes the currently selected record. The amazing thing about this command is that because it follows the naming rules listed above, you don't have to worry about supplying a value. Instead, you simply define the parameter as shown below, and the DetailsView will use the CustomerID from the currently displayed record:

```
<asp:SqlDataSource ID="SingleCustomerSource" Runat="server"
 DeleteCommand="DELETE Customers WHERE CustomerID=@original_CustomerID"
 ... >
   <DeleteParameters>
     <asp:Parameter Name="CustomerID">
     </asp:Parameter>
   </DeleteParameters>
   ...
</asp:SqlDataSource>
```

Example 4-2 shows a completed SqlDataSource that defines commands for update, insert, and delete operations in this way.

In this example, some of the commands are split over multiple lines to fit the margins of the page. This isn't acceptable in the real .aspx web page markup.

Example 4-2. A SqlDataSource tag

```
<asp:SqlDataSource ID="SingleCustomerSource" Runat="server"
  ConnectionString=
"Data Source=127.0.0.1;Integrated Security=SSPI;Initial Catalog=Northwind"
  SelectCommand=
"SELECT CustomerID,CompanyName,ContactName,ContactTitle,Address,
City,Country FROM Customers"
  FilterExpression="CustomerID='@CustomerID'"
  DeleteCommand="DELETE Customers WHERE CustomerID=@original_CustomerID"
  InsertCommand=
"INSERT INTO Customers (CustomerID,CompanyName,ContactName,ContactTitle,Address,
City,Country) VALUES
(@CustomerID,@CompanyName,@ContactName,@ContactTile,@Address,
@City,@Country)"
  UpdateCommand=
  "UPDATE Customers SET CompanyName=@CompanyName,ContactName=@ContactName,
ContactTitle=@ContactTitle,Address=@Address,City=@City,Country=@Country WHERE
CustomerID=@original_CustomerID">

  <FilterParameters>
    <asp:ControlParameter Name="CustomerID" Type="String" ControlID="GridView1"
     PropertyName="SelectedValue">
    </asp:ControlParameter>
  </FilterParameters>

  <DeleteParameters>
    <asp:Parameter Name="CustomerID">
    </asp:Parameter>
  </DeleteParameters>

  <InsertParameters>
    <asp:Parameter Name="CustomerID"></asp:Parameter>
    <asp:Parameter Name="CompanyName"></asp:Parameter>
    <asp:Parameter Name="ContactName"></asp:Parameter>
    <asp:Parameter Name="ContactTitle"></asp:Parameter>
    <asp:Parameter Name="Address"></asp:Parameter>
    <asp:Parameter Name="City"></asp:Parameter>
    <asp:Parameter Name="Country"></asp:Parameter>
  </InsertParameters>

  <UpdateParameters>
    <asp:Parameter Name="CompanyName"></asp:Parameter>
    <asp:Parameter Name="ContactName"></asp:Parameter>
    <asp:Parameter Name="ContactTitle"></asp:Parameter>
    <asp:Parameter Name="Address"></asp:Parameter>
    <asp:Parameter Name="City"></asp:Parameter>
    <asp:Parameter Name="Country"></asp:Parameter>
    <asp:Parameter Name="CustomerID"></asp:Parameter>
  </UpdateParameters>

</asp:SqlDataSource>
```

This tag is a long one, but the parameter definitions are surprisingly simple. Even better, Visual Studio wizards can help you build insert, update, and delete commands quickly. Just click the ellipsis next to the property name in the Properties window (e.g., the DeleteCommand property), and then type in the parameterized command and click Refresh Parameters. Refreshing automatically generates all the parameter tags based on your command.

To configure the DetailsView so that it uses these commands, just click the smart tag and add a checkmark next to the options Enable Inserting, Enable Deleting, and Enable Updating. This sets Boolean properties like AutoGenerateInsertButton, AutoGenerateDeleteButton, and AutoGenerateEditButton.

Figure 4-8 shows a DetailsView in edit mode.

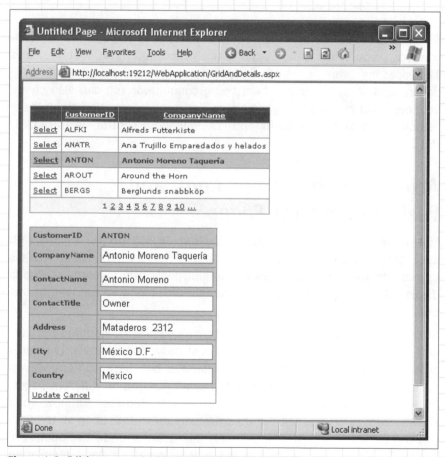

Figure 4-8. Editing a record with the DetailsView

What about...

...updating the GridView so it stays synchronized with the DetailsView? If you don't take any extra steps you'll notice a little inconsistency; changes you make editing, inserting, or deleting records with the DetailsView won't appear in the GridView until you manually refresh the page. To get around this problem, you need to add a little event-handling code. In this case, the important DetailsView events are ItemInserted, ItemDeleted, and ItemUpdated, which fire after each of these edit operations has completed. Here's code you can add to each event handler to refresh the grid when an item is inserted, deleted, or updated:

```
Sub DetailsView1_ItemUpdated(ByVal sender As Object, _
  ByVal e As System.Web.UI.WebControls.DetailsViewUpdatedEventArgs)
    GridView1.DataBind()
End Sub
```

The DetailsView has much more functionality that you can harness. For example, you can handle the ItemInserting, ItemDeleting, and ItemUpdating events to check the requested change, perform data validation, and stop the update from being committed. You can also create your own edit controls using templates. For more information about these techniques, look up the index entry "DetailsView control" in the MSDN Help.

Achieve a Consistent Look and Feel with Master Pages

Need to enforce a regular design across all the pages in a web site? ASP.NET 2.0 has a new master pages feature that allows you to create page templates.

Most professional web sites standardize their layout. On the O'Reilly web site (*http://www.oreilly.com*), for example, a navigation bar always appears on the left-hand side of a content page, and a company logo is displayed at the top. These details remain consistent as the user moves from page to page.

In ASP.NET 1.0 and 1.1, you can create web sites with standardized layouts, but there aren't any tools to make it easy. For example, with user controls you can reuse blocks of user interface, but there isn't any way to ensure that they always end up in the same position on different pages. Using HTML frames, you can break up a web browser window so it shows multiple web pages, but it's extremely difficult to keep all the web pages properly coordinated. In ASP.NET 2.0, these imperfect solutions are replaced with a new feature called *master pages*, a page templating system.

How do I do that?

To create a basic master page in Visual Studio, select Website → Add New Item from the menu, select Master Page, and click OK to add the item.

Master pages are similar to ordinary ASP.NET pages in the sense that they can contain HTML, web controls, and code. However, they have a different extension (.*master* instead of .*aspx*), and they can't be requested directly by a browser. Instead, other pages (known as *content pages*) can use the master page.

You design the master page as you would a normal ASP.NET web page, adding the text and controls you need to get a consistent look across all pages of your site. The elements you add to the master page cannot be modified by the content pages that make use of it. You use the new ContentPlaceHolder control to mark off areas reserved for content that will vary from page to page. In these regions of the master page, content pages can add their own controls and HTML.

Consider the sample master page whose source is shown in Example 4-3. It creates two tables. The topmost table holds the header region, and the second table contains the rest of the page. The second table is split into two cells, a cell on the left for a navigation bar, and a cell on the right that contains a ContentPlaceHolder tag. Any content page that uses (i.e., inherits from) this master page can completely control the content of that cell, but not of any other cell in that table or other tables on the master page.

Example 4-3. A master page that uses a table

```
<%@ Master language="VB" %>

<html>
  <head id="Head1" runat="server">
    <title>Master Page</title>
  </head>

  <body>
    <form id="Form1" runat="server">
      <table id="header" width="100%" height="80px"
       cellspacing="1" cellpadding="1" border="1">
        <tr>
          <td width="100%" style="TEXT-ALIGN: center">
            This is the Master Page fixed header.
          </td>
        </tr>
      </table>
```

Example 4-3. *A master page that uses a table (continued)*

```
<table id="main" width="100%" height="100%"
 cellspacing="1" cellpadding="1" border="1">
  <tr>
    <td valign=top width="100px">
     Put the site map here (on left). </td>
    <td valign=top >
      <asp:ContentPlaceHolder id="content" runat="Server">
        Put your content here.
      </asp:ContentPlaceHolder>
    </td>
  </tr>
</table>

  </form>
 </body>

</html>
```

Figure 4-9 shows the master page at design time. For more advanced layout, you could use nested tables, or put the ContentPlaceHolder tag inside a single cell of a more complex table, which includes multiple columns and rows.

To create a new content page, right-click the Solution Explorer and select Add New Item. Choose the Web Form option, give the file a name, and then select the "Select master page" checkbox. When you click Add, a dialog box will appear, prompting you to select one of the master pages in the current web application. Select the master page in Example 4-3, and click OK.

When you create a content page, it automatically gets the same look as the master page from which it derives. You can add content only inside the content areas designated by a ContentPlaceHolder control. The predefined header and sitemap regions of the master page will appear grayed out in Visual Studio.

The actual markup for content pages looks a little different than ordinary pages. First of all, the Page directive links to the master page you're using, as shown here:

```
<%@ Page MasterPageFile="Site.master" %>
```

In order to add content to the page, you need to enter it inside a special Content tag. The Content tag links to one of the ContentPlaceHolder tags you created in the master page. For example, if you want to add content to the master page example shown earlier, you need a Content tag that looks like this:

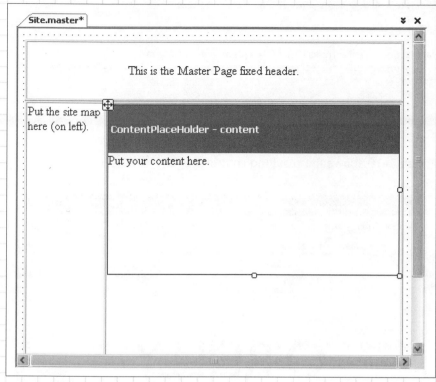

Figure 4-9. A simple master page

```
<asp:Content ContentPlaceHolderID="content" Runat="server">
    ...
</asp:Content>
```

This ContentPlaceHolderID attribute must match the id attribute of one of the ContentPlaceHolder tags in the master page. Note that you do not need to add Content tags to the content page in the same order as the ContentPlaceHolder tags appear in the master page. Visual Studio will create the content tag automatically as you add controls to the content page.

Example 4-4 shows the code you need to implement a very simple content page based on the master page shown in Example 4-3. Note that the page doesn't include tags like <html>, <header>, <body>, and <form>, because these tags are only defined once for a page, and they're already included in the master page.

You don't need to specify content for each placeholder. If you don't, ASP.NET shows whatever content is in the ContentPlaceHolder tag on the master page (if any).

Example 4-4. A content page with a picture and text

```
<%@ page language="VB" MasterPageFile="Site.master" %>

<asp:Content ContentPlaceHolderID=content Runat=server>
    <asp:Image ID="image1" ImageUrl="oreilly_header.gif" Runat="server" />
    <br />
    <br />
    <i>This is page-specific content!</i>
    <hr />
</asp:Content>
```

Figure 4-10 shows the resulting content page.

Figure 4-10. A simple content page

You can create master pages that use other previously defined master pages, effectively nesting one master page inside another. Such a nested design might make sense if you need to define some content that appears on every page in a web site (like a company header) and some content that appears on many but not all pages (like a navigation bar).

One good reason to use master pages is to dedicate some web page real estate for some sort of navigation controls. The next lab, "Add Navigation to Your Site," explores this topic in more detail.

What about...

...other ways to help ensure consistency? ASP.NET 2.0 introduces another feature for standardizing web sites called *control theming*. While master pages ensure a regular layout and allow you to repeat certain elements over an entire site, theming helps to make sure web page controls have the same "look and feel." Essentially, a control theme is a set of style attributes (such as fonts and colors) that can be applied to different controls.

Where can I learn more?

For more information, look for the index entry "themes" in the MSDN Help.

Add Navigation to Your Site

Most web sites include some type of navigation bar that lets users move from one page to another. In ASP.NET 1.0 and 1.1, it's easy enough to create these navigation controls, but you need to do so by hand. In ASP.NET 2.0, a new *sitemap* feature offers a much more convenient pre-built solution. The basic principle is that you define the structure of your web site in a special XML file. Once you've taken that step, you can configure a list or tree control to use the sitemap data—giving you a clickable navigation control with no code required.

ASP.NET 2.0 provides new navigation features that let you create a sitemap and bind it to different controls.

How do I do that?

The first step in using ASP.NET's new sitemap feature is to define the structure of your web site in an XML file named *web.sitemap*. To add this file to your site in Visual Studio, right-click the Solution Explorer and select Add New Item. Select the Site Map file type and click Add.

The first ingredient you need in the *web.sitemap* file is the root `<siteMap>` tag:

```
<siteMap>
</siteMap>
```

In the `<siteMap>` tag, you add one `<siteMapNode>` child element for each entry you want to show in the sitemap. You can then give a title, description, and URL link for each entry using attributes. Here's an example:

```
<siteMapNode title="Home" description="Home Page" url="default.aspx" />
```

Notice that this tag ends with the characters /> instead of just >. This indicates that it's an *empty element*—in other words, it doesn't contain any other elements. However, if you want to build a multi-level sitemap, you have to nest one <siteMapNode> element inside another. Here's an example:

```
<siteMapNode title="Home" description="Home Page" url="default.aspx" >
    <siteMapNode title="Products"
      description="Order Products" url="produ.aspx" />
</siteMapNode>
```

Example 4-5 shows a sitemap with six links in three levels.

Example 4-5. A multi-level sitemap

```
<?xml version="1.0" ?>
<siteMap>
  <siteMapNode title="Home" description="Home" url="default.aspx">
    <siteMapNode title="Personal" description="Personal Services"
     url="personal.aspx">
      <siteMapNode title="Resume" description="Download Resume"
       url="resume.aspx" />
    </siteMapNode>

    <siteMapNode title="Business" description="Business Services"
     url="business.aspx">
      <siteMapNode title="Products" description="Order Products"
       url="products.aspx" />
      <siteMapNode title="Contact Us" description="Contact Information"
       url="contact.aspx" />
    </siteMapNode>
  </siteMapNode>
</siteMap>
```

Once you create a sitemap, it's easy to use it on a web page, thanks to the new SiteMapDataSource control. This control works much like the other data source controls discussed in "Bind to Data Without Writing Code." However, it doesn't require any properties at all. Once you add the SiteMapDataSource, ASP.NET automatically reads the *web.sitemap* file and makes its data available to your other controls:

```
<asp:SiteMapDataSource ID="SiteMapDataSource1" Runat="server" />
```

Now you can bind just about any other control to the SiteMapDataSource. Because sitemaps are, by default, hierarchical, they work particularly well with the new TreeView control. Here's a TreeView control that binds to the sitemap data:

```
<asp:TreeView ID="TreeView1" Runat="server"
DataSourceID="SiteMapDataSource1"
  Font-Names="Verdana" Font-Size="8pt" ForeColor="Black"
ImageSet="BulletedList"
```

```
        Width="149px" Height="132px">
    </asp:TreeView>
```

The resulting TreeView doesn't just show the sitemap, it also renders
each node as a hyperlink that, if clicked, sends the user to the appropriate page. Figure 4-11 shows a content page that's based on a master
page that uses a TreeView with a sitemap. (Refer to the lab "Achieve a
Consistent Look and Feel with Master Pages" for more information about
master pages.)

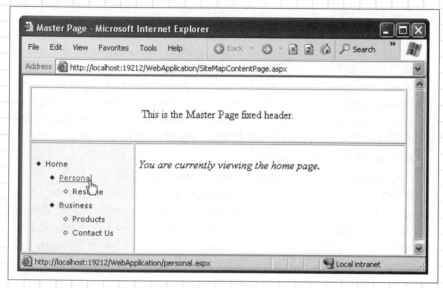

Figure 4-11. Using a sitemap in a master page

What about...

...customizing the sitemap? There's a lot more you can do to control the
look of a site as well as its behavior. Here are some starting points:

Show a sitemap in a non-hierarchical control
> Controls like the ListBox and GridView don't support the sitemap's
> tree-based view. To solve this problem, set the SiteMapDataSource.
> SiteMapViewType property to Flat instead of Tree so that the multi-
> layered sitemap is flattened into a single-level list. You can also use
> the Flat option with a TreeView to save screen real estate (because
> subsequent levels won't be indented).

Vary the sitemap displayed in different pages
> To accomplish this, put all the sitemap information you need into the
> same *web.sitemap* file, but in different branches. Then, set the

`SiteMapDataSource.StartingNodeUrl` to the URL of the page you want to use as the root of your sitemap. The `SiteMapDataSource` will only get the data from that node, and all the nodes it contains.

Make the sitemap collapsible

If you have a large sitemap, just set the `TreeView.ShowExpandCollapse` to `True`, and the familiar plus boxes will appear next to Home, Personal, and Business, allowing you to show just part of the sitemap at a time.

Fine-tune the appearance of the `TreeView`

It's remarkably easy. In the previous example, the `TreeView` used the bullet style, which shows different bullet icons next to each item. By setting the `TreeView.ImageSet` to different values available within the `TreeViewImageSet` enumeration, you can show square bullets, arrows, folder and file icons, and much more. For even more information about tweaking the `TreeView` (or using it in other scenarios that don't involve sitemaps), look up the reference for the `System.Web.UI.WebControls.TreeView` class.

Retrieve the sitemap information from another location

Maybe you want to store your sitemap in a different file, a database, or some other data source. Unfortunately, the `SiteMapProvider` doesn't have the ability to retrieve information from these locations—at least not yet. Instead, you'll need to create your own custom sitemap provider. Refer to the MSDN help under the index entry "site map."

Easily Authenticate Users

Tired or writing your own authentication code? ASP.NET 2.0 will take care of the drudgery, maintaining user credentials in a database and validating a user login when you ask for it.

In ASP.NET 1.0 and 1.1, developers had a handy tool called *forms authentication*. Essentially, forms authentication kept track of which users had logged in by using a special cookie. If ASP.NET noticed a user who hadn't logged in trying to access a secured page, it automatically redirected the user to your custom login page.

On its own, forms authentication worked well, but it still required some work on your part. For example, you needed to create the login page and write the code that examined the user's login name and password and compared it to values in a custom database. Depending on how your application worked, you may also have needed to write code for adding new users and removing old ones. This code wasn't complicated, but it could be tedious.

ASP.NET 2.0 dramatically reduces your work with its new *membership* features. Essentially, all you need to do is use the methods of the membership classes to create, delete, and validate user information. ASP.NET automatically maintains a database of user information behind the scenes on your behalf.

How do I do that?

The first step in adding authentication to your site is to choose a *membership provider*, which determines where the user information will be stored. ASP.NET includes membership providers that allow you to connect to a SQL Server database, and several additional providers are planned.

The membership provider is specified in the *web.config* configuration file. However, rather than typing this information in by hand, you'll almost certainly use the WAT, described in the lab "Administer a Web Application." Just click the Security tab, and click the "Use the security Setup Wizard" link to walk through a wizard that gives you all the options you need. The first question is the access method—in other words, how your visitors will authenticate themselves. Choose "From the internet" to use forms authentication rather than Windows authentication.

The following step allows you to choose the membership provider. You can choose a single provider to use for all ASP.NET features, or separate providers for different features (such as membership, role-based security, and so on). If you choose to use a SQL Server database, you must also run the *aspnet_regsql.exe* utility, which will walk you through the steps needed to install the membership database. You'll find the *aspnet_regsql.exe* utility in the *c:\[WinDir]\Microsoft.NETframework\[Version] directory*.

Next, you'll have the chance to create users and roles. Roles are discussed in a later lab ("Use Role-Based Authentication"), so you don't need to create them yet. You don't need to create a test user, because you'll do that through your web site in the next step.

You can choose the name of your login page by modifying the <authentication> section in the *web.config* file, as shown here:

```
<?xml version="1.0"?>
<configuration>
  <system.web>
    <authentication mode="Forms">
      <forms loginUrl="Login.aspx" />
    </authentication>

    <!-- Other settings ommitted. -->
  </system.web>
</configuration>
```

In this case, the login page for the application is named *Login.aspx* (which is the default). In this page, you can use the shared methods and properties of the `System.Web.Security.Membership` class to authenticate your users. However, you don't need to, because ASP.NET includes a set of security-related controls that you can drag and drop into your web pages effortlessly. The security controls include:

`Login`

> Shows the controls needed for a user to log in, including username and password text boxes, and a Login button. Optionally, you can show an email address text box, and you can configure all the text labels in the control by modifying properties like `UserNameLabelText` and `PasswordLabelText`.

`LoginView`

> Shows one template out of a group of templates, depending on who is currently logged in. This gives you a way to customize content for different users and roles without using any custom code.

`PasswordRecovery`

> Provides a mechanism through which users can have a forgotten password mailed to them. This feature is disabled by default and requires some tweaking of *web.config* settings.

`LoginStatus`

> Displays a Login link if the user isn't currently logged in, or a Logout link if the user is logged in.

`LoginName`

> Shows the name of the currently logged-in user in a label.

`CreateUserWizard`

> Allows the user to step through creating a new user account.

`ChangePassword`

> Allows the user to change his or her current password, by specifying the current and new passwords.

You'll find the security controls in the Login tab of the Visual Studio toolbox. To try them out, create a new page named *RegisterUser.aspx*. Drop a `CreateUserWizard` control onto the web page. Now run the page and use the wizard to create a new user with the username *testuser* and the password *test*.

By default, the `CreateUserWizard` control uses two steps (shown in Figure 4-12). The first step allows you to specify all your user information, and the second step simply displays a confirmation message.

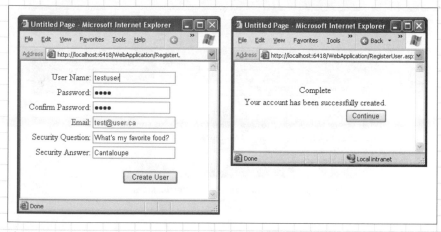

Figure 4-12. Adding a new user with the CreateUserWizard control

If you like, you can dig into the backend database to confirm that your user information was saved (after all, it happened automatically, without requiring any custom code). But a better test is to actually create a restricted area of your web page.

First, add the *Login.aspx* page. To create this page, just drag a Login control onto the page, and you're finished.

Now, it's time to restrict access to a portion of the web site. Select Website → New Folder to create a subdirectory in your web application directory, and name the new directory *Secured*. Next, create a new page in this directory named *Private.aspx*, and add the text "This is a secured page."

Now, run the WAT by selecting Website → ASP.NET Configuration. Choose the Security tab. Using this tab, you can examine the list of users (including the test user you added in the previous step) and modify their information. What you really need to do, however, is click the "Create access rules" link to restrict access to the *Secured* directory. Select the directory in the list, choose the Deny Permission option, and select Anonymous users, as shown in Figure 4-13. Then, click OK to add this rule.

Now you're ready to test this simple security example. Right-click on the *Private.aspx*, file and choose "Set As Start Page." Then, run your application. ASP.NET will immediately detect that your request is for a secured page and you haven't authenticated yourself. Because you've configured forms authentication, it redirects you to the *Login.aspx* page.

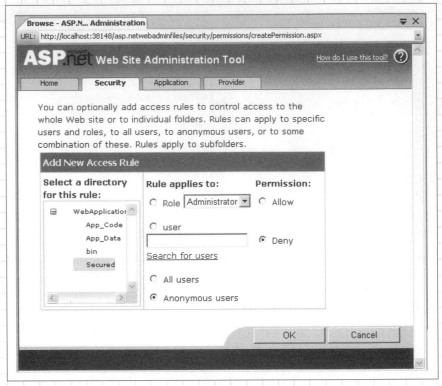

Figure 4-13. Creating a rule to prevent anonymous access to the Secured directory

Now enter the username *testuser* and the password *test* in the login control. ASP.NET will validate you using the membership provider and redirect you to the originally requested *Private.aspx* page.

In other words, by using the CreateUserWizard and Login controls in conjunction with the WAT, you've created an authentication system that restricts access to a specific portion of your web site—all without a single line of code.

What about…

…ways to customize the authentication process? If you need to control how authentication, user creation, and other security tasks work, you'll be happy to find that the security controls are easily extensible. You can add new steps to the CreateUserWizard to collect additional data, respond to events that fire when the user is logged in (or denied access), and even convert the steps to editable templates so that you can fine-tune the user interface, adding new controls or removing existing ones.

If you want to go a step further, you can abandon the security controls altogether, but still create almost no-code solutions using the static methods of the System.Web.Security.Membership class. Here are some of the methods you can call:

CreateUser( )
> Creates a new user record in the data store with a username, a password, and (optionally) an email address.

DeleteUser( )
> Removes the user record from the data store that has the indicated username.

GeneratePassword( )
> Creates a random password of the specified length. You can suggest this to the user as a default password when creating a new user record.

GetUser( )
> GetUser( ) retrieves a MembershipUser record for a user with the given username. You can then examine the MembershipUser properties to find out details such as the user's email address, when the account was created, when the user last logged in, and so on. If you don't specify a username, the GetUser( ) method retrieves the current user for the page.

GetUserNameByEmail( )
> If you know a user's email address but you don't know the username, you can use this method to get it.

UpdateUser( )
> After you've retrieved a MembershipUser object, you can modify its properties and then submit the object to the UpdateUser( ) method, which commits all your changes to the user database.

ValidateUser( )
> This accepts a username and password, and verifies that it matches the information in the database (in which case it returns True). ASP.NET doesn't actually store the unencrypted password in the database—instead, it uses a hashing algorithm to protect this information.

Using these methods, you can quickly construct basic login and user registration pages without needing to write any database code. All you need to do is create the user interface for the page (in other words, add labels, text boxes, and other controls).

For example, to design a customized login page, just create a page with two text boxes (named txtUser and txtPassword) and a button (named cmdLogin). When the button is clicked, run this code:

```
Sub cmdLogin_Click(ByVal sender As Object, ByVal e As System.EventArgs)

    If Membership.ValidateUser(txtUser.Text, txtPassword.Text) Then
        ' ASP.NET validated the username and password.
        ' Send the user to page that was originally requested.
        FormsAuthentication.RedirectFromLoginPage(txtUser.Text, False)
    Else
        ' The user's information is incorrect.
        ' Do nothing (or just display an error message).
    End If

End Sub
```

Notice how simple the code is for this page. Instead of manually validating the user by connecting to a database, reading a record, and checking the fields, this code simply calls the Membership.ValidateUser() method, and ASP.NET takes care of the rest.

Just as easily, you can create a page that generates a new user record with the Membership class:

```
Sub cmdRegister_Click(ByVal sender As Object, ByVal e As System.EventArgs)

    Dim Status As MembershipCreateStatus
    Dim NewUser As MembershipUser = Membership.CreateUser(_
      txtUser.Text, txtPassword.Text, txtEmail.Text, Status)

    ' If the user was created successfully, redirect to the login page.
    If Status = MembershipCreateStatus.Success Then
        Response.Redirect("Login.aspx")
    Else
        ' Display an error message in a label.
        lblStatus.Text = "Attempt to create user failed with error " & _
          Status.ToString()
    End If

End Sub
```

For more information, look up the index entry "Membership class" in the MSDN Help. You can also refer to the next three labs, which build up the basic membership framework with new features:

"Determine How Many People Are Currently Using Your Web Site"
Explains how additional membership features can track who's online.

"Use Role-Based Authorization"
Describes how you can enhance your authorization logic by assigning users to specific roles, essentially giving them different sets of

privileges. This feature isn't handled by the membership service, but by a complementary role manager service.

"Store Personalized Information"

Shows how you can store other types of user-specific information in a data store, instead of just usernames, passwords, and email addresses. This feature isn't handled by the membership service, but by a complementary personalization service.

Determine How Many People Are Currently Using Your Web Site

The Web uses HTTP, a stateless protocol that rarely maintains a connection longer than a few seconds. As a result, even as users are reading through your web pages, they aren't connected directly to your server. However, ASP.NET gives you a way to estimate how many people are using your web site at any given moment using *timestamps*. This information makes a great addition to a community site (e.g., a web discussion forum), and it can also be useful for diagnostic purposes.

Ever wondered how many people are using your site right now? If you're using ASP.NET's personalization features, it's remarkably easy to set a reasonable estimate.

How do I do that?

Every time a user logs in using a membership provider (described in the lab "Easily Authenticate Users"), ASP.NET records the current time in the data store. When the same user requests a new page, ASP.NET updates the timestamp accordingly. To make a guess at how many people are using your web site, you can count the number of users who have a timestamp within a short window of time. For example, you might consider the number of users who have requested a page in the last 15 minutes.

You can retrieve this information from ASP.NET using the new GetNumberOfUsersOnline() method of the Membership class. You can also configure the time window that will be used by setting the UserIsOnlineTimeWindow property (which reflects a number of minutes). It's set to 15 by default.

Here's a code snippet that counts the online users and displays the count in a label:

```
Sub Page_Load(ByVal sender As Object, ByVal e As System.EventArgs)
    lblStatus.Text &= "<br>There are " &_
    Membership.GetNumberOfUsersOnline() & _
        " users online right now. That is an estimate based" &_
        " on looking at timestamps that fall in the last " &_
```

```
        Membership.UserIsOnlineTimeWindow & _
        " minutes."
    End Sub
```

Keep in mind that this count doesn't include anonymous users.

What about...

...getting information about exactly which users are online? Unfortunately, ASP.NET doesn't currently provide any way to determine which users are online. The only alternative is to add your own tracking code. For example, you could store this information in a database or add it to an in-memory object such as the Application collection whenever a user logs in. You would also need to store the login time and discard old entries periodically.

Use Role-Based Authorization

Do you need to give different privileges to different types of users? The easiest way to implement this logic is by using ASP.NET's new role-management service.

In many web applications, all users are not equal. Some might be allowed to perform a carefully restricted set of actions, while others are given free reign to perform more advanced administrative tasks. ASP.NET 2.0 makes it easier than ASP.NET 1.x to assign permissions to different groups of users using the new role-management service.

How do I do that?

ASP.NET uses a role-management service to manage the storage and retrieval of role-based information. ASP.NET gives you the flexibility to use different *role-manager providers* to store the role information in different data sources. Usually, you'll use the same data store that you use for membership (as described in the lab "Easily Authenticate Users"). Because the membership provider and the role-manager provider use different tables, you don't need to worry about a conflict.

Role management is not enabled by default. You can enable it by using the WAT, as described in the lab "Administer a Web Application." Just select Website → ASP.NET Configuration and choose the Security tab. Then click the "Enable roles" link in the Roles box. This modifies the *web.config* as needed. However, you'll still need to configure the roles you want to use.

The easiest way to add role information is also through the WAT. To do so, click the "Create or Manage roles" link in the Roles box on the Security page. This presents a page where you can add new roles and assign users to existing roles. To add a new role, type in the role name and click Add Role. You'll see the role appear in the list below. Figure 4-14 shows an example with two groups, Administrators and Sales Officials. Note that you won't see group membership on this page.

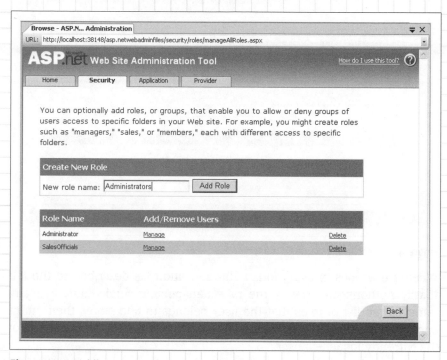

Figure 4-14. Adding a new role

To change group membership, click the Manage link next to the appropriate role. Because a typical system could easily have hundreds of users, the WAT does not attempt to show all the users at once. Instead, it allows you to specify the user that you want to add to the role by typing in the name, browsing an alphabetical directory, or using a search with wild cards (as in John* to find usernames starting with John). Once you've found the appropriate user, place a checkmark in "User Is In Role" column to add the user to the role, or clear the checkbox to remove the user, as shown in Figure 4-15.

Using this tab, you can examine the list of users (including the test user you added in the previous step) and modify their information. What you really need to do, however, is click the "Create access rules" link to restrict access to the *Secured* directory. Select the directory in the list, choose the Deny Permission option, and select Anonymous users, as shown in Figure 4-13. Then, click OK to add this rule.

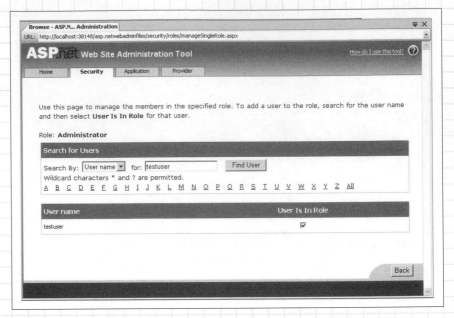

Figure 4-15. Assigning a role to a user

When a user logs in using forms authentication (as described in the lab "Easily Authenticate Users"), the role-management service automatically retrieves the list of roles that the user belongs to and stores them in an encrypted cookie. After this point, it's easy to test the role membership of the currently logged-in user.

For example, the following code checks if the user is an Administrator. In order for this to work, the user must have logged in:

```
If Roles.IsUserInRole("Administrator") Then
    ' (Allow the code to continue, or show some content
    ' that would otherwise be hidden or disabled.)
End If
```

And, finally, this code displays a list of all the roles that the user belongs to:

```
For Each Role As String In Roles.GetRolesForUser()
    lblRoles.Text &= Role & " "
Next
```

Clearly, none of these tasks requires much work!

You can also set and retrieve role information using the System.Web. Security.Roles class. Here are the core methods you'll want to use:

CreateRole( )
:   This creates a new role with the designated name in the database. Remember, roles are just labels (like *Administrator* or *Guest*). It's up to your code to decide how to respond to that information.

DeleteRole( )
:   Removes a role from the data source.

AddUserToRole( )
:   Adds a record in the data store that indicates that the specified user is a member of the specified role. You can also use other methods that work with arrays and allow you to add a user to several different roles at once, or add several different users to the same role. These methods include AddUserToRoles( ), AddUsersToRole( ), and AddUsersToRoles( ).

RemoveUserFromRole( )
:   Removes a user from a role.

GetRolesForUser( )
:   Retrieves an array of strings that indicate all the roles a specific user belongs to. If you're retrieving roles for the currently logged-in user, you don't need to specify a username.

GetUsersInRole( )
:   Retrieves an array of strings with all of the usernames that are in a given role.

IsUserInRole( )
:   Tests if a user is in a specific role. This is the cornerstone of role-based authorization. Depending on whether this method returns True or False, your code should decide to allow or restrict certain actions. If you're testing the group membership of the currently logged-in user, you don't need to specify a username.

The following code snippet creates a role and adds a user to that role:

```
Roles.CreateRole("Administrator")
Roles.AddUserToRole("testUser", "Administrator")
```

What about...

...performance? At first glance, role management might not seem very scalable. Reading the role information for each web request is sure to

---

slow down the speed of your application, and it may even introduce a new bottleneck as ASP.NET threads wait to get access to the database. Fortunately, the role-management service is quite intelligent. It won't make a trip to the database with each web request; instead, it retrieves role information once, encrypts it, and stores it in a cookie. For all subsequent requests, ASP.NET reads the roles from the encrypted cookie. You can remove this cookie at any time by calling Roles.DeleteCookie( ), or you can configure settings in the *web.config* file to determine when it should expire on its own.

If you have an extremely large number of roles, the cookie might not contain them all. In this case, ASP.NET flags the cookie to indicate this fact. When your code performs a role check, ASP.NET will try to match one of the roles in the cookie first, and if it can't find a match, it will double-check the data source next.

Where can I learn more?

For more information, look up the index entry "role-based security → ASP. NET" in the MSDN Help.

Store Personalized Information

Need to store some custom user-specific information for long periods of time? Why not use the membership data provider to save and retrieve information without resorting to database code.

ASP.NET applications often have the need to store user-specific information beyond the bare minimum username and password. One way to solve this problem is to use the Session collection. Session state has two limitations: it isn't permanent (typically, a session times out after 20 minutes of inactivity), and it isn't strongly typed (in other words, you need to know what's in the session collection and manually cast references to the appropriate data types). ASP.NET 2.0 addresses these limitations with a new framework for storing user-specific data called *profile settings*.

How do I do that?

Profiles build on the same provider model that's used for membership and role management. Essentially, the *profile provider* takes care of storing all the user-specific information in some backend data store. Currently, ASP.NET includes a profile provider that's tailored for SQL Server.

Before you start using profiles, you should have a system in place for authenticating users. That's because personalized information needs to be linked to a specific user, so that you can retrieve it on subsequent visits. Typically, you'll use forms authentication, with the help of the ASP.NET membership services described in the lab "Easily Authenticate Users."

With profiles, you need to define the type of user-specific information you want to store. In early builds, the WAT included a tool for generating profile settings. However, this tool has disappeared in later releases, and unless (or until) it returns, you need to define your profile settings in the *web.config* file by hand. Here's an example of a profile section that defines a single string named `Fullname`:

```xml
<?xml version="1.0"?>
<configuration>
  <system.web>

    <profile>
      <properties>
        <add name="FullName" type="System.String" />
      </properties>
    </profile>

    <!-- Other settings ommitted. -->
  </system.web>
</configuration>
```

Initially, this doesn't seem any more useful than an application setting. However, Visual Studio automatically generates a new class based on your profile settings. You can access this class through the `Page.Profile` property. The other benefit is the fact that ASP.NET stores this information in a backend database, automatically retrieving it from the database at the beginning of the request and writing it back at the end of the request (if these operations are needed). In other words, profiles give you a higher-level model for maintaining user-specific information that's stored in a database.

In other words, assuming you've defined the `FullName` property in the `<profile>` section, you can set and retrieve a user's name information using code like this:

```
Profile.FullName = "Joe Smythe"
...
lblName.Text = "Hello " & Profile.FullName
```

Note that the Profile class is strongly typed. There's no need to convert the reference, and Visual Studio's IntelliSense springs into action when you type `Profile` followed by the period.

Life gets even more interesting if you want to store a full-fledged object. For example, imagine you create specialized classes to track the products in a user's shopping basket. Example 4-6 shows a `Basket` class that contains a collection of `BasketItem` objects, each representing a separate product.

ASP.NET does include basic features that allow you to use personalization with anonymous users (see the "What about..." section of this lab for more information).

Example 4-6. Custom classes for a shopping cart

```vb
Imports System.Collections.Generic

Public Class Basket
    Private _Items As New List(Of BasketItem)
    Public Property Items() As List(Of BasketItem)
        Get
            Return _Items
        End Get
        Set(ByVal value As List(Of BasketItem))
            _Items = value
        End Set
    End Property
End Class

Public Class BasketItem
    Private _Name As String
    Public Property Name() As String
        Get
            Return _Name
        End Get
        Set(ByVal value As String)
            _Name = value
        End Set
    End Property

    Private _ID As String = Guid.NewGuid().ToString()
    Public Property ID() As String
        Get
            Return _ID
        End Get
        Set(ByVal value As String)
            _ID = value
        End Set
    End Property

    Public Sub New(ByVal name As String)
        _Name = name
    End Sub

    Public Sub New()
        ' Used for serialization.
    End Sub
End Class
```

To use this class, you need to add it to the *Code* subdirectory so that it's compiled automatically. Then, to make it a part of the user profile, you need to define it in the *web.config* file, like this:

```xml
<profile>
    <properties>
        <add name="Basket" type="Basket" />
    </properties>
</profile>
```

With this information in place, it's easy to create a simple shopping cart test page. Figure 4-16 shows an example that lets you add and remove items. When the page is first loaded, it checks if there is a shopping basket for the current user, and if there isn't, it creates one. The user can then add items to the cart or remove existing items, using the Add and Remove buttons. Finally, the collection of shopping basket items is bound to a listbox every time the page is rendered, ensuring the page shows the current list of items in the basket. Example 4-7 shows the complete code.

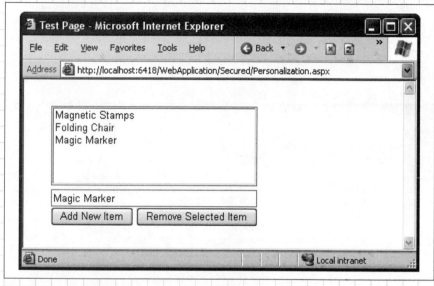

Figure 4-16. Adding items to a shopping basket

Example 4-7. Testing a personalized shopping basket

```
<%@ Page language="VB" %>

<script runat="server">
    Sub Page_Load(ByVal sender As Object, ByVal e As System.EventArgs)
        If Profile.Basket Is Nothing Then Profile.Basket = New Basket()
    End Sub

    ' Put a new item in the basket.
    Sub cmdAdd_Click(ByVal sender As Object, ByVal e As System.EventArgs)
        Profile.Basket.Items.Add(New BasketItem(txtItemName.Text))
    End Sub

    ' Remove the selected item.
    Sub cmdRemove_Click(ByVal sender As Object, ByVal e As System.EventArgs)
        For Each Item As BasketItem In Profile.Basket.Items
            If Item.ID = lstItems.SelectedItem.Value Then
```

Example 4-7. Testing a personalized shopping basket (continued)

```
                Profile.Basket.Items.Remove(Item)
                Return
            End If
        Next
    End Sub

    ' The page is being rendered. Create the list using data binding.
    Sub Page_PreRender(ByVal sender As Object, ByVal e As System.EventArgs)
        lstItems.DataSource = Profile.Basket.Items
        lstItems.DataTextField = "Name"
        lstItems.DataValueField = "ID"
        lstItems.DataBind()
    End Sub

</script>

<html>
<head runat="server">
    <title>Test Page</title>
</head>
<body>
    <form id="form1" runat="server">
        <br />
        <br />
        <asp:ListBox ID="lstItems" Runat="server" Width="266px"
            Height="106px"></asp:ListBox><br />
        <asp:TextBox ID="txtItemName" Runat="server"
            Width="266px"></asp:TextBox><br />
        <asp:Button ID="cmdAdd" Runat="server" Width="106px"
            Text="Add New Item" OnClick="cmdAdd_Click" />
        <asp:Button ID="cmdRemove" Runat="server" Width="157px"
            Text="Remove Selected Item" OnClick="cmdRemove_Click" />
    </form>
</body>
</html>
```

Remember, profile information doesn't time out. That means that even if you rebuild and restart the web application, the shopping cart items will still be there, unless your code explicitly clears them. This makes profiles perfect for storing permanent user-specific information without worrying about the hassle of ADO.NET code.

What about...

...anonymous users? By default, you can only access profile information once a user has logged in. However, many web sites retain user-specific information even when users aren't logged in. For example, most online e-commerce shops let users start shopping immediately, and only force them to log in at checkout time. To implement this design (without resorting to session state), you need to use another new feature in ASP.NET— *anonymous identification*.

With anonymous identification, ASP.NET assigns a unique ID to every new user. This ID is stored in a persistent cookie, which means that even if a user waits several days before making a repeat visit, ASP.NET will still be able to identify the user and find the personalized information from the user's last visit. (The default expiration settings remove the cookie after about one week if the user hasn't returned.)

In order to use anonymous identification, you need to add the <anonymousIdentification> tag to the *web.config* file, and you need to explicitly indicate what profile information can be tracked anonymously by flagging these properties with the allowAnonymous attribute.

Here's an example with a revised *web.config* that stores shopping basket information for anonymous users:

```xml
<?xml version="1.0"?>
<configuration>
  <system.web>
    <anonymousIdentification enabled="true">

    <profile>
      <properties>
        <add name="Basket" type="Basket" allowAnonymous="true"/>
      </properties>
    </profile>

    <!-- Other settings ommitted. -->
  </system.web>
</configuration>
```

Anonymous identification raises a few new considerations. The most significant occurs in systems where an anonymous user needs to log in at some point to complete an operation. In order to make sure information isn't lost, you need to handle the PersonalizationModule. MigrateAnonymous event in the *global.asax* file. You can then transfer information from the anonymous profile to the new authenticated profile.

Where can I learn more?

For more information about various profile options, including transferring anonymous profile information into an authenticated profile, look for the index entry "profiles" in the MSDN Help.

Files, Databases, and XML

.NET 1.0 revolutionized Visual Basic data access with a whole new object model for interacting with files, connecting to databases, and manipulating XML. In .NET 2.0, the revolution continues with a slew of minor improvements, some new features, and a tool for generating data access code automatically, all designed to make life better for the VB programmer.

In this chapter, you'll start out by considering how VB 2005 streamlines common file IO tasks with the My object. Next, you'll learn about some of the new frills in ADO.NET, the data-access framework at the heart of .NET. Finally, you'll learn about the revamped XPathNavigator class, which adds new support for working with XML documents.

Most of the labs in this chapter use console applications. Console applications allow you to quickly try out new features without a clutter of Windows forms or ASP.NET web pages. Of course, you can easily integrate these examples into any type of .NET application.

TIP

What you *won't* learn about in this chapter are the new .NET Framework features designed for SQL Server 2005. These include using .NET code to program user-defined data types and stored procedures, SQL Server 2005 notifications, and multiple active recordsets (MARS). For more information about these SQL Server 2005 features, please pay a visit to the MSDN SQL Server 2005 Developer Center at *http://msdn.microsoft.com/SQL/2005*.

In this chapter:
- *Get Drive Information*
- *Get File and Directory Information*
- *Copy, Move, and Delete Files*
- *Read and Write Files*
- *Compress and Decompress Data*
- *Collect Statistics on Your Data Connections*
- *Batch DataAdapter Commands for Better Performance*
- *Bulk-Copy Rows from One Table to Another*
- *Write Database-Agnostic Code*
- *Use the New XPathDocument and XPathNavigator*

The DriveInfo
class lets you
easily retrieve
information about
the drives on your
computer.

Get Drive Information

.NET includes handy `DirectoryInfo` and `FileInfo` classes for gathering information about files and directories. However, in .NET 1.x there wasn't any way to get a list of all the drives on your computer without using unmanaged calls to the Windows API. Thankfully, the `DriveInfo` class finally debuts in .NET 2.0.

TIP

Before going any further, start by importing the `System.IO` namespace. The file access classes in .NET 2.0 (`FileInfo`, `DirInfo`, and `DriveInfo`) all exist there. Whether you access them directly or through the My object, you'll need to import this namespace.

How do I do that?

The `My.Computer.FileSystem` provides a quick way to get a list of all the drives on the current computer. All you need to do is loop through the `Drives` collection, which exposes a collection of `System.IO.DriveInfo` objects.

For example, to see all the drive letters on the current computer, enter the following code:

```
' Display a list of drives.
For Each Drive As DriveInfo In My.Computer.FileSystem.Drives
    Console.WriteLine(Drive.Name)
Next
```

This writes a list of drive letter names ("A:\", "C:\", "D:\", and so on). You can also create a `DriveInfo` object for a specific directory by using the `My.Computer.FileSystem.GetDriveInfo()` method, and specifying the letter of the drive you want to examine as a string. For example, try the following code to take a closer look at drive C:

```
Console.WriteLine("The label for drive C:\ is " & _
    My.Computer.FileSystem.GetDriveInfo("C").VolumeLabel
```

This example displays the volume label that's set for the drive. You can also examine other properties of the `DriveInfo` object to get more information (such as the `DriveType`, `TotalFreeSpace`, and `TotalSize`). But keep in mind that you can't retrieve this information for a removable drive if there's no media present (for example, if the CD or diskette isn't in the drive). To guard against this possibility, check to make sure the `DriveType` doesn't include `DriveType.Fixed` before trying to get more detail.

Example 5-1 puts these concepts together with a complete, simple console application that displays information about all the drives on your computer.

Example 5-1. Displaying information about all the drives on a computer

```
Imports System.IO

Module DriveInfoTest

    Public Sub Main()
        Console.WriteLine("Drives on this computer: ")
        For Each Drive As DriveInfo In My.Computer.FileSystem.Drives
            ' Display drive information.
            Console.WriteLine(Drive.Name)

            Console.WriteLine(vbTab & "Type: " & Drive.DriveType.ToString())

            If (Drive.DriveType And DriveType.Fixed) = DriveType.Fixed Then
                Console.WriteLine(vbTab & "Format: " & _
                  Drive.DriveFormat.ToString())
                Console.WriteLine(vbTab & "Label: " & Drive.VolumeLabel)
                Console.WriteLine(vbTab & "Total Size: " & Drive.TotalSize)
                Console.WriteLine(vbTab & "Free Space: " & Drive.TotalFreeSpace)
            End If
            Console.WriteLine()
        Next
    End Sub

End Module
```

When you run this code, you'll see the following output:

```
Drives on this computer:
A:\
        Type: Removable

C:\
        Type: Fixed
        Format: NTFS
        Label: Applications
        Total Size: 15726702592
        Free Space: 2788483072

D:\
...
```

What about...

...getting information about the rest of the filesystem? The .NET Framework has always made it easy to get directory and file information using DirectoryInfo and FileInfo objects. Once you have instantiated a

DriveInfo object, you can use its RootDirectory property to get a DirectoryInfo object that wraps the root directory (e.g., *C:*). You can then use methods like DirectoryInfo.GetFiles() and DirectoryInfo.GetDirectories() to retrieve the files and subdirectories contained in the root directory.

Where can I learn more?

For more information about all the properties of the filesystem information classes, look for the "DriveInfo," "DirectoryInfo," and "FileInfo" index entries in the MSDN class library reference. You can also refer to other labs in this chapter, which show new shortcuts available with the My.Computer.FileSystem object. These include:

- "Get File and Directory Information," which shows how you can quickly get information about a specific file or directory without directly creating a FileInfo or DirectoryInfo object.
- "Copy, Move, and Delete Files," which shows how you can easily shuffle files and directories from one place to another.
- "Read and Write Files," which shows the quickest way to extract text content from a file or write to a file.

Get File and Directory Information

The new My.Computer. FileSystem object lets you get file and directory information with a bare minimum of code.

In VB 2005, you can access all the file and directory information you need from a single starting point: the new My.Computer.FileSystem object.

How do I do that?

Here are four key methods of My.Computer.FileSystem that you can use to get file and directory information. Every method has the same signature—it takes a single string parameter whose value is the complete path of the file or directory that's the subject of your query. The methods are:

FileExists()
  Returns True if the file exists.

DirectoryExists()
  Returns True if the directory exists.

GetFileInfo( )

> Returns a FileInfo object. You can examine its various properties to get information such as file size, attributes, and so on.

GetDirectoryInfo( )

> Returns a DirectoryInfo object. You can examine its various properties to get information such as directory size, attributes, and so on.

The code snippet shown in Example 5-2 first determines whether a file exists and then displays some information when it does.

Example 5-2. Retrieving information about a specific file

```
Imports System.IO

Module FileInfoTest

    Public Sub Main( )
        ' Get a file in a "special directory."
        Dim Info As FileInfo
        Info = My.Computer.FileSystem.GetFileInfo("c:\Windows\explorer.exe")

        ' Show the access/update times.
        Console.WriteLine("Created: " & Info.CreationTime)
        Console.WriteLine("Last Modified: " & Info.LastWriteTime)
        Console.WriteLine("Last Accessed: " & Info.LastAccessTime)

        ' Check if the file is read-only. When testing file attributes,
        ' you need to use bitwise arithmetic, because the FileAttributes
        ' collection usually contains more than one attribute at a time.
        Dim ReadOnlyFile As Boolean
        ReadOnlyFile = Info.Attributes And FileAttributes.ReadOnly
        Console.WriteLine("Read-Only: " & ReadOnlyFile)

        ' Show the size.
        Console.WriteLine("Size (bytes): " & Info.Length)
    End Sub

End Module
```

Here's the type of output you'll see:

```
Created: 3/30/2004 7:35:17 PM
Last Modified: 8/29/2002 4:41:24 AM
Last Accessed: 4/28/2004 10:59:38 AM
Read-Only: False
Size (bytes): 104032
Version: 6.0.1106
```

In early beta versions, Visual Basic included new FolderProperties and FileProperties classes that duplicated the DirectoryInfo and FileInfo classes. Fortunately, Microsoft decided not to reinvent the wheel, and went back to the .NET 1.x standards.

What about...

...searching for directories and files? The `My.Computer.FileSystem` object also provides a `GetDirectories()` method to retrieve the names of all the subdirectories in a directory and a `GetFiles()` method to retrieve the names of all files in a given directory.

Both methods offer additional flexibility via an overloaded version that accepts additional parameters. You can specify an array with one or more filter strings (for example, use `*.doc` to find all the files with the extension *.doc*). You can also supply a Boolean `includeSubFolders` parameter that, if `True`, searches for matching files or directories in every contained subdirectory.

Here's an example of an advanced search that finds all the *.exe* files in the *c:\windows* directory:

```
' Get all the EXE files in the Windows directory.
For Each File As String In My.Computer.FileSystem.GetFiles( _
  "c:\windows\", True, "*.exe")
    Info = My.Computer.FileSystem.GetFileInfo(File)
    Console.WriteLine(Info.Name & " in " & Info.Directory.Name)
Next
```

Note that the `GetFiles()` and `GetDirectories()` methods just return strings. If you want more information, you need to create a `FileInfo` or `DirectoryInfo` object for the file or directory, as shown above.

There is one caveat: when you perform a search with the `GetFiles()` method, the matching file list is first created and *then* returned to your code. In other words, if you're performing a time-consuming search, you won't receive a single result until the entire search is finished.

In VB 2005, you can perform common file-management tasks with a single line of code.

Copy, Move, and Delete Files

In addition to helping you gather information about the directories and files on your system, the `My.Computer.FileSystem` object also gives you quick access to a number of methods for performing common file-management tasks, such as copying, moving, and deleting files.

How do I do that?

The `My.Computer.FileSystem` object provides several self-contained methods for performing common file-management operations. They are:

- `CopyFile()` and `CopyDirectory()`
- `MoveFile()` and `MoveDirectory()`

- RenameFile( ) and RenameDirectory( )
- DeleteFile( ) and DeleteDirectory( )

The way you use each of these methods is fairly straightforward. You supply two parameters: a source path and, if required, a target filename or path. For example, you can rename a file with this line of code:

```
My.Computer.FileSystem.RenameFile("c:\myfile.txt", "newname.txt")
```

These methods are also available in overloaded versions that give you additional features. We'll take a look at those next.

The move and copy methods of FileSystem are available in a variety of overloaded versions. If you need to overwrite an existing file or directory, be sure to use a version that includes the Boolean parameter overwrite and set it to True. Otherwise, you'll receive an exception and the operation won't be completed. Here's an example of one such option:

```
My.Computer.FileSystem.CopyDirectory("c:\MyFiles", _
    "c:\CopyOfMyFiles", True)
```

Interestingly, among the copying and deleting methods are versions that accept the showUI Boolean parameter. If that parameter is set to True, the operation works exactly as if a user had initiated the delete or copy operation in Windows Explorer: dialog boxes appear asking the user to confirm the request to overwrite or delete files, and a progress indicator appears with a Cancel button when a file copy or delete operation is in progress (unless the operation completes very quickly). You can even specify what should happen when the user clicks Cancel (either an exception is thrown or nothing at all happens) using the onUserCancel parameter.

In some beta versions, the user interface for moving or deleting a file doesn't appear, even when you choose to see it. However, the underlying task (moving or deleting a file) is always performed correctly.

Example 5-3 provides a complete console application that lets you test this behavior.

Example 5-3. Moving and deleting files with Windows UI

```
Imports System.IO

Module FileManagement

    Public Sub Main()
        ' Create a large test file (100 MB).
        Dim TestFile As String = "c:\test.bin"
        Console.WriteLine("Creating file...")
        Dim fs As FileStream = File.OpenWrite(TestFile)
        For i As Integer = 1 To 100000000
            fs.WriteByte(0)
        Next
        fs.Close()
```

Example 5-3. Moving and deleting files with Windows UI (continued)

```
        ' Create the target directory.
        Console.WriteLine("Creating directory...")
        Dim TargetDir As String = "c:\TestDir"
        My.Computer.FileSystem.CreateDirectory(TargetDir)
        Dim TargetFile As String = Path.Combine(TargetDir, "test.bin")

        Console.WriteLine("Moving file...")
        ' Try moving the file. Set the following parameters:
        '    showUI = UIOption.AllDialogs
        ' (Show all the Windows UI, not just error messages.)
        '    onUserCancel = UICancelOption.ThrowException
        ' (Generate an error if the user clicks Cancel.)
        Try
            My.Computer.FileSystem.MoveFile(TestFile, TargetFile, _
                UIOption.AllDialogs, UICancelOption.ThrowException)
            Console.WriteLine("File moved.")
        Catch Err As Exception
            Console.WriteLine("You canceled the operation.")

            ' Remove the original file.
            My.Computer.FileSystem.DeleteFile(TestFile)
        End Try

        Console.WriteLine("Press Enter to continue.")
        Console.ReadLine( )

        ' Delete the target directory. Set the following parameters:
        '    showUI = UIOption.AllDialogs
        ' (Show the confirmation and Windows UI dialog box.)
        '    sendToRecycleBin = RecycleOption.SendToRecycleBin
        ' (Delete the file permanently.
        '    onUserCancel = UICancelOption.DoNothing
        ' (Allow the user to cancel this operation.)
        My.Computer.FileSystem.DeleteDirectory(TargetDir, _
            UIOption.AllDialogs, RecycleOption.SendToRecycleBin, _
            UICancelOption.DoNothing)

        Console.WriteLine("Cleanup finished.")
    End Sub

End Module
```

As shown in this example, the DeleteFile( ) and DeleteDirectory( ) methods have one additional frill available. By default, when you delete a file, it bypasses the Windows recycle bin. However, you can use an overloaded version of DeleteFile( ) or DeleteDirectory( ) that accepts a sendToRecycleBin parameter. Set this to True to keep your file around as a safeguard.

What about...

...file operations that use special folders? The new My.Computer.
FileSystem object allows you to retrieve references to many system-
defined folders through the SpecialDirectories class. For example, you
can quickly retrieve the path for temporary files, user documents, and the
desktop. Here's an example:

```
Dim Desktop As String = My.Computer.FileSystem.SpecialDirectories.Desktop
Console.WriteLine("Your desktop is at: " & Desktop)

Console.Write("It's size is: ")
Console.Write(My.Computer.FileSystem.GetDirectoryInfo(Desktop).Size)
Console.WriteLine(" bytes")
Console.Write("It contains: ")
Console.Write(My.Computer.FileSystem.GetFiles(Desktop).Count)
Console.WriteLine(" files")
```

The SpecialDirectories class includes all the following properties, each
of which returns a string with the corresponding fully qualified path:

```
AllUsersApplicationData
CurrentUserApplicationData
Desktop
MyDocuments
MyMusic
MyPictures
Programs
Temp
```

Read and Write Files

If you need to work with text files or raw binary data, VB 2005 provides
a new solution that bypasses the lower-level classes of System.IO for
small files. Now you can read and write text in a single atomic operation
using the My.Computer.FileSystem object. Best of all, you no longer need
to create streams, track your position, or clean up afterward.

At last, a way to read and write files without the complexities of streams and stream readers.

How do I do that?

The My.Computer.FileIO object provides the absolute quickest way to
read or write the contents of a file. Its secret lies in a few self-contained
methods. These include:

ReadAllText( )
    Reads the content of a text file and returns it as a single string.

ReadAllBytes( )
> Reads the content of any file and returns it as an array of bytes.

WriteAllText( )
> Writes text as a string to a file in one atomic operation. You can either add to an existing file or create a new file, depending on whether you supply True or False for the Boolean append parameter.

WriteAllBytes( )
> Writes a byte array to a file in a single operation. You can either add to an existing file or create a new file, depending on whether you supply True or False for the Boolean append parameter.

Example 5-4 creates a simple text file and then reads it back into memory.

Example 5-4. Write a file in one step and read a file in one step

```
Imports System.IO

Module FileReadAndWrite

    Public Sub Main()
        Dim Text As String = "This is line 1" & _
          vbNewLine & "This is line 2" & _
          vbNewLine & "This is line 3" & _
          vbNewLine & "This is line 4"

        ' Write the file.
        My.Computer.FileSystem.WriteAllText("c:\test.txt", Text, False)

        ' Read the file.
        Console.WriteLine(My.Computer.FileSystem.ReadAllText("c:\test.txt"))
    End Sub

End Module
```

What about...

...the limitations of this approach? The methods that you'll find in the My.Computer.FileSystem object are unmatched for sheer convenience, but they aren't always appropriate. Here are some reasons you might be better off using the lower-level classes of the System.IO namespace:

- You have an extremely large file, and you want to read and process its contents one piece at a time, rather than load the entire file into memory at once. This is a reasonable approach it you're dealing with a long document, for example.

- You want to use other data types, like numbers or dates. In order to use the My.Computer.FileIO methods to handle numeric data, you'll need to first convert the numbers into strings or byte arrays manually using other .NET classes. On the other hand, if you use a FileStream instead, you simply need to wrap it with a BinaryReader or BinaryWriter.

- You want to use other stream-based .NET features, such as compression (explained in the next lab, "Compress and Decompress Data"), object serialization, or encryption.

The core .NET classes for reading and writing files are found in the System.IO namespace and haven't changed in .NET 2.0. The most useful of these are FileStream (allows you to open a file directly for reading or writing), StreamReader and StreamWriter (used for reading and writing text, one line at a time), and BinaryReader and BinaryWriter (used for converting basic .NET data types to binary data and back). Look these classes up in the MSN Help for the traditional file-access techniques. Also, in the next lab, you'll see a more advanced example that uses FileStream to encrypt data in a file.

Compress and Decompress Data

Even with the ever-increasing capacity of hard drives and the falling price of computer memory, it still pays to save space. In .NET 2.0, a new System.IO.Compression namespace makes it easy for a VB 2005 programmer to compress data as she writes it to a stream, and decompress data as she reads it from a stream.

Need to save space before you store data in a file or database? .NET 2.0 makes compression and decompression easy.

How do I do that?

The new System.IO.Compression namespace introduces two new stream classes: GZipStream and DeflateStream, which, as you'd guess, are used to compress and decompress streams of data.

The algorithms used by these classes are *lossless*, which means that when you compress and decompress your data, you won't lose any information.

To use compression, you need to understand that a compression stream *wraps* another stream. For example, if you want to write some compressed data to a file, you first create a FileStream for the file. Then, you wrap the FileStream with the GZipStream or DeflateStream. Here's how it works:

```
Dim fsWrite As New FileStream(FileName, FileMode.Create)
Dim CompressStream As New GZipStream(fsWrite, CompressionMode.Compress)
```

Now, if you want to write data to the file, you use the GZipStream. The GZipStream compresses that data, and then writes the compressed data to the wrapped FileStream, which then writes it to the underlying file. If you skip this process and write directly to the FileStream, you'll end up writing uncompressed data instead.

Like all streams, the GZipStream only allows you to write raw bytes. If you want to write strings or other data types, you need to create a StreamWriter. The StreamWriter accepts basic .NET data types (like strings and integers) and converts them to bytes. Here's an example:

```
Dim Writer As New StreamWriter(CompressStream)

' Put a compressed line of text into the file.
Writer.Write("This is some text")
```

Finally, once you're finished, make sure you flush the GZipStream so that all the data ends up in the file:

```
Writer.Flush()
CompressStream.Flush()
fsWrite.Close()
```

The process of decompression works in a similar way. In this case, you create a FileStream for the file you want to read, and then create a GZipStream that decompresses the data. You then read the data using the GZipStream, as shown here:

```
fsRead = New FileStream(FileName, FileMode.Open)
Dim DecompressStream As New GZipStream(fsRead, CompressionMode.Decompress)
```

Example 5-5 shows an end-to-end example that writes some compressed data to a file, displays the amount of space saved, and then decompresses the data.

Example 5-5. Compress and decompress a sample file

```
Imports System.IO

Module FileCompression

    Public Sub Main()
        ' Read original file.
        Dim SourceFile As String
        SourceFile = My.Computer.FileSystem.CurrentDirectory & "\test.txt"
        Dim fsRead As New FileStream(SourceFile, FileMode.Open)
        Dim FileBytes(fsRead.Length - 1) As Byte
        fsRead.Read(FileBytes, 0, FileBytes.Length)
        fsRead.Close()
```

Example 5-5. *Compress and decompress a sample file (continued)*

```
    ' Write to a new compressed file.
    Dim TargetFile As String
    TargetFile = My.Computer.FileSystem.CurrentDirectory & "\test.bin"
    Dim fsWrite As New FileStream(TargetFile, FileMode.Create)
    Dim CompressStream As New GZipStream(fsWrite, CompressionMode.Compress)
    CompressStream.Write(FileBytes, 0, FileBytes.Length)
    CompressStream.Flush()
    CompressStream.Close()
    fsWrite.Close()

    Console.WriteLine("File compressed from " & _
      New FileInfo(SourceFile).Length & " bytes to " & _
      New FileInfo(TargetFile).Length & " bytes.")

    Console.WriteLine("Press Enter to decompress.")
    Console.ReadLine()

    fsRead = New FileStream(TargetFile, FileMode.Open)
    Dim DecompressStream As New GZipStream(fsRead, CompressionMode.Decompress)
    Dim Reader As New StreamReader(CType(DecompressStream, Stream))
    Console.WriteLine(Reader.ReadToEnd())
    Reader.Close()
    fsRead.Close()
  End Sub

End Module
```

What about...

...unzipping *.zip* files? Unfortunately, the .NET 2.0 compression streams can't deal with ZIP files, file archives that are commonly used to shrink batches of files (often before storing them for the long term or attaching them to an email message). If you need this specific ability, you'll probably be interested in the freely downloadable #ziplib (available at *http:// www.icsharpcode.net/OpenSource/SharpZipLib*).

Where can I learn more?

For more information about the GZipStream and DeflateStream algorithms, look them up in the MSDN Help. You can also look up the "compression" index entry for a Windows application example that uses these classes.

Want to find out what's really going on while you're connected to a database? In .NET 2.0, you can get ahold of much more information, but only if you're using SQL Server.

Collect Statistics on Your Data Connections

Most programmers like to look at statistics. Considered carefully, they can suggest the underlying cause of a long-standing problem, explain the performance problems of an application, or suggest possible optimization techniques. If you're using the SQL Server provider, you can make use of a new SqlConnection.RetrieveStatistics() method to get a hashtable with a slew of diagnostic details about your database connection.

How do I do that?

Before you can call RetrieveStatistics(), you need to instruct it to collect statistics by setting the SqlConnection.StatisticsEnabled property to True. Once you take this step, the SqlConnection class will gather statistics for every database command you execute over the connection. If you perform multiple operations with the same connection, the statistics will be cumulative, even if you close the connection between each operation.

To take a look at the statistics at any time, you call the RetrieveStatistics() method to retrieve a hashtable containing the accumulated data. The hashtable indexes its members with a descriptive name. For example, to retrieve the number of transactions you've performed, you'd write this code:

```
Dim Stats as Hashtable = con.RetrieveStatistics()
Console.Writeline(Stats("Transactions"))
```

To get a good idea of the different statistics available, try running Example 5-6, a console application that iterates over the statistics collection and displays the key name and value of each statistic it contains.

Example 5-6. Retrieving all the connection statistics

```
Imports System.Data.SqlClient

Module StatisticsTest

    Private ConnectString As String = _
      "Data Source=localhost;Initial Catalog=Northwind;Integrated Security=SSPI"
    Private con As New SqlConnection(ConnectString)

    Public Sub Main()
        ' Turn on statistics collection.
        con.StatisticsEnabled = True
```

Example 5-6. *Retrieving all the connection statistics (continued)*

```
        ' Perform two sample commands.
        SampleCommand()
        SampleCommand()

        ' Retrive the hashtable with statistics.
        Dim Stats As Hashtable = con.RetrieveStatistics()

        ' Display all the statistics.
        For Each Key As String In Stats.Keys
            Console.WriteLine(Key & " = " & Stats(Key))
        Next
    End Sub

    Private Sub SampleCommand()
        con.Open()
        Dim cmd As New SqlCommand("SELECT * FROM Customers", con)
        Dim reader As SqlDataReader = cmd.ExecuteReader()
        reader.Close()
        con.Close()
    End Sub

End Module
```

Here's the complete list of statistics produced by this code:

```
    NetworkServerTime = 18
    BytesReceived = 46248
    Transactions = 0
    SumResultSets = 2
    SelectCount = 2
    PreparedExecs = 0
    ConnectionTime = 13
    CursorFetchCount = 0
    CursorUsed = 0
    Prepares = 0
    CursorFetchTime = 0
    UnpreparedExecs = 2
    SelectRows = 182
    ServerRoundtrips = 2
    CursorOpens = 0
    BuffersSent = 2
    ExecutionTime = 725
    BytesSent = 108
    BuffersReceived = 6
    IduRows = 0
    IduCount = 0
```

To reset the values of the statistics collection to zero at any time, simply call the ResetStatistics() method:

```
    con.ResetStatistics()
```

What about...

...making sense of the various statistics gathered and putting them to use? Unfortunately, the MSDN Help doesn't yet provide the full lowdown on the SQL Server statistics. However, several statistics are particularly useful and not too difficult to interpret:

BytesReceived
> Gives a snapshot of the total number of bytes retrieved from the database server.

ServerRoundtrips
> Indicates the number of distinct commands you've executed.

ConnectionTime
> Indicates the cumulative amount of time the connection has been open.

SumResultSets
> Indicates the number of queries you've performed.

SelectRows
> Records the total number of rows retrieved in every query you've executed. (In the previous example this is 182, because each query retrieved 91 rows.)

And for an example where statistics are used to profile different approaches to database code, refer to the next lab, "Batch DataAdapter Commands for Better Performance."

If you need an easy way to optimize DataSet updates, ADO.NET's new batching can help you out.

Batch DataAdapter Commands for Better Performance

Many databases are able to execute commands in batches, reducing the total number of calls you need to make. For example, if you submit 10 update commands in a single batch, your code only needs to make 1 trip to the server (instead of 10). Cutting down the number of round-trips can increase performance, particularly on networks that have a high degree of latency. In .NET 2.0, the SqlDataAdapter is enhanced to use batching for updating, inserting, and deleting records.

How do I do that?

In previous versions of .NET, you could batch direct commands by concatenating them in a single string, and separating each with a semicolon. This syntax requires support from the database provider, but it works

perfectly well with SQL Server. Here's an example that inserts two rows
into a table:

```
Dim TwoInserts As String ="INSERT INTO Shippers" &_
    "(CompanyName, Phone) VALUES "ACME", "212-111-1111;" & _
    "INSERT INTO Shippers (CompanyName, Phone)" &_
    VALUES "Grey Matter", "416-123-4567"

Dim cmd As New SqlCommand(TwoInsert)
cmd.ExecuteNonQuery( )
```

As useful as this feature is, previous versions of .NET didn't provide any
way to batch commands to one of the most important ADO.NET provider
objects—the data adapter. The data-adapter object scans a DataSet, and
executes insert, delete, and update commands whenever it finds a new,
removed, or changed row. Each of these commands is executed separately, which means that if your DataSet contains three new rows, the
data adapter will make three round-trips to the server.

It makes good sense to have batching support in the data adapter, because the data adapter is often used to commit more than one modification at a time.

.NET 2.0 improves the picture with a new SqlDataAdapter.
UpdateBatchSize property. By default, the value of this property is set to
1, which causes each insert, update, or delete command to be executed
separately. If you set the UpdateBatchSize to a larger number, the data
adapter will group its commands into batches.

Example 5-7 is a console application, BatchedDataAdapterTest, that puts
this technique to the test. BatchedDataAdapterTest retrieves data from
the Orders table in the Northwind database and then makes changes to
each row. To make life interesting, the module applies this update not
once, but twice—once without batching, and once with batch sizes set to
15. BatchedDataAdapterTest displays connection statistics for each
approach, allowing you to compare their performance.

Example 5-7. Updates with and without batching

```
Imports System.Data.SqlClient

Module BatchedDataAdapterTest

    Private ConnectString As String = _
        "Data Source=localhost;Initial Catalog=Northwind;Integrated Security=SSPI"
    Private con As New SqlConnection(ConnectString)

    Public Sub Main( )
        ' Turn on statistics collection.
        con.StatisticsEnabled = True

        Dim Query As String = "SELECT * FROM Orders"
        Dim cmd As New SqlCommand(Query, con)
        Dim Adapter As New SqlDataAdapter(cmd)
```

Example 5-7. Updates with and without batching (continued)

```
Dim CommandBuilder As New SqlCommandBuilder(Adapter)

Dim ds As New DataSet
con.Open()
Adapter.Fill(ds, "Orders")
con.Close()

' Perform an update without batching.
ChangeRows(ds)
con.ResetStatistics()
Adapter.Update(ds, "Orders")
Console.WriteLine("Statistics without batching....")
DisplayStatistics()

' Perform an update with batching (15 row batches).
ChangeRows(ds)
con.ResetStatistics()
Adapter.UpdateBatchSize = 15
' When performing a batch update you must explicitly
' open the connection.
con.Open()
Adapter.Update(ds, "Orders")
con.Close()

Console.WriteLine("Statistics with batching....")
DisplayStatistics()
    End Sub

    Public Sub ChangeRows(ByVal ds As DataSet)
        For Each Row As DataRow In ds.Tables("Orders").Rows
            Row("ShippedDate") = DateTime.Now
        Next
    End Sub

    Public Sub DisplayStatistics()
        ' Retrive the hasthable with statistics.
        Dim Stats As Hashtable = con.RetrieveStatistics()

        ' Display all the statistics.
        For Each Key As String In Stats.Keys
            Console.WriteLine(Key & " = " & Stats(Key))
        Next
        Console.WriteLine()
    End Sub

End Module
```

When you run this application, the rows will be updated, and a list of statistics will appear. Take a close look at these statistics, paying special attention to the number of round-trips made to the database, the total connection time, and the amount of data required to complete the updates. Here's a portion of the output generated by one run of the application that highlights some of the more important numbers:

```
Statistics without batching....
ConnectionTime = 5682
UnpreparedExecs = 831
ServerRoundtrips = 831
BytesSent = 2637094

Statistics with batching....
ConnectionTime = 6319
UnpreparedExecs = 56
ServerRoundtrips = 56
BytesSent = 1668160
```

This listing reports that, in the batched update, 831 rows were updated in 56 batches of 15 commands each. As you can see, batching reduced the amount of data that needed to be sent (by packing it more effectively into batches), which is one of the most important metrics of database scalability. On the other hand, the overall performance of the application hardly changed at all, and the connection time even increased slightly. Clearly, to make a meaningful decision about whether to use batching, you need to profile your application in a real-world scenario.

What about...

...the quirks and limitations of batched updates? Currently, only the SqlDataAdapter supports batching, although other providers may implement this functionality in the future. The actual implementation details will differ for each provider—in the case of the SqlDataAdapter, the provider uses the sp_executesql system stored procedure to execute the batch. As for quirks, you'll notice a change to how the RowUpdated and RowUpdating events of the SqlDataAdapter work. When batching is enabled, these events fire once for every batch, not once for every row. That means that when the RowUpdated event fires, you can determine the number of rows affected, but not the row-by-row details of the changes made. This loss of information can make it more difficult to handle errors that occur somewhere inside a batch.

The ideal batch size depends on a variety of low-level factors, including the network architecture and the size of the rows. The best advice is to test your application with different batch settings. If you want all updates to be done in a single batch of unlimited size, set the UpdateBatchSize property to 0.

Bulk-Copy Rows from One Table to Another

Most SQL Server gurus are familiar with the BCP command-line utility, which allows you to move vast amounts of information from one SQL Server database to another. BCP comes in handy any time you need to load a large number of records at once, but it's particularly useful when you need to transfer data between servers. In .NET 2.0, the SqlClient namespace includes a new SqlBulkCopy class that allows you to perform a bulk-copy operation programmatically.

How do I do that?

The key ingredient in a bulk-copy operation is the new SqlBulkCopy class. It performs all of its work when you call the WriteToServer( ) method, which can be used in two ways:

- You can submit your data as a DataTable or an array of DataRow objects. This makes sense if you want to insert a batch of records from a file you created earlier. It also works well if you're creating a server-side component (like a web service) that receives a disconnected DataSet with the records that need to be loaded into a table.

- You can submit your data as an open DataReader that draws records from another SqlConnection. This approach is ideal if you want to transfer records from one database server to another.

Before you call WriteToServer( ), you need to create the connections and commands you need and set up *mapping* between the destination and source table. If your source and destination tables match exactly, no mapping is required. However, if the table names differ, you need to set the SqlBulkCopy.DestinationTableName property to the name of the target table. Additionally, if the column names don't match or if there are fewer columns in the target table than there are in the source data, you also need to configure column mapping. To set column mapping, you add one mapping object for each column to the SqlBulkCopy.ColumnMappings collection. Each mapping object specifies the name of the source column and the name of the corresponding target column.

To try this out, create a new SQL Server database named *NorthwindCopy* and a table named *CustomersShort*. The *CustomersShort* table is designed to offer a subset of the information in the *Customers* table. You can create it by using a tool like SQL Server Enterprise Manager (see the column settings in Figure 5-1), or you can use the script included with the down-

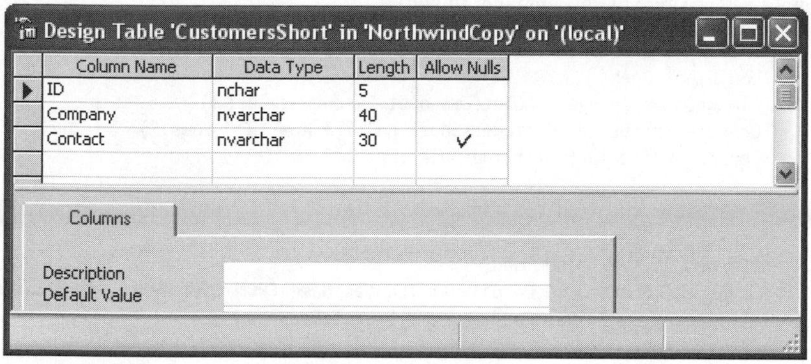

Figure 5-1. Creating a CustomersShort table

loadable content for this chapter to create it automatically (look for the file *GenerateNorthwindCopy.sql*).

Once you've created *CustomersShort*, you have a perfect table for testing a SQL Server bulk-copy operation. All you need to do is create two connections, define the mapping, and start the process. Example 5-8 has the code you need.

Example 5-8. Using SQLBulkCopy

```
Imports System.Data.SqlClient

Module Module1

    Private ConnectSource As String = _
      "Data Source=localhost;Initial Catalog=Northwind;Integrated Security=SSPI"
    Private ConnectTarget As String = _
      "Data Source=localhost;Initial Catalog=NorthwindCopy;" &_
      "Integrated Security=SSPI"

    Public Sub Main()
        ' Create the source and target connections.
        Dim conSource As New SqlConnection(ConnectSource)
        Dim conTarget As New SqlConnection(ConnectTarget)

        ' Create a command for counting the number of rows in a table.
        Dim cmdCount As New SqlCommand("SELECT COUNT(*) FROM CustomersShort", _
            conTarget)

        ' Initialize the SqlBulkCopy class with mapping information.
        Dim BCP As New SqlClient.SqlBulkCopy(conTarget)
        BCP.DestinationTableName = "CustomersShort"
        BCP.ColumnMappings.Add("CustomerID", "ID")
        BCP.ColumnMappings.Add("CompanyName", "Company")
        BCP.ColumnMappings.Add("ContactName", "Contact")
```

Example 5-8. Using SQLBulkCopy (continued)

```
        ' Count the rows in CustomersShort.
        conTarget.Open()
        Dim Rows As Integer = CInt(cmdCount.ExecuteScalar())
        Console.WriteLine("CustomersShort has " & Rows & " rows.")
        Console.WriteLine("Starting bulk copy...")

        ' Retrieve the rows you want to transfer.
        conSource.Open()
        Dim cmd As New SqlCommand( _
          "SELECT CustomerID,CompanyName,ContactName FROM Customers", conSource)
        Dim reader As SqlDataReader = cmd.ExecuteReader()

        ' Write the data to the destination table.
        BCP.WriteToServer(reader)

        ' Clean up.
        BCP.Close()
        reader.Close()
        conSource.Close()

        ' Count the rows in CustomersShort again.
        conSource.Open()
        Rows = CInt(cmdCount.ExecuteScalar())
        Console.WriteLine("Finished bulk copy.")
        Console.WriteLine("CustomersShort has " & Rows & " rows.")

        conTarget.Close()
        Console.ReadLine()
    End Sub

End Module
```

When you run the code, you'll see output like this, indicating that the bulk-copy operation completed successfully:

```
CustomersShort has 0 rows.
Starting bulk copy...
Finished bulk copy.
CustomersShort has 91 rows.
```

What about...

...other SqlBulkCopy properties? SqlBulkCopy provides two useful properties: BulkCopyTimeout (which allows you to set how long you'll wait for an unresponsive server) and BatchSize (which allows you to set how many operations are batched together, as described in the lab "Batch DataAdapter Commands for Better Performance"). Errors are handled in the same way as when you directly execute a `SqlCommand`. In other words, if an error happens on the server side (like a unique value conflict), the process will be interrupted immediately, and you'll receive a `SqlClient` exception with the full details.

Where can I learn more?

For a complete list of class members, look up the `SqlBulkCopy` class in the MSDN help library reference. Or, for information about the original BCP utility, look for the index entry "bcp utility" in the SQL Server Books Online help.

Write Database-Agnostic Code

In developing ADO.NET, Microsoft set out to create a new data access architecture that would be more flexible, better performing, and more easily extensible than its previous COM-based OLE DB and ADO architectures. They did this by creating a model where every data source must supply its own *data provider*: a set of managed classes that allow you to connect to a particular data source (e.g., SQL Server, Oracle), execute commands, and retrieve data. In order to ensure that these providers are consistent, each implements a standard set of interfaces. However, this approach creates major challenges for developers who want to write *provider-agnostic* code—for example, a basic database routine that can be used equally well with the SQL Server provider or the Oracle provider. Usually, you use provider-agnostic code because you aren't sure what type of database the final version of an application will use, or because you anticipate the need to migrate to a different database in the future.

.NET 2.0 takes major steps to facilitate generic database coding by introducing a new *factory model*. (A factory model is a pattern where one class has the exclusive responsibility for creating instances of other classes.) In this model, you can use a database provider factory to build the ADO.NET connections, commands, and many other types of objects required for a particular database. The factory automatically returns the type of object that you need for your data source (e.g., a `SqlCommand` or an `OracleCommand`), but when you write your code, you don't worry about these details. Instead, you write generic commands without regard to the particular details of the data source.

Want a way to write database code that isn't bound to a specific data source? This challenge becomes a whole lot easier in .NET 2.0.

Because provider-agnostic code attempts to be as generic as possible, it's more difficult to properly optimize a database. As a result, this technique isn't suitable for most large-scale enterprise applications.

How do I do that?

In provider-agnostic code, you still use all the same strongly typed objects. However, your code manipulates these objects using common interfaces. For example, every command object, whether it's used for SQL Server or Oracle, implements the common IDbCommand interface, which guarantees a basic set of methods and properties.

Provider-agnostic code is structured so that you specify the type of database you're using early on, usually by reading some information from a configuration file. You use this information to retrieve a DbProviderFactory for your database. Here's an example where the factory string is hardcoded:

```
Dim Factory As String = "System.Data.SqlClient"
Dim Provider As DbProviderFactory
Provider = DbProviderFactories.GetFactory(Factory)
```

In this example, the code uses the shared GetFactory( ) method of the System.Data.Common.DbProviderFactories class. It specifies a string that identifies the provider name. For example, if you use the string System.Data.SqlClient, the GetFactory( ) method returns a System.Data.SqlClient.SqlClientFactory object. The DbProviderFactories class can create factories for all the data providers included with .NET, because they are explicitly configured in the *machine.config* configuration file on the current computer. Essentially, the configuration record tells the DbProviderFactories class to create a SqlClientFactory when the programmer passes the exact string "System.Data.SqlClient." If you develop your own provider, you can also register it to work in this way (although that task is beyond the scope of this lab).

The SqlClientFactory object has the built-in smarts to create all the objects used by the SQL Server provider. However, your code can be completely generic. Instead of interacting with the specific SqlClientFactory class type, it should use the generic base class DbProviderFactory. That way, your code can work with any type of DbProviderFactory, and therefore support any database provider.

Once you have the DbProviderFactory, you can create other types of strongly typed ADO.NET objects using a set of common methods by using the CreateXxx( ) methods. These include:

```
CreateConnection( )
CreateCommand( )
CreateParameter( )
CreateDataAdapter( )
CreateCommandBuilder( )
```

All these methods create a provider-specific version of the object they name.

To get a better understanding of how generic database code works, it helps to try out a complete example that can switch from one data provider to another on the fly. First of all, you need to create an application configuration file that stores all the provider-specific details. To do this, create a console application and open the *app.config* file. Add the following three settings, which specify the factory name, the connection string for the database, and the query to perform:

```xml
<?xml version="1.0" encoding="utf-8" ?>
<configuration>
  <appSettings>
    <add key="Factory" value="System.Data.SqlClient" />
    <add key="Connection" value=
 "Data Source=localhost;Initial Catalog=Northwind;Integrated Security=SSPI"
/>
    <add key="Query" value="SELECT * FROM Orders" />
  </appSettings>
</configuration>
```

This example uses the SQL Server provider to connect to the Northwind database and retrieve a list of all the records in the Orders table.

Now you can retrieve the configuration file information and use it with the DbProviderFactories class to create every ADO.NET provider object you need. In Example 5-9, the query is executed, a DataSet is filled, and a list of OrderID values is displayed in the console window.

Example 5-9. Using DbProviderFactories to write database-agnostic code

```vb
Imports System.Data.Common
Imports System.Configuration

Module GenericDatabaseTest

    Public Sub Main()
        ' Get all the information from the configuration file.
        Dim Factory, Connection, Query As String
        Factory = ConfigurationManager.AppSettings("Factory")
        Connection = ConfigurationSettings.AppSettings("Connection")
        Query = ConfigurationManager.AppSettings("Query")

        ' Get the factory for this provider.
        Dim Provider As DbProviderFactory
        Provider = DbProviderFactories.GetFactory(Factory)

        ' Use the factory to create a connection.
        Dim con As DbConnection = Provider.CreateConnection()
        con.ConnectionString = Connection
```

Example 5-9. Using DbProviderFactories to write database-agnostic code (continued)

```
        ' Use the factory to create a data adapter
        ' and fill a DataSet.
        Dim Adapter As DbDataAdapter = Provider.CreateDataAdapter
        Adapter.SelectCommand = Provider.CreateCommand( )
        Adapter.SelectCommand.Connection = con
        Adapter.SelectCommand.CommandText = Query
        Dim ds As New DataSet
        Adapter.Fill(ds, "Orders")

        ' Display the retrieved information.
        For Each Row As DataRow In ds.Tables("Orders").Rows
            Console.WriteLine(Row("OrderID"))
        Next
    End Sub

End Module
```

Mostly, this is a fairly pedestrian piece of data access logic. The only exciting part is that you can switch from one provider to another without modifying any of the code or recompiling. You just need to modify the provider information and connection string in the configuration file. For example, make these changes to the configuration file to access the same table through the slower OLE DB provider interface:

```
<?xml version="1.0" encoding="utf-8" ?>
<configuration>
  <appSettings>
    <add key="Factory" value="System.Data.OleDb" />
    <add key="Connection" value=
 "Provider=SQLOLEDB;Data Source=localhost;Initial
Catalog=Northwind;Integrated Security=SSPI" />
    <add key="Query" value="SELECT * FROM Orders" />
  </appSettings>
</configuration>
```

After saving the configuration file, you can run the application again. It will work just as well, displaying the same list of order records.

What about...

...the challenges you'll encounter in writing database-agnostic programs? The new factory approach is a giant leap forward for those who want to write provider-agnostic code. However, a slew of problems (some minor and some more significant) still remain. These include:

Handling errors
> Every database provider has its own exception object (like `SqlException` and `OracleException`), and these objects don't derive from a common base class. That means there's no way to write an

exception handler that catches database exceptions generically. All you can do is write exception handlers that catch the base Exception object.

Provider-specific functionality

Some features aren't exposed through the common interfaces. For example, SQL Server has the ability to execute FOR XML queries that return XML documents. To execute this type of query, you use the SqlCommand.ExecuteXmlReader() method. Unfortunately, this isn't a standard command method, so there's no way to access it through the IDbCommand interface.

Handling parameters

Some providers (like SQL Server) recognize command parameters by their name. Others (like OLE DB) recognize command parameters by the order of their appearance. Minor differences like this can thwart provider-agnostic programming.

Where can I learn more?

Unfortunately, there isn't much documentation yet in the MSDN Help about provider-agnostic coding. However, you can get a good overview with additional examples from the Microsoft whitepaper at *http://msdn. microsoft.com/library/en-us/dnvs05/html/vsgenerics.asp*.

Use the New XPathDocument and XPathNavigator

.NET provides a range of options for dealing with XML in the System.Xml namespaces. One common choice is XmlDocument, which lets you navigate in-memory XML as a collection of node objects. For more efficient performance, the XmlWriter and XmlReader classes offer a streamlined way to read and write a stream of XML. Unfortunately, neither solution is perfect. The XmlDocument consumes too much memory, and navigating its structure requires too much code. Furthermore, because the XmlDocument is based on a third-party standard (the XML DOM, or *document object model*), it's difficult to improve it without breaking compatibility. On the other hand, the XmlWriter and XmlReader are too restrictive, forcing you to access information linearly from start to finish. They also make it pro-hibitively difficult for a developer to provide an XML interface to non-XML data.

Talk about an improvement! The revamped XPathDocument sets a new standard for XML parsing in .NET.

.NET 2.0 proposes a solution with the System.Xml.XPath.XPathDocument. The XPathDocument is a cursor-based XML reader that aims to become the only XML interface you need to use. It gives you the freedom to move to any position in a document, and it provides blistering speed when used with other XML standards such as XQuery, XPath, XSLT, and XML Schema validation.

How do I do that?

To use an XPathDocument, you begin by loading the document from a stream, XmlReader, or URI (which can include a file path or an Internet address). To load the content, you can use the Load( ) method or a constructor argument—they both work in the same way. In this example, the XPathDocument is filled with the content from a local file:

```
Dim Doc As New XPathDocument("c:\MyDocument.xml")
```

To actually move around an XPathDocument, you need to create an XPathNavigator by calling the CreateNavigator( ) method.

```
Dim Navigator As XPathNavigator = Doc.CreateNavigator( )
```

The XPathNavigator includes a generous group of methods for navigating the structure of the XML document. Some of the methods include:

MoveToRoot( )
> Jumps to the root, or document element that contains all the other elements.

MoveToID( )
> Moves to an element that has a specific ID, as identified with the ID attribute.

MoveToNext( )
> Moves to the next node at the same level (technically called a sibling).

MoveToPrevious( )
> Moves to the previous node at the same level (technically called a sibling).

MoveToFirstChild( )
> Moves down a level to the first node contained by the current node.

MoveToParent( )
> Moves up a level to the parent that contains the current node.

Once you're positioned on an element, you can read the element name from the Name property. You can retrieve the contained text content from the Value property.

Now that you've learned this much, it's worth trying a basic example. In it, we'll use an XML document that contains a product catalog based on Microsoft's ASP.NET Commerce Starter Kit. This XML file (which is available with the downloadable content for this chapter) has the structure shown in Example 5-10.

Example 5-10. Sample XML for a product catalog

```
<?xml version="1.0" standalone="yes"?>
<Products>
  <Product>
    <ProductID>356</ProductID>
    <ModelName>Edible Tape</ModelName>
    <ModelNumber>STKY1</ModelNumber>
    <UnitCost>3.99</UnitCost>
    <CategoryName>General</CategoryName>
  </Product>
  <Product>
    <ProductID>357</ProductID>
    <ModelName>Escape Vehicle (Air)</ModelName>
    <ModelNumber>P38</ModelNumber>
    <UnitCost>2.99</UnitCost>
    <CategoryName>Travel</CategoryName>
  </Product>
  ...
</Products>
```

Example 5-11 loads this document, creates an XPathNavigator, and moves through the nodes, looking for the <ModelName> element for each <Product>. When that element is found, its value is displayed.

Example 5-11. Navigating an XML document with XPathNavigator

```
Imports System.Xml.XPath
Imports System.Xml

Module XPathNavigatorTest

    Sub Main( )
        ' Load the document.
        Dim Doc As New XPathDocument( _
          My.Computer.FileSystem.CurrentDirectory & _
          "\ProductList.xml")

        ' Navigate the document with an XPathNavigator.
        Dim Navigator As XPathNavigator = Doc.CreateNavigator( )

        ' Move to the root <Products> element.
        Navigator.MoveToFirstChild( )

        ' Move to the first contained <Product> element.
        Navigator.MoveToFirstChild( )
```

Example 5-11. Navigating an XML document with XPathNavigator (continued)

```
    ' Loop through all the <Product> elements.
    Do
        ' Search for the <ModelName> element inside <Product>
        ' and display its value.
        Navigator.MoveToFirstChild( )
        Do
            If Navigator.Name = "ModelName" Then
                Console.WriteLine(Navigator.Value)
            End If
        Loop While Navigator.MoveToNext( )

        ' Move back to the <Product> element.
        Navigator.MoveToParent( )
    Loop While Navigator.MoveToNext( )
End Sub

End Module
```

When you run this code, you'll see a display with a list of model names for all the products.

Interestingly, the XPathNavigator also provides *strong typing* for data values. Instead of retrieving the current value as a string using the Value property, you can use one of the properties that automatically converts the value to another data type. Supported properties include:

```
ValueAsBoolean
ValueAsDateTime
ValueAsDouble
ValueAsInt
ValueAsLong
```

To try this out, you can rewrite the loop in Example 5-11 so that it converts the price to a double value and then displays a total with added sales tax:

```
Do
    If Navigator.Name = "ModelName" Then
        Console.WriteLine(Navigator.Value)
    ElseIf Navigator.Name = "UnitCost" Then
        Dim Price As Double = Navigator.ValueAsDouble * 1.15
        Console.WriteLine(vbTab & "Total with tax: " & Math.Round(Price, 2))
    End If
Loop While Navigator.MoveToNext( )
```

What about...

...other ways to search an XML document with the XPathNavigator? To simplify life, you can select a portion of the XML document to work with in an XPathNavigator. To select this portion, you use the Select() or SelectSingleNode() methods of the XPathNavigator class. Both of these methods require an XPath expression that identifies the nodes you want to retrieve. (For more information about the XPath standard, see the "Introducing XPath" sidebar.)

For example, the following code selects the <ModelName> element for every product that's in the Tools category:

```
' Use an XPath expression to get just the nodes that interest you
' (in this case, all product names in the Tools category).
Dim XPathIterator As XPathNodeIterator
XPathIterator = Navigator.Select ( _
  "/Products/Product/ModelName[../CategoryName='Tools']")

Do While (XPathIterator.MoveNext())
    ' XPathIterator.Current is an XPathNavigator object pointed at the
    ' current node.
    Console.WriteLine(XPathIterator.Current.Value)
Loop
```

TIP

The examples in this lab use an XML document with no namespace. However, namespaces are often used in programming scenarios to allow your program to uniquely identify the type of document it references. If your document uses namespaces, you need to use the XmlNamespaceManager class and rewrite your XPath expressions to use a namespace prefix. If you'd like an example of this technique, refer to the downloadable samples for this lab, which demonstrate an example with a product catalog that uses XML namespaces.

Where can I learn more?

The XPathNavigator class is too detailed to cover completely in this lab. For more information, refer to both classes in the MSDN Help. Additionally, you can learn about XML standards like XPath, XQuery, and XML Schema from the excellent online tutorials at *http://www.w3schools.com*.

In addition, you'll find one more lab that can help you extend your XPathDocument skills: "Edit an XML Document with XPathDocument," which explains the editing features of the XPathDocument.

Introducing XPath

Basic XPath syntax uses a path-like notation to describe locations in a document. For example, the path /Products/Product/ModelName indicates a ModelName element that is nested inside a Product element, which, in turn, is nested in a root Products element. This is an absolute path (indicated by the fact that it starts with a single slash, representing the root of the document).

You can also use relative paths, which search for nodes with a given name regardless of where they are. Relative paths start with two slashes. For example, //ModelName will find all ModelName elements no matter where they are in the document hierarchy. Other path characters that you can use include the period (.), which refers to the current node; the double period (..) to move up one level; and the asterisk (*) to select any node.

XPath gets really interesting when you start to add filter conditions. Filter conditions are added to a path in square brackets. For example, the XPath expression //Product[CategoryName='Tools'] finds all Product elements that contain a CategoryName element with the text "Tools." You can use the full range of logical operators, such as less than and greater than (< and >) or not equal to (!=). For much more information about the wonderful world of XPath, refer to *XML in a Nutshell* (O'Reilly).

WARNING

The editable XPathNavigator has undergone extensive changes, and the features demonstrated in the next lab ("Edit an XML Document with XPathNavigator") weren't working in the last build we tested. Although it's expected to return, features are sometimes cut even at this late stage. If the coding model changes, you'll find updated code in the downloadable examples for the book.

The best feature of the XPathNavigator is its new support for editing and inserting content.

Edit an XML Document with XPathNavigator

The XPathNavigator is the XML interface of choice for Visual Basic 2005 applications. And in .NET 2.0, it doesn't just work as a view onto read-only XML data—it also allows you to change XML documents, such as by modifying text content, inserting new elements, or removing a branch of nodes.

Chapter 5: Files, Databases, and XML

How do I do that?

In the previous lab, "Use the New XPathDocument and XPathNavigator," you learned how to load XML data into an XPathDocument, and then browse and search through it using an XPathNavigator. If you want to make changes, you still start with the same XPathDocument. The secret is that you also use a couple of additional methods in the XPathNavigator:

SetValue( )
> This method inserts a new value in the current element, replacing the existing value.

DeleteCurrent( )
> This method removes the current node from the document.

Remember, you have two basic choices for creating an XPathNavigator:

Use the XPathDocument.CreateNavigator( ) *method*
> This method returns an XPathNavigator for the whole document. You can then move to the portion of the document you want to change.

Use the XPathDocument.Select( ) *method with an XPath expression*
> This returns an XPathNodeIterator that allows you to move through your results, retrieving an XPathNavigator for each selected node.

Example 5-12 modifies the XML document shown in Example 5-10. It increases all the prices by 10% and then deletes nodes that don't fall into the Tools category. Finally, it displays the altered XML document.

Example 5-12. Modifying an XML document with XPathNavigator

```
Imports System.Xml.XPath
Imports System.Xml

Module XPathNavigatorTest

    Sub Main( )
        ' Load the document.
        Dim Doc As New XPathDocument(My.Computer.FileSystem.CurrentDirectory & _
          "\ProductList.xml")

        ' Use the XPathNavigator to make updates.
        Dim XPathIterator As XPathNodeIterator = Doc.Select("//UnitCost")

        ' Increase the price by 10%.
        For Each Editor As XPathNavigator In XPathIterator
            Editor.SetValue((1.1 * Editor.ValueAsDouble).ToString( ))
        Next
```

Example 5-12. Modifying an XML document with XPathNavigator (continued)

```
        ' Delete nodes that aren't in the Tools category.
        XPathIterator = Doc.Select("/Products/Product[CategoryName!='Tools']")
        For Each Editor As XPathNavigator In XPathIterator
            Editor.DeleteCurrent()
        Next

        ' Show changes.
        XPathEditor.MoveToRoot()
        Console.WriteLine(XPathEditor.OuterXml)
    End Sub

End Module
```

When you run this application, the XML for the changed document is displayed in the console window. You can also open the *ProductList_new. xml* file where the changes are saved.

In many cases, you won't just want to change a value—you'll need a way to insert new elements or entire sections. The XPathNavigator includes a handful of methods for inserting new elements and attributes in one shot. However, the easiest way to add a block of XML is to use an XmlWriter. If you've worked with XML and .NET before, you probably recognize the XmlWriter. The XmlWriter was commonly used to write XML content directly to a file in .NET 1.x applications. The difference in .NET 2.0 is that the XPathEditor allows you to use the XmlWriter to write directly to your in-memory XPathDocument.

All you need to do is start by calling one of the XPathEditor methods that returns an XmlWriter. These include the following, which differ on where each places the inserted XML:

AppendChild( )
> Adds a new element inside the current element, after all existing child elements.

PrependChild( )
> Adds a new element inside the current element, before any existing child elements.

InsertAfter( )
> Adds a new element after the current element (and at the same level).

InsertBefore( )
> Adds a new element just before the current element (and at the same level).

Example 5-13 uses the AppendChild( ) method to add a new product to the product list XML document.

Example 5-13. Using the AppendChild( ) method to add a new element to an XML document

```
Imports System.Xml.XPath
Imports System.Xml

Module XPathNavigatorTest

    Sub Main( )
        ' Load the document.
        Dim Doc As New XPathDocument(My.Computer.FileSystem.CurrentDirectory & _
          "\ProductList.xml")

        ' Create a new product.
        Dim XPathEditor As XPathNavigator = Doc.CreateEditor( )
        XPathEditor.MoveToRoot( )
        XPathEditor.MoveToFirstChild( )

        ' Use the XmlWriter to add a new <Product> complete with
        ' all child elements.
        Dim Writer As XmlWriter = XPathEditor.AppendChild

        ' Insert the opening <Product> tag.
        Writer.WriteStartElement("Product", _
          "http://www.ibuyspy.com/ProductCatalog")

        ' The WriteElementString( ) method inserts a whole element at once.
        Writer.WriteElementString("ProductID", "999")
        Writer.WriteElementString("ModelName", "Rubber Pants")
        Writer.WriteElementString("ModelNumber", "NOZ999")
        Writer.WriteElementString("UnitCost", "12.99")
        Writer.WriteElementString("CategoryName", "Clothing")

        ' Insert the closing </Product> tag and close the writer.
        Writer.WriteEndElement( )
        Writer.Close( )

        ' Show changes.
        XPathEditor.MoveToRoot( )
        Console.WriteLine(XPathEditor.OuterXml)
    End Sub

End Module
```

Running Example 5-13 generates the following XML, which is displayed in the console window and saved to the newly generated XML file:

```
...
  <Product>
    <ProductID>999</ProductID>
    <ModelName>Rubber Pants</ModelName>
    <ModelNumber>NOZ999</ModelNumber>
    <UnitCost>12.99</UnitCost>
    <CategoryName>Clothing</CategoryName>
  </Product>
...
```

You can create multiple navigator and editor objects to work with the same XPathDocument. However, the editors don't perform any lockings, so you can't edit an XPathDocument on multiple threads at the same time unless you take your own safeguards.

What about...

...validating your XML? The XPathNavigator and the XmlWriter both force you to write valid XML. However, it's also important to check XML documents to make sure they match specific rules. The best tool for this task is an XML *schema document* that defines the elements, structure, data types, and constraints for a document.

The actual schema standard is beyond the scope of this chapter. (For a good introduction, refer to the tutorial at *http://www.w3schools.com/schema*.) However, assuming you have a schema for your XML, you can validate your document at any time by calling XPathNavigator. CheckValidity( ). This method returns True if the document conforms to the schema. Here's how to do it:

```
' Load the document.
Dim Doc As New XPathDocument("c:\ProductList.xml")

' (Make updates).

' Load the schema.
' Technically, you can load a collection of schemas,
' one for each namespace in the document that you want to validate.
Dim Schemas As New XmlSchemaSet( )
Schemas.Add("http://www.ibuyspy.com/ProductCatalog", "c:\ProductListSchema.
xsd")
Schemas.Compile( )

' Validate with the schema.
' Instead of submitting a null reference (Nothing), you can supply
' a delegate that points to a callback method that will be triggered
' every time an error is found when the validation check is performed.
Dim Valid As Boolean
Valid = Doc.CreateNavigator( ).CheckValidity(Schemas, Nothing)
```

Where can I learn more?

For more information about editing the XPathDocument, look up the "XPathNavigator class" index entry in the MSDN Help. If you've used earlier betas of .NET 2.0, which included the same features in a different class (XPathEditableNavigator), you may want to refer to *http://blogs.msdn.com/dareobasanjo/archive/2004/09/03/225070.aspx* for some explanation straight from Microsoft bloggers.

Chapter 5: Files, Databases, and XML

.NET 2.0 Platform Services

In earlier chapters, you learned about the most profound changes in .NET 2.0, including new features in Windows Forms, ASP.NET web applications, and ADO.NET data access. These changes are impressive, but they're only part of the story. In fact, Microsoft developers have been hard at work tweaking and fine-tuning the *entire* .NET class library. If you look around, you'll find new members, types, and namespaces cropping up everywhere.

This chapter explores some of the additions to the .NET class library that previous chapters haven't explored, and a few more convenient quick-access shortcuts provided by the My object. The chapter ends with a look at ClickOnce, a remarkable new technology that promises to simplify the way you distribute and update Windows clients.

Easily Log Events

When something goes wrong in your application, the user is rarely in a position to fix the problem. Instead of showing a detailed message box, it's much more important to make sure all the details are recorded somewhere permanent, so you can examine them later to try to diagnose the problem. In previous versions of .NET, logging was straightforward but tedious. In VB 2005, life becomes much easier thanks to the My.Application.Log object.

How do I do that?

You can use the new My.Application.Log object to quickly write to an XML file, an ordinary text file, or the Windows event log.

When something
bad happens in
your application,
you want an easy
way to log it to a
file or event log.
Look no further
than the My.
Application.Log
object.

To write a log message with My.Application.Log, you simply need to use the WriteEntry() method. You supply a string message as the first parameter, and (optionally) two more parameters. The second parameter is the event type, which indicates whether the message represents information, a warning, an error, and so on. The third parameter is an exception object, the details of which will also be copied into the log entry.

To try this out, create and run the console application in Example 6-1, which writes a short string of text to the log.

Example 6-1. Simple logging

```
Module LogTest

    Sub Main( )
      My.Application.Log.WriteEntry("This is a test!", _
        TraceEventType.Information)
    End Sub

End Module
```

Clearly, the logging code is extremely simple—but where are the log entries recorded? It all depends on the configuration of your application. .NET uses *trace listeners*, which are dedicated classes that listen to log messages and then copy them to another location (such as a file, event log, and so on). When you call the WriteEntry() method, the entry is written to the current set of trace listeners (which are exposed through the My.Application.TraceSource collection). By default, these listeners include the FileLogTraceListener, which writes to a user logfile. This file is stored under a user-specific directory (which is defined by the user's APPDATA environment variable) in a subdirectory of the form *[CompanyName]\[ProductName]\[FileVersion]*, where *CompanyName*, *ProductName*, and *FileVersion* refer to the information defined in the application assembly. For example, if the Windows user *JoeM* runs the application LogTestApp, the logfile will be created in a directory such as *c:\Documents and Settings\JoeM\Application Data\ MyCompany\LogTestApp\1.0.0.0\LogTestApp.log*.

To configure
assembly informa-
tion, double-click
the My Project
item in the
Solution Explorer,
select the
Application tab,
and then click
the Assembly
Information
button.

Once you've found the right directory, you can open the logfile in Notepad to examine the text contents. You'll see the following information:

```
Microsoft.VisualBasic.MyServices.Log.WindowsFormsSource    Information
   0    This is a test!
```

The number 0 represents the information log type. Subsequent entries append data to this logfile. Data is never removed (unless you delete the file by hand).

What about...

...logging to other locations? .NET includes a number of pre-built trace listeners that you can use. They include:

DefaultTraceListener

> This listener writes information into the debug portion of the window in Visual Studio. It's primarily useful while testing.

FileLogTraceListener

> This listener writes information to the application logfile named *[AssemblyName].log*. The default location of the logfile depends on the user's environment settings and the application information.

EventLogTraceListener

> This listener writes information to the Windows event log.

XmlWriterTraceListener

> This listener writes information to a file in XML format. You specify the location where the file should be stored. If needed, the directory will be created automatically.

By default, every new Visual Basic application you create starts its life with two trace listeners: a DefaultTraceListener and a FileLogTraceListener. To add new trace listeners, you need to modify the application configuration file. In Visual Studio, you can double-click the *app.config* item in the Solution Explorer. Trace-listener information is specified in two subsections of the <system.diagnostics> section.

WARNING

The logging configuration settings have changed with newer builds. For a version of the code that's updated to work with the latest build, download the samples from this book's web site.

In the <sharedListeners> subsection, you define the trace listeners you want to have the option of using, specify any related configuration properties, and assign a descriptive name. Here's an example that defines a new listener for writing XML data to a logfile:

Remember, after the application is built, the app.config file is renamed to have the name of the application, plus the extension .config.

```
<sharedListeners>
  <add name="MyXmlLog" type="System.Diagnostics.XmlWriterTraceListener"
     initializeData="c:\MyLog.xml" />
</sharedListeners>
```

In the `<sources>` subsection, you name the trace listeners you want to use, choosing from the `<sharedListeners>` list:

```
<source name="Microsoft.VisualBasic.MyServices.Log.WindowsFormsSource">
  <listeners>
    <add name="Xml"/>
  </listeners>
</source>
```

This separation between the `<sharedListeners>` section and the `<sources>` section allows you to quickly switch trace listeners on and off, without disturbing their configuration settings.

You can now re-run the application shown in Example 6-1. Now it will write the message to an XML file named *MyLog.xml* in the root *C:* directory. Here's what the contents look like (with the schema information removed for better readability):

```
<E2ETraceEvent>
  <System>
    <EventID>0</EventID>
    <Type>0</Type>
    <TimeCreated SystemTime="2004-07-26T16:14:04.7533392Z" />
    <Source Name="Microsoft.VisualBasic.MyServices.Log.WindowsFormsSource" />
    <Execution ProcessName="LogSample.vshost" ProcessID="3896" ThreadID="8" />
    <Computer>FARIAMAT</Computer>
  </System>
  <ApplicationData>
    <System.Diagnostics>
      <Message>This is a test!</Message>
      <Severity>Information</Severity>
    </System.Diagnostics>
  </ApplicationData>
</E2ETraceEvent>
```

Example 6-2 shows a complete configuration file example. It enables file tracing, event log tracing, and XML log tracing. Notice that the `EventLogTraceListener` is fine-tuned with a filter that ensures only error messages are logged.

Example 6-2. Logging data to three different trace listeners

```
<?xml version="1.0" encoding="utf-8" ?>
<configuration>
  <system.diagnostics>

    <!-- Enable all three trace listeners
         (from the <sharedListeners> section). -->
```

Example 6-2. *Logging data to three different trace listeners (continued)*

```xml
<sources>
  <source name="Microsoft.VisualBasic.MyServices.Log.WindowsFormsSource"
    switchName="DefaultSwitch">
    <listeners>
      <add name="FileLog"/>
      <add name="EventLog"/>
      <add name="Xml"/>
    </listeners>
  </source>
</sources>
<switches>
  <add name="DefaultSwitch" value="Information" />
</switches>

<!-- Define three trace listeners that you might want to use. -->
<sharedListeners>
  <add name="FileLog" type="System.Diagnostics.FileLogTraceListener"
    initializeData="FileLogWriter" delimiter=";" />
  <add name="EventLog" type="System.Diagnostics.EventLogTraceListener"
    initializeData="MyApplicationLog">
    <filter type="System.Diagnostics.SeverityFilter" initializeData="Error" />
  </add>
  <add name="Xml" type="System.Diagnostics.XmlWriterTraceListener"
    initializeData="c:\SampleLog.xml" delimiter=";"/>
</sharedListeners>
</system.diagnostics>
</configuration>
```

You can now use the same simple application to simultaneously write the ordinary logfile, an XML logfile, and an entry in the Windows event log named Application.

Unfortunately, there isn't any high-level .NET API for retrieving information from a log. If the log information is stored in a file, you can use the FileStream and StreamReader classes from the System.IO namespace to read the file one line at a time. If you've entered information in the Windows event log, you'll need to rely on the EventLog class, which you can find in the System.Diagnostics namespace.

> The event log is a list of messages stored by the operating system for a specific period of time. To view the event log, choose Event Viewer from the Administrative Tools section of the Control Panel.

Where can I learn more?

For more information, look up the following classes in the MSDN help: DefaultTraceListener, FileLogTraceListener, EventLogTraceListener, and XmlWriterTraceListener.

Need to find out if a computer is reachable over the Internet? With the new Ping class, you can make this simple request without a tangle of low-level socket code.

Ping Another Computer

The Internet is a dynamic network where computers appear and drop out of sight without warning. One simple test an application can always perform to check if a computer is reachable is to send a *ping* message. Technically, a ping is the equivalent of asking another computer, "Are you there?" To get its answer, ping sends a special type of message over a low-level Internet protocol called ICMP (Internet Control Message Protocol).

Sending a ping message using the classes found in the System.Net namespaces is challenging and requires dozens of low-level code statements that deal with raw sockets. In .NET 2.0, there's a much simpler solution with the new Ping class in the System.Net.NetworkInformation namespace.

Windows includes a utility called ping.exe that you can use to ping other computers at the command line.

How do I do that?

To ping a computer, you use the Ping( ) method of the My.Computer. Network object. This approach gives you convenient access to the bare minimum ping functionality. The Ping( ) method returns True or False depending on whether it received a response from the computer you're trying to contact.

Example 6-3 uses this method in order to contact the web server at *www.yahoo.com.*

Example 6-3. Pinging a remote computer

```
Module PingTest

    Sub Main( )
        Dim Success As Boolean

        ' Try to contact www.yahoo.com (wait 1000 milliseconds at most,
        ' which is the default if you don't specify a timeout).
        Success = My.Computer.Network.Ping("www.yahoo.com", 1000)
        Console.WriteLine("Did the computer respond? " & Success)
    End Sub

End Module
```

When you call Ping( ), you specify two parameters: the URL or IP address for the computer you're trying to reach (e.g., *www.microsoft.com* or 123. 4.123.4) and, optionally, a maximum wait time in milliseconds. Once this limit is reached, the request times out, and the Ping( ) method returns False to indicate the failure.

What about...

...getting more information from the remote computer? The My.Computer. Network object doesn't return any additional information about the results of the ping test. For example, you won't find out how long it took to receive a response, which is a key statistic used by some applications, such as peer-to-peer software, to rank the connection speed of different computers.

To get more information, you need to head directly to the Ping class in the System.Net.NetworkInformation namespace. It returns a PingResult object with several pieces of information, including the time taken for a response. The following code snippet puts this approach to the test. It assumes that you've imported the System.Net.NetworkInformation namespace:

```
Dim Pinger As New Ping
Dim Reply As PingReply = Pinger.Send("www.yahoo.com")
Console.WriteLine("Time (milliseconds): " & Reply.RoundTripTime)
Console.WriteLine("Exact status: " & Reply.Status.ToString())
Console.WriteLine("Adress contacted: " & Reply.Address.ToString())
```

Here's some sample output:

```
Time (milliseconds): 61
Exact status: Success
Adress contacted: 216.109.118.78
```

The Ping class also provides a SendAsync( ) method you can use to ping a computer without stalling your code (you can handle the response in another thread when a callback fires), and other overloaded versions of the Send( ) method that allow you to set low-level options (like the number of hops the ping message will travel before expiring).

Where can I learn more?

To use this added networking muscle, read up on the Ping class in the MSDN Help.

Need to find out if your computer's currently online? With the My class, this test is just a simple property away.

Get Information About a Network Connection

Some applications need to adjust how they work based on whether a network connection is present. For example, imagine a sales reporting tool that runs on the laptop of a traveling sales manager. When the laptop is plugged into the network, the application needs to run in a *connected mode* in order to retrieve the information it needs, such as a list of products, directly from a database or web service. When the laptop is disconnected from the network, the application needs to gracefully degrade to a *disconnected mode* that disables certain features or falls back on slightly older data that's stored in a local file. To make the decision about which mode to use, an application needs a quick way to determine the network status of the current computer. Thanks to the new My.Computer.Network object, this task is easy.

How do I do that?

The My.Computer.Network object provides a single IsAvailable property that allows you to determine if the current computer has a network connection. The IsAvailable property returns True as long as at least one of the configured network interfaces is connected, and it serves as a quick-and-dirty test to see if the computer is online. To try it out, enter the following code in a console application:

```
If My.Computer.Network.IsAvailable Then
    Console.WriteLine("You have a network interface.")
End If
```

If you want more information, you need to turn to the System.Net and System.Net.NetworkInformation namespaces, which provide much more fine-grained detail. For example, to retrieve and display the IP address for the current computer, you can use the System.Net.Dns class by entering this code:

```
' Retrieve the computer name.
Dim HostName As String = System.Net.Dns.GetHostName()
Console.WriteLine("Host name: " & HostName)

' Get the IP address for this computer.
' Note that this code actually retrieves the first
' IP address in the list, because it assumes the
' computer only has one assigned IP address
' (which is the norm).
Console.WriteLine("IP: " & _
    System.Net.Dns.GetHostByName(HostName).AddressList(0).ToString())
```

Here's the output you might see:

```
Host name: FARIAMAT
IP: 192.168.0.197
```

In addition, you can now retrieve even more detailed information about your network connection that wasn't available in previous versions of .NET. To do so, you need to use the new `System.Net.NetworkInformation.IPGlobalProperties` class, which represents network activity on a standard IP network.

The `IPGlobalProperties` class provides several methods that allow you to retrieve different objects, each of which provides statistics for a specific type of network activity. For example, if you're interested in all the traffic that flows over your network connection using TCP, you can call `IPGlobalProperties.GetTcpIPv4Statistics()`. For most people, this is the most useful measurement of the network. On the other hand, if you're using a next-generation IPv6 network, you need to use `IPGlobalProperties.GetTcpIPv6Statistics()`. Other methods exist for monitoring traffic that uses the UPD or ICMP protocols. Obviously, you'll need to know a little bit about networking to get the best out of these methods.

TIP

IP (Internet Protocol) is the core building block of most networks and the Internet. It uniquely identifies computers with a four-part IP address, and allows you to send a basic packet from one machine to another (without any frills like error correction, flow control, or connection management). Many other networking protocols, such as TCP (Transmission Connection Protocol) are built on top of the IP infrastructure, and still other protocols are built on top of TCP (e.g., HTTP, the language of the Web). For more information about networking, refer to a solid introduction such as *Internet Core Protocols* (O'Reilly).

The following code retrieves detailed statistics about the network traffic. It assumes that you've imported the `System.Net.NetworkInformation` namespace:

```
Dim Properties As IPGlobalProperties = IPGlobalProperties.
GetIPGlobalProperties()
Dim TcpStat As TcpStatistics
TcpStat = Properties.GetTcpIPv4Statistics()

Console.WriteLine("TCP/IPv4 Statistics:")
Console.WriteLine("Minimum Transmission Timeout... : " & _
    TcpStat.MinimumTransmissionTimeOut)
```

```vbnet
Console.WriteLine("Maximum Transmission Timeout... : " & _
    TcpStat.MaximumTransmissionTimeOut)

Console.WriteLine("Connection Data:")
Console.WriteLine("  Current  .................... : " & _
    TcpStat.CurrentConnections)
Console.WriteLine("  Cumulative .................. : " & _
    TcpStat.CumulativeConnections)
Console.WriteLine("  Initiated ................... : " & _
    TcpStat.ConnectionsInitiated)
Console.WriteLine("  Accepted .................... : " & _
    TcpStat.ConnectionsAccepted)
Console.WriteLine("  Failed Attempts ............. : " & _
    TcpStat.FailedConnectionAttempts)
Console.WriteLine("  Reset ....................... : " & _
    TcpStat.ResetConnections)

Console.WriteLine()
Console.WriteLine("Segment Data:")
Console.WriteLine("  Received  ................... : " & _
    TcpStat.SegmentsReceived)
Console.WriteLine("  Sent ........................ : " & _
    TcpStat.SegmentsSent)
Console.WriteLine("  Retransmitted ............... : " & _
    TcpStat.SegmentsResent)
```

Statistics are kept from the time the connection is established. That means every time you disconnect or reboot your computer, you reset the networking statistics.

Here's the output you might see:

```
TCP/IPv4 Statistics:
Minimum Transmission Timeout... : 300
Maximum Transmission Timeout... : 120000
Connection Data:
  Current  .................... : 6
  Cumulative .................. : 29
  Initiated ................... : 10822
  Accepted .................... : 41
  Failed Attempts ............. : 187
  Reset ....................... : 2271

Segment Data:
  Received  ................... : 334791
  Sent ........................ : 263171
  Retransmitted ............... : 617
```

What about...

...other connection problems, like a disconnected router, erratic network, or a firewall that's blocking access to the location you need? The network connection statistics won't give you any information about the rest of the network (although you can try to ping a machine elsewhere on the network, as described in the previous lab, "Ping Another Computer"). In other words, even when a network connection is available there's no way to make sure it's working. For that reason, whenever you need to access a resource over the network—whether it's a web service, database, or application running on another computer—you need to wrap your call in proper exception-handling code.

Where can I learn more?

For more information on advanced network statistics, look up the "IPGlobalProperties" index entry in the MSDN help, or look for the "network information sample" for a more sophisticated Windows Forms application that monitors network activity.

Upload and Download Files with FTP

Earlier versions of .NET didn't include any tools for FTP (File Transfer Protocol), a common protocol used to transfer files to and from a web server. As a result, you either had to purchase a third-party component or write your own (which was easy in principle but difficult to get right in practice).

In .NET 2.0, a new FtpWebRequest class neatly fills the gap. However, the FtpWebRequest class has its own complexities, so Microsoft programmers simplified life for VB developers even further by extending the My.Computer.Network object to provide two quick access methods for completing basic FTP operations. These are UploadFile( ), which sends a file to a remote server, and DownloadFile( ), which retrieves a file and stores it locally.

How do I do that?

Whether you use the FtpWebRequest class or the My.Computer.Network object, all FTP interaction in .NET is *stateless*. That means that you connect to the FTP site, perform a single operation (like transferring a file or retrieving a directory listing), and then disconnect. If you need to perform another operation, you need to reconnect. Fortunately, this process of connecting and logging in is handled automatically by the .NET Framework.

The easiest way to use FTP in a VB application is to do so through the My.Computer.Network object. If you use its FTP methods, you never need to worry about the tedious details of opening, closing, and reading streams. To download a file, the bare minimum information you need is

Need to upload files to an FTP site or download existing content? New support is available in VB 2005.

the URL that points to the FTP site and the path that points to the local file. Here's an example:

```
My.Computer.Network.DownloadFile( _
    "ftp://ftp.funet.fi/pub/gnu/prep/gtk.README", "c:\readme.txt")
```

This command retrieves the file that is on the FTP site *ftp.funet.fi* in the path */pub/gnu/prep/gtk.README* and copies it to the local file *c:\readme.txt*.

Uploading uses similar parameters, but in reverse:

```
My.Computer.Network.UploadFile("c:\newfile.txt", _
    "ftp://ftp.funet.fi/pub/newfile.txt")
```

This command copies the local file *newfile.txt* from the directory *c:* to the FTP site *ftp.funet.fi*, in the remote directory */pub*.

Both `DownloadFile( )` and `UploadFile( )` support several overloads that take additional parameters, including credentials (the username and password information you might need to log on to a server) and a time-out parameter to set the maximum amount of time you'll wait for a response before giving up (the default is 1,000 milliseconds).

Unfortunately, the `DownloadFile()` and `UploadFile()` methods haven't been too robust in beta builds of Visual Basic 2005, and the methods may fail to work. An option that works better is the more sophisticated `FtpWebRequest` class. Not only does it perform more reliably, but it also fills a few glaring gaps in the FTP support provided by the `My.Network.Computer`. Because `FtpWebRequest` allows you to execute any FTP command, you can use it to retrieve directory listings, get file information, and more.

To use the `FtpWebRequest` class, you need to follow several steps. First, pass the URL that points to the FTP site to the shared `WebRequest.Create( )` method:

```
Dim Request As FtpWebRequest
Request = CType(WebRequest.Create("ftp://ftp.microsoft.com/MISC"), _
    FtpWebRequest)
```

The `WebRequest.Create( )` method examines the URL and returns the appropriate type of `WebRequest` object. Because FTP URLs always start with the scheme *ftp://*, the `Create( )` method will return a new `FtpWebRequest` object.

Once you have the `FtpWebRequest`, you need to choose what FTP operation you want to perform by setting the `FtpWebRequest.Method` property with the text of the FTP command. Here's an example for retrieving directory information with the `LIST` command:

```
Request.Method = "LIST"
```

Internet Explorer has its own built-in FTP browser. Just type a URL that points to an FTP site (like ftp://ftp.microsoft.com) into the IE address bar to browse what's there. You can use this tool to verify that your code is working correctly.

Chapter 6: .NET 2.0 Platform Services

Once you've chosen the FTP operation you want to perform, the last step is to execute the command and read the response. The tricky part is the fact that the response is returned to you as a stream of text. It's up to you to move through this block of text line by line with a StreamReader and parse the information.

For example, the following code reads through a returned directory listing and displays each line in a Console window:

```
Dim Response As FtpWebResponse = CType(Request.GetResponse( ), FtpWebResponse)
Dim ResponseStream As Stream = Response.GetResponseStream( )
Dim Reader As New StreamReader(ResponseStream, System.Text.Encoding.UTF8)

Dim Line As String
Do
    Line = Reader.ReadLine( )
    Console.WriteLine(Line)
Loop Until Line = ""
```

The output looks like this:

```
dr-xr-xr-x    1 owner      group                   0 Jul  3  2002 beckyk
-r-xr-xr-x    1 owner      group               15749 Apr  8  1994 CBCP.TXT
dr-xr-xr-x    1 owner      group                   0 Jul  3  2002 csformat
dr-xr-xr-x    1 owner      group                   0 Aug  1  2002 DAILYKB
-r-xr-xr-x    1 owner      group                 710 Apr 12  1993 DISCLAIM.TXT
dr-xr-xr-x    1 owner      group                   0 Jul  3  2002 FDC
dr-xr-xr-x    1 owner      group                   0 Jul  3  2002 friKB
dr-xr-xr-x    1 owner      group                   0 Jul  3  2002 FULLKB
dr-xr-xr-x    1 owner      group                   0 Jul  3  2002 Homenet
-r-xr-xr-x    1 owner      group                  97 Sep 28  1993 INDEX.TXT
...
```

Clearly, if you want to manipulate individual pieces of information (like the file size) or distinguish files from directories, you'll need to do extra work to parse the text returned by the StreamReader.

Finally, when you're finished with the FTP request and response, you need to close the streams:

```
Reader.Close( )
Response.Close( )
```

To put it all in context, it helps to consider a simple FTP browsing application. Figure 6-1 shows a sample application that's included with the downloadable samples for this chapter.

This Windows application includes the following controls:

- A TextBox where you can enter a URL that points to a file or directory in an FTP site.

- A Button named Query Directory that retrieves the folders and files at a given URL. This task requires the FtpWebRequest class.

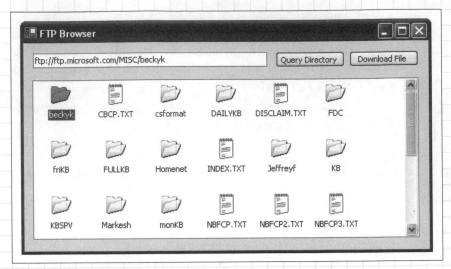

Figure 6-1. A simple FTP Browser application

- A Button named Download File that downloads the file at a given URL. This task uses the My.Computer.Network.DownloadFile() method.

- A FolderBrowserDialog that allows you to choose a folder where the downloaded file will be saved.

- A ListView that shows the directory and file listing for the URL. This list is refreshed every time you click the Query Directory button. In addition, every time you click to select an item in the ListView, that information is automatically added to the URL in the text box. This allows you to quickly browse through an FTP site, drilling down several layers into the directory structure and selecting the file that interests you.

Example 6-4 shows code for the FTP browser form

Example 6-4. The FTP browser form

```
Public Class FtpForm
    Inherits System.Windows.Forms.Form

    ' Stores the path currently shown in the ListView.
    Private CurrentPath As String

    Private Sub cmdQuery_Click(ByVal sender As System.Object, _
      ByVal e As System.EventArgs) Handles cmdQuery.Click
        ' Check the URI is valid.
        Dim RequestUri As Uri = ValidateUri(txtFtpSite.Text)
        If RequestUri Is Nothing Then Return
```

Example 6-4. The FTP browser form (continued)

```vb
        ' Clear the ListView.
        listDir.Items.Clear()

        ' Create a new FTP request using the URI.
        Dim Request As FtpWebRequest
        Request = CType(WebRequest.Create(RequestUri), FtpWebRequest)

        ' Use this request for getting full directory details.
        Request.Method = "LIST"
        Request.UsePassive = False

        Dim Response As FtpWebResponse
        Dim ResponseStream As Stream
        Dim Reader As StreamReader
        Try
            ' Execute the command and get the response.
            Response = CType(Request.GetResponse(), FtpWebResponse)
            Debug.WriteLine("Status: " & Response.StatusDescription)

            ' Read the response one line at a time.
            ResponseStream = Response.GetResponseStream()
            Reader = New StreamReader(ResponseStream, System.Text.Encoding.UTF8)
            Dim Line As String
            Do
                Line = Reader.ReadLine()
                If Line <> "" Then
                    Debug.WriteLine(Line)

                    ' Extract just the file or directory name from the line.
                    Dim ListItem As New ListViewItem(Line.Substring(59).Trim())
                    If Line.Substring(0, 1) = "d" Then
                        ListItem.ImageKey = "Folder"
                    Else
                        ListItem.ImageKey = "File"
                    End If
                    listDir.Items.Add(ListItem)
                End If
            Loop Until Line = ""

            ' Operation completed successfully. Store the current FTP path.
            CurrentPath = RequestUri.ToString()

        Catch Ex As Exception
            MessageBox.Show(Ex.Message)

        Finally
            ' Clean up.
            Reader.Close()
            Response.Close()

        End Try
```

Example 6-4. The FTP browser form (continued)

```
End Sub

Private Sub cmdDownload_Click(ByVal sender As System.Object, _
   ByVal e As System.EventArgs) Handles cmdDownload.Click

     ' Check the URI is valid.
     Dim RequestUri As Uri = ValidateUri(txtFtpSite.Text)
     If RequestUri Is Nothing Then Return

     ' Prompt the user to choose a destination folder.
     ' Default the file name to the same file name used on the FTP server.
     dlgSave.FileName = Path.GetFileName(txtFtpSite.Text)
     If dlgSave.ShowDialog() <> Windows.Forms.DialogResult.OK Then
          Return
     End If

     ' Create a new FTP request using the URI.
     Dim Request As FtpWebRequest
     Request = CType(WebRequest.Create(RequestUri), FtpWebRequest)

     ' Use this request for downloading the file.
     Request.UsePassive = False
     Request.Method = "RETR"

     Dim Response As FtpWebResponse
     Dim ResponseStream, TargetStream As Stream
     Dim Reader As StreamReader
     Dim Writer As StreamWriter
     Try
          ' Execute the command and get the response.
          Response = CType(Request.GetResponse(), FtpWebResponse)
          Debug.WriteLine("Status: " & Response.StatusDescription)
          Debug.WriteLine("File Size: " & Response.ContentLength)

          ' Create the destination file.
          TargetStream = New FileStream(dlgSave.FileName, FileMode.Create)
          Writer = New StreamWriter(TargetStream)

          ' Write the response to the file.
          ResponseStream = Response.GetResponseStream()
          Reader = New StreamReader(ResponseStream, System.Text.Encoding.UTF8)
          Writer.Write(Reader.ReadToEnd())

     Catch Err As Exception
          MessageBox.Show(Err.Message)

     Finally
          ' Clean up.
          Reader.Close()
          Response.Close()
          Writer.Close()
     End Try
End If
```

Example 6-4. The FTP browser form (continued)

```
    End Sub

    Private Function ValidateUri(ByVal uriText As String) As Uri
        Dim RequestUri As Uri
        Try
            ' Check that the string is interpretable as a URI.
            RequestUri = New Uri(uriText)

            ' Check that the URI starts with "ftp://"
            If RequestUri.Scheme <> Uri.UriSchemeFtp Then
                RequestUri = Nothing
            End If
        Catch
            RequestUri = Nothing
        End Try

        If RequestUri Is Nothing Then
            MessageBox.Show("Invalid Uri.")
        Else

        End If
        Return RequestUri
    End Function

    Private Sub listDir_SelectedIndexChanged(ByVal sender As System.Object, _
      ByVal e As System.EventArgs) Handles listDir.SelectedIndexChanged
        ' When a new item is selected in the list, add this
        ' to the URI in the text box.
        If listDir.SelectedItems.Count <> 0 Then
            CurrentPath = CurrentPath.TrimEnd("/")
            txtFtpSite.Text = CurrentPath & "/" & listDir.SelectedItems(0).Text
        End If
    End Sub

End Class
```

The most complex code found in this example occurs in the event handler for the cmdQuery button, which retrieves a directory listing, parses out the important information, and updates the ListView.

Where can I learn more?

In previous builds, the MSDN help included much more information on FTP access and different FTP operations under the index entry "FtpMethods," complete with useful demonstrations of the different methods. This entry has disappeared in recent builds (along with the FtpMethods class), but check for it to return. In the meantime, you can read up on the FTP protocol and supported commands at *www.vbip.com/ winsock/winsock_ftp_ref_01.asp*.

Find out who's using your application, and the groups a mystery user belongs to.

Test Group Membership of the Current User

The .NET Framework has always provided security classes that let you retrieve basic information about the account of the current user. The new My.User object provided by Visual Basic 2005 makes it easier than ever to access this information.

How do I do that?

Applications often need to test who is running the application. For example, you might want to restrict some features to certain groups, such as Windows administrators. You can accomplish this with the My.User object.

The My.User object provides two key properties that return information about the current user. These are:

IsAuthenticated

>   Returns True if the current user account information is available in the My.User object. The only reason this information wouldn't be present is if you've created a web application that allows anonymous access, or if the current Windows account isn't associated with the application domain.

Username

>   Returns the current username. Assuming you're using a Windows security policy, this is the Windows account name for the user, in the form *ComputerName\UserName* or *DomainName\UserName*.

To check the user and group list for the current computer (or make changes), select Computer management from the Administrative Tools section of the Control Panel. Then, expand the System Tools → Local Users and Groups node.

The My.User object also provides a single method, IsInRole( ). This method accepts the name of a group (as a string) and then returns True if the user belongs to that group. For example, you could use this technique to verify that the current user is a Windows administrator before performing a certain task.

To try this out, use the following console application in Example 6-5, which displays some basic information about the current user and tests if the user is an Administrator.

Example 6-5. Testing the current user identity

```
Module SecurityTest

    Sub Main( )
        ' Use Windows security. As a result, the User object will
```

Example 6-5. *Testing the current user identity (continued)*

```
        ' provide the information for the currently logged in user
        ' who is running the application.
        My.User.InitializeWithWindowsUser()

        Console.WriteLine("Authenticated: " & My.User.Identity.IsAuthenticated)
        Console.WriteLine("User: " & My.User.Identity.Username)

        Console.WriteLine("Administrator: " & My.User.IsInRole("Administrators"))
    End Sub

End Module
```

Here's the sort of output you'll see when you run this test:

```
Authenticated: True
User: FARIAMAT\Matthew
Administrator: True
```

Encrypt Secrets for the Current User

Applications often need a way to store private data in a file or in memory. The obvious solution is *symmetric encryption*, which scrambles your data using a random series of bytes called a *secret key*. The problem is that when you want to decrypt your scrambled data, you need to use the same secret key you used to encrypt. This introduces serious complications. Either you need to find a secure place to safeguard your secret key (which is tricky at best), or you need to derive the secret key from some other information, like a user-supplied password (which is much more insecure, and can break down entirely when users forget their passwords).

The ideal solution is to have the Windows operating system encrypt the data for you. To accomplish this, you need the DPAPI (Data Protection API), which encrypts data using a symmetric key that's based on a piece of user-specific or machine-specific information. This way, you don't need to worry about key storage or authentication. Instead, the operating system authenticates the user when he logs in. Data stored by one user is automatically inaccessible to other users.

In previous versions of .NET, there were no managed classes for using the DPAPI. This oversight is corrected in .NET 2.0 with the new ProtectedData class in the System.Security.Cryptography namespace.

Need a quick way to encrypt secret information, without needing to worry about key management? The long awaited solution appears in .NET 2.0 with the Protected-Data class.

How do I do that?

The `ProtectedData` class provides two shared methods. `ProtectData()` takes a byte array with source data and returns a byte array with encrypted data. `UnprotectData()` performs the reverse operation, taking an encrypted byte array and returning a byte array with the decrypted data.

The only trick to using the `ProtectData()` and `UnprotectData()` methods is that you can only encrypt or decrypt data in a byte array. That means that if you want to encrypt strings, numbers, or something else, you need to write it to a byte array before you perform the encryption.

To see this in action, you can run the console application code in Example 6-6.

Example 6-6. Storing an encrypted string of text in a file

```
Imports System.Security.Cryptography
Imports System.IO

Module ProctedData

    Sub Main()
        ' Get the data.
        Console.WriteLine("Enter a secret message and press enter.")
        Console.Write(">")
        Dim Input As String = Console.ReadLine()

        Dim DataStream As MemoryStream
        If Input <> "" Then
            Dim Data(), EncodedData() As Byte

            ' Write the data to a new MemoryStream.
            DataStream = New MemoryStream()
            Dim Writer As New StreamWriter(DataStream)
            Writer.Write(Input)
            Writer.Close()

            ' Convert the MemoryStream into a byte array,
            ' which is what you need to use the ProtectData() method.
            Data = DataStream.ToArray()

            ' Encrypt the byte array.
            EncodedData = ProtectedData.Protect(Data, Nothing, _
              DataProtectionScope.CurrentUser)

            ' Store the encrypted data in a file.
            My.Computer.FileSystem.WriteAllBytes("c:\secret.bin", _
              EncodedData, False)
        End If
    End Sub

End Module
```

When you run this application, you'll be prompted to type in some text, which will be encrypted using your current user account information and stored in the file *secret.bin*. The data won't be accessible to any other user.

To verify that the data is encrypted, you have two choices. You can open the file and take a look for yourself, or you can modify the code so that it reads the data directly from the encrypted memory stream. This code tries the latter, and displays a string of meaningless gibberish as a result:

```
' Verify the data is encrypted by reading and displaying it
' without performing any decryption.
DataStream = New MemoryStream(EncodedData)
Dim Reader As New StreamReader(DataStream)
Console.WriteLine("Encrypted data: " & Reader.ReadToEnd())
Reader.Close()
```

To decrypt the data, you need to place it into a byte array and then use the UnprotectData() method. To extract your data out of the unencrypted byte array, you can use a StreamReader. To add decryption support to the previous example, insert the following code, which opens the file and displays the secret message that you entered earlier:

```
If My.Computer.FileSystem.FileExists("c:\secret.bin") Then
    Dim Data(), EncodedData() As Byte

    EncodedData = My.Computer.FileSystem.ReadAllBytes("c:\secret.bin")
    Data = ProtectedData.Unprotect(EncodedData, Nothing, _
        DataProtectionScope.CurrentUser)

    Dim DataStream As New MemoryStream(Data)
    Dim Reader As New StreamReader(DataStream)

    Console.WriteLine("Decoded data from file: " & Reader.ReadToEnd())
    Reader.Close()
End If
```

Remember, because the data is encrypted using the current user profile, you can decrypt the data at any time. The only restriction is that you need to be logged on under the same user account.

Note that when you protect data, you must choose one of the values from the DataProtectionScope enumeration. There are two choices:

LocalMachine

> Windows will encrypt data with a machine-specific key, guaranteeing that no one can read the data unless they log in to the same computer. This works well for server-side applications that run without user intervention, such as Windows services and web services.

CurrentUser

> Windows will encrypt data with a user-specific key, so that it's inaccessible to any other user.

No matter which DataProtectionScope you choose, the encrypted information will be stored in a specially protected area of the Windows registry.

In the current example, user-specific data is stored. However, you could modify the DataProtectionScope to store data that's accessible to any user on the current computer.

What about...

...protecting data before you put it in a database? Once you use the ProtectedData class to encrypt your data, you can put it anywhere you want. The previous example wrote encrypted data to a file, but you can also write the binary data to a database record. To do so, you simply need a binary field in your table with enough room to accommodate the encrypted byte array. In SQL Server, you use the varbinary data type.

At last, a Console class with keyboard-handling and screen-writing features.

Unleash the Console

.NET 1.0 introduced the Console class to give programmers a convenient way to build simple command-line applications. The first version of the Console was fairly rudimentary, with little more than basic methods like Write(), WriteLine(), Read(), and ReadLine(). In .NET 2.0, new features have been added, allowing you to clear the window, change foreground and background colors, alter the size of the window, and handle special keys.

How do I do that?

The best way to learn the new features is to see them in action. Example 6-7 shows a simple application, *ConsoleTest*, which lets the user move a happy face character around a console window, leaving a trail in its wake. The application intercepts each key press, checks if an arrow key was pressed, and ensures that the user doesn't move outside of the bounds of the window.

WARNING

In order for the advanced console features to work, you must disable the Quick Console window. The Quick Console is a console window that appears in the design environment, and it's too lightweight to support features like reading keys, setting colors, and copying characters. To disable it, select Tools → Options, make sure the "Show all settings checkbox" is checked, and select the Debugging → General tab. Then, turn off the "Redirect all console output to the Quick Console window."

Example 6-7. Advanced keyboard handling with the console

```
Module ConsoleTest

    Private NewX, NewY, X, Y As Integer
    Private BadGuyX, BadGuyY As Integer

    Public Sub Main()
        ' Create a 50 column x 20 line window.
        Console.SetWindowSize(50, 20)
        Console.SetBufferSize(50, 20)

        ' Set up the window.
        Console.Title = "Move The Happy Face"
        Console.CursorVisible = False
        Console.BackgroundColor = ConsoleColor.DarkBlue
        Console.Clear()

        ' Display the happy face icon.
        Console.ForegroundColor = ConsoleColor.Yellow
        Console.SetCursorPosition(X, Y)
        Console.Write("˘")

        ' Read key presses.
        Dim KeyPress As ConsoleKey
        Do
            KeyPress = Console.ReadKey().Key

            ' If it's an arrow key, set the requested position.
            Select Case KeyPress
                Case ConsoleKey.LeftArrow
                    NewX -= 1
                Case ConsoleKey.RightArrow
                    NewX += 1
                Case ConsoleKey.UpArrow
                    NewY -= 1
                Case ConsoleKey.DownArrow
                    NewY += 1
            End Select

            MoveToPosition()
        Loop While KeyPress <> ConsoleKey.Escape

        ' Return to normal.
        Console.ResetColor()
        Console.Clear()
    End Sub

    Private Sub MoveToPosition()
        ' Check for an attempt to move off the screen.
        If NewX = Console.WindowWidth Or NewX < 0 Or _
          NewY = Console.WindowHeight Or NewY < 0 Then
            ' Reset the position.
            NewY = Y
```

Example 6-7. Advanced keyboard handling with the console (continued)

```
            NewX = X
            Console.Beep()
        Else
            ' Repaint the happy face in the new position.
            Console.MoveBufferArea(X, Y, 1, 1, NewX, NewY)

            ' Draw the trail.
            Console.SetCursorPosition(X, Y)
            Console.Write("*")

            ' Update the position.
            X = NewX
            Y = NewY
            Console.SetCursorPosition(0, 0)
        End If
    End Sub

End Module
```

To try this out, run the application and use the arrow keys to move about. Figure 6-2 shows the output of a typical *ConsoleTest* session.

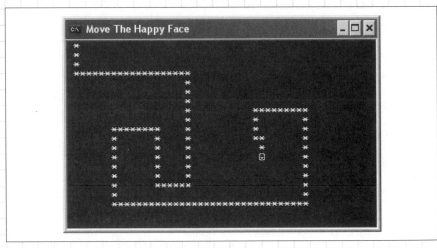

Figure 6-2. A fancy console application

Some of the new Console methods used in *ConsoleTest* include the following:

Clear()
>   Erases everything in the console window and positions the cursor in the top-left corner.

SetCursorPosition( )
> Moves the cursor to the designated x- and y-coordinates (measured from the top-left corner). Once you've moved to a new position, you can use Console.Write( ) to display some characters there.

SetWindowSize( ) and SetBufferSize( )
> Allow you to change the size of the window (the visible area of the console) and the buffer (the scrollable area of the console, which is equal to or greater than the window size).

ResetColor( )
> Resets the foreground and background colors to their defaults.

Beep( )
> Plays a simple beep, which is often used to indicate invalid input.

ReadKey( )
> Reads just a single key press and returns it as a ConsoleKeyInfo object. You can use this object to easily tell what key was pressed (including extended key presses like the arrow keys) and what other keys were held down at the time (like Alt, Ctrl, or Shift).

MoveBufferArea( )
> Copies a portion of the console window to a new position, and erases the original data. This method offers a high-performance way to move content around the console.

The new Console properties include:

Title
> Sets the window caption.

ForegroundColor
> Sets the text color that will be used the next time you use Console.Write( ) or Console.WriteLine( ).

BackgroundColor
> Sets the background color that will be used the next time you use Console.Write( ) or Console.WriteLine( ). To apply this background color to the whole window at once, call Console.Clear( ) after you set the background color.

CursorVisible
> Hides the blinking cursor when set to False.

WindowHeight and WindowWidth
> Returns or sets the dimensions of the console window.

CursorLeft and CursorTop
> Returns or moves the current cursor position.

What about...

...reading a character from a specified position of the window? Sadly, the new Console class provides no way to do this. That means that if you wanted to extend the happy face example so that the user must navigate through a maze of other characters, you would need to store the position of every character in memory (which could get tedious) in order to check the requested position after each key press, and prevent the user from moving into a space occupied by another character.

Where can I learn more?

To learn more about the new Console class and its new properties and methods, look for the Console and ConsoleKeyInfo classes in the MSDN help library reference.

Time Your Code

The new Stopwatch class allows you to track how fast your code executes with unparalleled precision.

Timing code isn't difficult. You can use the DateTime.Now property to capture the current date and time down to the millisecond. However, this approach isn't perfect. Constructing the DateTime object takes a short time, and that little bit of latency can skew the time you record for short operations. Serious profilers need a better approach, one that uses low-level systems calls and has no latency.

How do I do that?

In .NET 2.0, the best way to time your code is to use the new Stopwatch class in the System.Diagnostics namespace. The Stopwatch class is refreshingly simple to use. All you need to do is create an instance and call the Start( ) method. When you're finished, call Stop( ).

Example 6-8 shows a simple test that times how long a loop takes to finish. The elapsed time is then displayed in several different ways, with different degrees of precision.

Example 6-8. Timing a loop

```
Module TimeCode

    Sub Main( )
        Dim Watch As New Stopwatch( )

        Watch.Start( )
```

Example 6-8. Timing a loop (continued)

```
        ' Delay for a while.
        For i As Integer = 1 To 1000000000
        Next

        Watch.Stop()

        ' Report the elasped time.
        Console.WriteLine("Milliseconds " & Watch.ElapsedMilliseconds)
        Console.WriteLine("Ticks: " & Watch.ElapsedTicks)
        Console.WriteLine("Frequency: " & Stopwatch.Frequency)
        Console.WriteLine("Whole Seconds: " & Watch.Elapsed.Seconds)
        Console.WriteLine("Seconds (from TimeSpan): " & Watch.Elapsed.
TotalSeconds)
        Console.WriteLine("Seconds (most precise): " & _
            Watch.ElapsedTicks / Stopwatch.Frequency)
    End Sub

End Module
```

Here's the output you'll see:

```
Milliseconds 10078
Ticks: 36075265
Frequency: 3579545
Whole Seconds: 10
Seconds (from TimeSpan): 10.0781705
Seconds (most precise): 10.078170549609
```

You can retrieve the elapsed time in milliseconds from the Stopwatch.
ElapsedMilliseconds property. (One second is 1,000 milliseconds.) The
ElapsedMilliseconds property returns a 64-bit integer (a Long), making
it extremely precise. If it's more useful to retrieve the time as a number of
seconds or minutes, use the Stopwatch.Elapsed property instead, which
returns a TimeSpan object.

On the other hand, if you want the greatest possible precision, retrieve
the number of ticks that have elapsed from the Stopwatch.ElapsedTicks
property. Stopwatch *ticks* have a special meaning. When you use the
TimeSpan or DateTime object, a tick represents 0.0001 of a millisecond. In
the case of a Stopwatch, however, ticks represent the smallest measur-
able increment of time, and depend on the speed of the CPU. To convert
Stopwatch ticks to seconds, divide ElapsedTicks by Frequency.

What about...

...pausing a timer? If you want to record the total time taken to complete
multiple operations, you can use Stop() to pause a timer and Start() to

resume it later. You can then read the total time taken for all the operations you timed from the Elasped and ElaspedMilliseconds properties.

You can also run multiple timers at once. All you need to do is create one Stopwatch object for each distinct timer you want to use.

Deploy Your Application with ClickOnce

Want the functionality of a rich client application with the easy deployment of a web application? ClickOnce offers a new solution for deploying your software.

One of the driving forces behind the adoption of browser-based applications is the fact that organizations don't need to deploy their applications to the client. Most companies are willing to accept the limitations of HTML in order to avoid the considerable headaches of distributing application updates to hundreds or thousands of users.

Deploying a .NET client application will never be as straightforward as updating a web site. However, .NET 2.0 includes a new technology called ClickOnce that simplifies deployment dramatically.

How do I do that?

ClickOnce includes a few remarkable features:

- ClickOnce can automatically create a setup program that you can distribute on a CD or launch over a network or through a web page. This setup program can install prerequisites and create the appropriate Start menu icons.

- ClickOnce can configure your application to check for updates automatically every time it starts (or periodically in the background). Depending on your preference, you can give the user the option of downloading and running the new updated version, or you can just install it by force.

- ClickOnce can configure your application to use an online-only mode. In this case, the user always runs the latest version of your application from a web page URL. However, the application itself is cached locally to improve performance.

ClickOnce is tightly integrated with Visual Studio 2005, which allows you to deploy a ClickOnce application to a web site using the Project → Publish menu command.

The following steps take you through the process of preparing your project for publication:

1. Using Visual Studio 2005, create a new project. A good choice is a Windows Forms application. Before continuing, save the project.

2. Choose Build → Publish *[ProjectName]* (or right-click your project in the Solution Explorer and choose Publish). This launches the Publish wizard, which gives you a chance to specify or change various settings.

3. The first dialog page of the Publish wizard (the "Where do you want to publish" dialog) prompts you to choose the location where you will publish the files to be deployed (see Figure 6-3). This location is the file path or the virtual directory on your web server where you want to deploy the application. For a simple test, use a URL that starts with *http://localhost/* (which refers to the current computer). Click Next to continue.

TIP

When Visual Studio publishes the application, it will automatically create a subdirectory named *publish* in the current application directory, and it will map this to the virtual directory path you've selected.

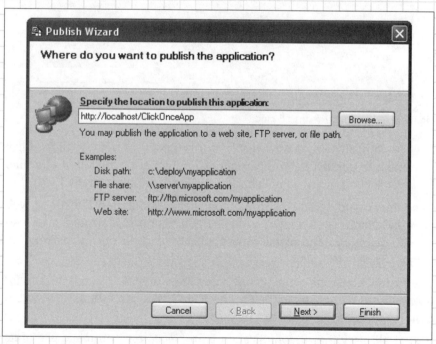

Figure 6-3. Choosing a deployment directory

4. Next, choose the install mode (see Figure 6-4) by clicking one of the buttons on the "Will the application be available offline" dialog page. Select "Yes, this application is available online or offline." This way, the setup will add application icons to the Start menu. If you choose "No, this application is only available online," the user will only be able to run it by surfing to the virtual directory to which it's been published. Click Next to continue.

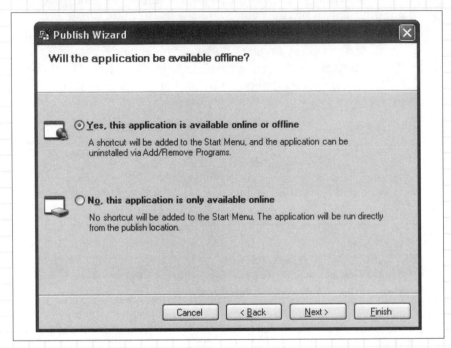

Figure 6-4. Choosing the install mode

5. The Publish wizard now displays a summary of your settings. Click Finish to publish it. (You can publish an updated version at any time by selecting Build → Publish [ProjectName] from the menu.)

Once the wizard completes, the automatically generated ClickOnce web page is launched, as shown in Figure 6-5. Using this page, a user can click to download and install your application. Try it out by clicking the Install [AppName] link.

The installation runs without any messages, unless it needs to ask for user consent. For example, before the installation can add an icon to the Start menu, it needs to prompt the user.

Best of all, now that the application is in place, you can make use of its automatic update ability. To test this out, return to the application in

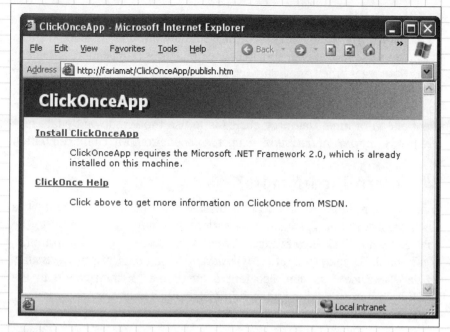

Figure 6-5. The ClickOnce installation page

Visual Studio .NET and change the main form (perhaps by adding a new button). Then, increment the version number of the application. (To do this, double-click the My Project item in the Solution Explorer, select the Application tab, and click the AssemblyInfo button. A dialog box will appear that lets you set assembly metadata, including the version number.) Finally, republish the application.

When a new version is available on the server, client applications will update themselves automatically, based on their update settings. If you run the installed sample application, it checks for updates when it starts. In this case, it will detect the new version and prompt you to install the update.

WARNING

The ClickOnce plumbing has been tweaked and refined continuously during the beta cycle. In some builds of Visual Studio, you may encounter an error when you try to publish a project using Click-Once. Unfortunately, there aren't any workarounds.

What about...

...computers that don't have the .NET Framework 2.0 installed? These machines can't download and install a ClickOnce application automatically. However, when they surf to the ClickOnce installation page, they will see a link that will install the required prerequisites. There are a number of other approaches you can pursue to get .NET 2.0 installed on the client ahead of time. One easy choice is to use the Windows Update feature (surf to *http://windowsupdate.microsoft.com* from the client computer).

Where can I learn more?

There are a number of articles that discuss the ClickOnce technology in much greater detail. For more information, you may want to refer to the book *Essential ClickOnce* (Addison Wesley, forthcoming), or the introduction from MSDN magazine at *http://msdn.microsoft.com/msdnmag/issues/04/05/ClickOnce*. You can also find a great deal of information in the MSDN help library, and online at *http://msdn.microsoft.com/clickonce*.

Index

Symbols

& (ampersand), required character, in
    mask, 75

''' (apostrophes, three), XML comments
    starting with, 22

* (asterisk), select any node,
    XPath, 192

\ (backslash), escapes masked
    character, 76

{} (braces) enclosing constraints, 41

: (colon), time separator, in mask, 75

, (comma), thousands placeholder, in
    mask, 75

$ (dollar sign), currency symbol, in
    mask, 75

\# (hash mark), optional character or
    space, in mask, 75

< (left angle bracket), convert
    characters to lowercase, 75

. (period)
  .. (move up one node level,
    XPath), 192
  current node, XPath, 192
  decimal placeholder, in mask, 75

? (question mark), optional letter, in
    mask, 75

> (right angle bracket), convert
    characters to uppercase, 76

/ (slash)
  /> (ending tag with), 140
  date separator, in mask, 75

[] (square brackets), XPath filters, 192

_ (underline)
  blue, indicating error found by
    AutoCorrect, 15
  green squiggly, indicating
    unsupported edit, 6

A

access levels, 57

AddUserToRole() method, Roles
    class, 153

Alignment property,
    DataGridViewCellStyle
    class, 104

AllowUserToAddRows property,
    DataGridView control, 101

AllowUserToDeleteRows property,
    DataGridView control, 101

ampersand (&), required character, in
    mask, 75

AndAlso operator, 58–59

animations, GDI+, increasing redraw
    speed for, 93–96

anonymous identification, 159

apostrophes, three ('''), XML comments
    starting with, 22

app.config file
  adding trace listeners to, 199
  for database-agnostic code, 185

APPDATA environment variable, 198

AppendChild() method, XPathEditor
    class, 194

We'd like to hear your suggestions for improving our indexes. Send email to *index@oreilly.com*.

Matthew MacDonald is an author, educator, and MCSD developer. He is the author of over a dozen books about programming with .NET, including *The Book of VB .NET* (No Starch), *Pro ASP.NET 1.1* (Apress), *Microsoft Visual Basic .NET Programmer's Cookbook* (Microsoft Press), and *Microsoft .NET Distributed Applications* (Microsoft Press). In a dimly remembered past life, he studied English literature and theoretical physics.

Our look is the result of reader comments, our own experimentation, and feedback from distribution channels. Distinctive covers complement our distinctive approach to technical topics, breathing personality and life into potentially dry subjects.

The *Developer's Notebook* series is modeled on the tradition of laboratory notebooks. Laboratory notebooks are an invaluable tool for researchers and their successors.

The purpose of a laboratory notebook is to facilitate the recording of data and conclusions as the work is being conducted, creating a faithful and immediate history. The notebook begins with a title page that includes the owner's name and the subject of research. The pages of the notebook should be numbered and prefaced with a table of contents. Entries must be clear, easy to read, and accurately dated; they should use simple, direct language to indicate the name of the experiment and the steps taken. Calculations are written out carefully and relevant thoughts and ideas recorded. Each experiment is introduced and summarized as it is added to the notebook. The goal is to produce comprehensive, clearly organized notes that can be used as a reference. Careful documentation creates a valuable record and provides a practical guide for future developers.

Sanders Kleinfeld was the production editor and proofreader for *Visual Basic 2005: A Developer's Notebook*, and Derek Di Matteo was the copyeditor. Marlowe Shaeffer and Claire Cloutier provided quality control. Angela Howard wrote the index.

Edie Freedman designed the cover of this book. Emma Colby produced the cover layout with QuarkXPress 4.1 using the Officina Sans and JuniorHandwriting fonts.

David Futato designed the interior layout, with contributions from Edie Freedman. This book was converted by Joe Wizda to FrameMaker 5.5.6 with a format conversion tool created by Erik Ray, Jason McIntosh, Neil Walls, and Mike Sierra that uses Perl and XML technologies. The text font is Adobe Boton; the heading font is ITC Officina Sans; the code font is LucasFont's TheSans Mono Condensed, and the hand-writing font is a modified version of JuniorHandwriting made by Tepid Monkey Foundry and modified by O'Reilly. The illustrations that appear in the book were produced by Robert Romano, Jessamyn Read, and Lesley Borash using Macromedia FreeHand MX and Adobe Photoshop CS. This colophon was written by Colleen Gorman.

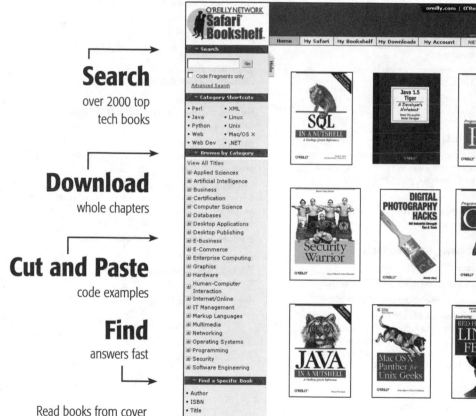

Part# 40421

Keep in touch with O'Reilly

1. Download examples from our books

To find example files for a book, go to:

www.oreilly.com/catalog

select the book, and follow the "Examples" link.

2. Register your O'Reilly books

Register your book at *register.oreilly.com*

Why register your books?
Once you've registered your O'Reilly books you can:

- Win O'Reilly books, T-shirts or discount coupons in our monthly drawing.
- Get special offers available only to registered O'Reilly customers.
- Get catalogs announcing new books (US and UK only).
- Get email notification of new editions of the O'Reilly books you own.

3. Join our email lists

Sign up to get topic-specific email announcements of new books and conferences, special offers, and O'Reilly Network technology newsletters at:

elists.oreilly.com

It's easy to customize your free elists subscription so you'll get exactly the O'Reilly news you want.

4. Get the latest news, tips, and tools

www.oreilly.com

- "Top 100 Sites on the Web"—PC Magazine
- CIO Magazine's Web Business 50 Awards

Our web site contains a library of comprehensive product information (including book excerpts and tables of contents), downloadable software, background articles, interviews with technology leaders, links to relevant sites, book cover art, and more.

5. Work for O'Reilly

Check out our web site for current employment opportunities:

jobs.oreilly.com

6. Contact us

O'Reilly Media
1005 Gravenstein Hwy North
Sebastopol, CA 95472 USA

TEL: 707-827-7000 or 800-998-9938
(6am to 5pm PST)

FAX: 707-829-0104

order@oreilly.com
For answers to problems regarding your order or our products. To place a book order online, visit:

www.oreilly.com/order_new

catalog@oreilly.com
To request a copy of our latest catalog.

booktech@oreilly.com
For book content technical questions or corrections.

corporate@oreilly.com
For educational, library, government, and corporate sales.

proposals@oreilly.com
To submit new book proposals to our editors and product managers.

international@oreilly.com
For information about our international distributors or translation queries. For a list of our distributors outside of North America check out:

international.oreilly.com/distributors.html

adoption@oreilly.com
For information about academic use of O'Reilly books, visit:

academic.oreilly.com

O'REILLY®

Our books are available at most retail and online bookstores.
To order direct: 1-800-998-9938 • *order@oreilly.com* • *www.oreilly.com*
Online editions of most O'Reilly titles are available by subscription at *safari.oreilly.com*